Project Earth Science:
Geology

Revised 2nd Edition

Project Earth Science: Geology

Revised 2nd Edition

by Paul D. Fullagar and Nancy W. West

National Science Teachers Association

Arlington, Virginia

National Science Teachers Association

Claire Reinburg, Director
Jennifer Horak, Managing Editor
Andrew Cooke, Senior Editor
Judy Cusick, Senior Editor
Wendy Rubin, Associate Editor
Amy America, Book Acquisitions Coordinator

Printing and Production
Catherine Lorrain, Director

National Science Teachers Association
Francis Q. Eberle, PhD, Executive Director
David Beacom, Publisher

Art and Design
Will Thomas Jr., Director
Tracey Shipley, Cover Design
Front Cover Photo: Punchstock.com
Back Cover Photo: Punchstock.com
Banner Art © Maite Lohmann / Dreamstime.com

Revised 2nd Edition developed, designed, illustrated,
and produced by
Focus Strategic Communications Inc.
www.focussc.com

Library of Congress Cataloging-in-Publication Data
Fullagar, Paul D., 1938-

Project Earth science. Geology / by Paul D. Fullagar and Nancy W. West. -- Rev. 2nd ed.

p. cm.

"One of the four-volume Project Earth Science series"--Introduction.

Includes bibliographical references and index.

ISBN 978-1-936137-30-5 -- eISBN 978-1-936137-54-1

1. Previous ed. by Brent A. Ford. 2. Geology--Experiments. 3. Geology--Study and teaching (Secondary) I. West, Nancy W., 1957- II. National Science Teachers Association. III. Title. IV. Title: Geology.

QE40.F85 2011

550.71'2--dc22

2011000488

NSTA is committed to publishing material that promotes the best in inquiry-based science education. However, conditions of actual use may vary, and the safety procedures and practices described in this book are intended to serve only as a guide. Additional precautionary measures may be required. NSTA and the authors do not warrant or represent that the procedures and practices in this book meet any safety code or standard of federal, state, or local regulations. NSTA and the authors disclaim any liability for personal injury or damage to property arising out of or relating to the use of this book, including any of the recommendations, instructions, or materials contained therein.

Featuring SciLinks—a new way of connecting text and the Internet. Up-to-the minute online content, classroom ideas, and other materials are just a click away. For more information go to www.scilinks.org/Faq.aspx.

Table of Contents

Readings

Acknowledgments

Many people played a role in the creation of this new edition of *Project Earth Science: Geology*. This volume was originally conceived as a collection of Activities and Readings for Project Earth Science (PES), a teacher enhancement program funded by the National Science Foundation. Principal investigators for this project were Iris R. Weiss, president of Horizon Research Inc.; Diana L. Montgomery, research associate at Horizon Research Inc.; Paul B. Hounshell, professor of education, University of North Carolina at Chapel Hill; and Paul D. Fullagar, professor of geosciences, University of North Carolina at Chapel Hill. PES provided in-service education for and by middle school Earth science teachers in North Carolina. Activities and Readings in this book underwent many revisions as a result of suggestions provided by PES teacher-leaders, principal investigators, and project staff and consultants. PES leaders made this book possible through their creativity and commitment to the needs of students and classroom teachers. Brent A. Ford was author of the first edition, and was part of the PES team.

We thank the many people who contributed to this revised second edition. One author (Paul D. Fullagar) benefited significantly from many discussions about plate tectonics with P. Sean Smith, Brent A. Ford, and Melanie J. Taylor of Horizon Research Inc. The other author (Nancy W. West) thanks P. Geoffrey Feiss of Quarter Dome Consulting, LLC, for constructive suggestions made during the writing of material for this volume. We also thank Adrianna Edwards and Ron Edwards of Focus Strategic Communications Inc., Oakville, Ontario, Canada, for their considerable efforts in preparing this volume for publication. We would also like to thank the rest of the Focus team for their efforts: Nancy Szostak, designer and formatter; Sarah Waterfield and Carolyn Tripp, illustrators; Linda Szostak, copyeditor and proofreader. The authors appreciate the helpful suggestions made by reviewer Catherine Oates-Bockenstedt.

Project Earth Science: Geology, Revised 2nd Edition, is published by NSTA Press. We thank everyone at NSTA who helped with this volume, and especially appreciate the efforts of the publisher, David Beacom. NSTA safety columnist, author, and consultant Ken Roy reviewed the entire manuscript for safety compliance. NSTA Press managing editor Jennifer Horak and project editor Mark Farrell led NSTA's in-house team for the revised second edition.

Introduction

Project Earth Science: Geology is one of the four-volume Project Earth Science series. The other three volumes in the series are *Astronomy, Meteorology,* and *Physical Oceanography.* Each volume contains a collection of hands-on Activities developed for middle-level students plus a series of Readings intended primarily for teachers, but that could also be useful to interested students.

Additions and Changes to Revised 2nd Edition

Activities and Readings have been rewritten to improve clarity and scientific currency, and to suggest additional teaching and learning strategies. The Resources section at the back of this book is almost entirely new. At the beginning of each Activity, there now is a Planner to quickly provide information about that Activity. Material specifically for students, and material specifically for teachers, is more clearly delineated. There are new sections for students within Activities titled What Can I Do? and Fast Fact. Additional new sections included for teachers are How Do We Know This?, Safety Alerts!, Connections, Differentiated Learning, and Assessment.

Within each Activity, there now is a section for teachers titled Preconceptions. A preconception is an opinion or view that a student might have prior to studying a particular topic. These opinions may not be accurate because the student does not have the correct information or does not understand that information. Each possible preconception that we list with each Activity actually is a misconception. Asking students about their preconceptions at the outset of a new instructional topic can provide useful information about what students already know and what misinformation needs to be corrected for them to have a good understanding of the topic. The preconceptions we list are, of course, only examples of incorrect ideas that some students might have. Most groups of students are imaginative enough to come up with many other preconceptions!

About *Project Earth Science: Geology*

Project Earth Science: Geology is built upon the unifying theory of plate tectonics. It explores how this concept can be used to explain the occurrences of volcanoes, earthquakes, and other geologic phenomena. The Activities herein also provide a link among plate tectonics, rock and mineral types, and the rock cycle. Integrated into this foundation are a variety of points regarding the process of scientific investigation and modeling. The intent is to increase student awareness of how scientific knowledge is created.

This book is divided into three sections: Activities, Readings, and Resources. The Activities emphasize the following: The outer part of Earth is composed of plates of rock. These plates move independently on top of a rock layer with different properties called the asthenosphere. Because of their motion, plates interact at their edges causing geological events and features (e.g., volcanic eruptions and earthquakes, volcanoes, mountain ranges). The rocks and minerals around us today are products of complex geological processes. Close study provides insights into the geological processes and environments to which they have been subjected.

An understanding of the concept of density is required for several of the Activities contained in this volume. The Activities are written with the assumption that students have this understanding. If students have not yet learned this concept, there are several activities in *Project Earth Science: Physical*

Oceanography and in *Project Earth Science: Meteorology* that could be used prior to conducting the Activities herein.

A series of overview Readings supports the Activities. By elaborating on concepts presented in the Activities, the Readings are intended to enhance teacher preparation and serve as additional resources for students. The Readings also introduce supplemental topics so that teachers can link contemporary science to broader subjects and other disciplines.

The Resources provide supplemental materials. The Resources section includes *Activities*—collections of hands-on activities and multidisciplinary units; *Audiovisual Materials*—media materials including DVDs and CDs; *Books and Booklets*—examples of useful textbooks and booklets; *Information and References*—additional resources such as periodicals, bibliographies, catalogs, maps, reference booklets, and reports; *Internet Resources*—starting points for exploration of online resources in geology, with an address (URL) for each website plus a brief annotation; *State Resources*—each of the 50 states has its own geological survey, and most can provide materials of use to teachers and students.

Creating Scientific Knowledge

Investigating plate tectonics offers a superb opportunity to encourage student thinking on two subjects: how scientific knowledge is created and how scientific knowledge evolves. The theory of plate tectonics gained wide acceptance only in the 1960s. Its implications produced a revolution within geology, forcing a complete reshaping of basic geological theories and understanding. *Project Earth Science: Geology* presents a variety of opportunities for teachers to discuss the creation and evolution of scientific knowledge.

For example, students might consider

- how models help develop—yet sometimes restrict—our conceptions of nature
- how scientific knowledge changes over time
- how our choice of measurement scale affects our perceptions of nature and of change

Models and analogies are extremely effective tools in scientific investigation, especially when the subject under study proves to be too large, too small, or too inaccessible for direct study. Although Earth scientists often use models, students must be reminded that models are not perfect representations of the object or phenomenon under study. It is essential that students learn to evaluate models for strengths and weaknesses, such as which phenomena are accurately represented and which are not. Preconceptions about geological processes can be introduced when models are used beyond their intended range of application. When using models, it is good to discuss both their advantages and their limitations.

As students learn science, it is easy for them to lose sight of the fact that scientific knowledge evolves. As scientists gather more data, test hypotheses, and develop more sophisticated means of investigation, their understanding of natural phenomena often changes. What is now known as the theory of plate tectonics, for example, has evolved significantly over the last century.

"Continental drift" was first proposed in the early 1900s to explain why the outlines of continents seemed to fit so well together— the western coast of Africa and the eastern coast of South America, for example—and to explain why fossils found in rocks on the coasts of different continents were so similar. Having no mechanism to explain how such "drifting" could occur, most geologists rejected these early proposals. In the 1950s, geologists studying patterns in the frequency and location of volcanoes and earthquakes suggested that continents were just parts of enormous "plates" that make up outer Earth. They proposed that as these plates moved and their edges interacted, earthquakes were generated, and magma rose to the surface between plates, producing volcanoes. Many geoscientists remained skeptical of this model, however, partly because they still were unsure what might drive such a process.

In the 1950s and 1960s, much information became available about the seafloor. Geologists found patterns in the relative ages and the magnetic orientations of rock formations on the seafloor. These patterns, combined with newer seismic studies of Earth's interior, provided compelling evidence that Earth's surface *is* composed of moving plates and that the continents are part of them. Since the late 1960s, plate tectonics has been accepted by virtually all scientists as an accurate account of how Earth's surface has changed and continues to change.

With growing information and expanded understanding, scientific knowledge changes; what seemed impossible to many at the start of the 20th century is accepted in the 21st century. Teachers should emphasize this changing nature of science—it is what makes scientific inquiry special as a form of knowledge—and encourage students to investigate in more detail how scientific knowledge evolves.

Because the development of the theory of plate tectonics—a new paradigm for understanding Earth processes—hinged on data, Activities in which students analyze evidence come first in this revised edition. Activities 1–8 allow students to discover tectonic plates and boundaries by examining data. In Activities 9–11, students explore how plate tectonics works. Activity 12 applies plate tectonics to drifting continents over geologic time. Finally, Activities 13–15 are other hands-on activities to help students understand geologic concepts.

Observing and the Problem of Scale

Central to understanding how science evolves is appreciating the limits of our perceptions of change. We observe the world as it *is*, and our thoughts about how it *was* and how it *could be* tend to be quite restricted. That our world is changing constantly can be a difficult concept for students to accept. In several respects, this is a function of the rate at which change sometimes occurs compared to the length of time available to humans for direct observation.

To illustrate this point, ask students to consider the life of an insect that spends its entire existence—from June to August of a single year—in an oak tree. As outside observers, humans can observe seasonal and annual changes in the tree's biology. Because of the relatively short duration of its life, the insect cannot observe these changes.

Likewise, due to the relatively short span of our lifetimes compared to geologic time, people have difficulty appreciating the changes taking place on a million-year scale, to say nothing of billions of years. Continents move at a rate of less than 10 cm per year; average global temperatures may change only a few degrees over thousands of years; mountain ranges can take millions of years to rise. Changes such as these may be imperceptible during a person's life span. It is important for students to understand that while observing these changes may be difficult, Earth's geologic features are continually changing. Comparing events and changes on different scales can be a difficult skill for students to acquire.

Also, diagrams and models often exaggerate or compress relative sizes to make a certain point more obvious or to make the model small enough to be practical. Sometimes one scale is changed, but others are not. For example, displays of our solar system often accurately depict the relative *distances* between planets but misrepresent planets' relative *sizes*. In geology, cross sections often exaggerate the vertical scale to emphasize surface topography or subsurface structures such as folds and faults. The result is that the horizontal axis is at one scale and the vertical at another. It is important for teachers to discuss the concept of scale and encourage students to raise questions about the various measurement scales used in these Activities.

Getting Ready for Classroom Instruction

The Activities in this volume are designed to be hands-on. In developing them, we tried to use materials that are either readily available in the classroom or inexpensive to purchase. Note that many of the Activities also could be done as demonstrations.

Each Activity has two sections: a Student section and a Teachers' Guide. Each Student section begins with Background information to explain briefly, in nontechnical terms, what the Activity is about; the Objective states what students will learn. Then there is Vocabulary, which includes important geological terms used in the Activity. This is followed by a list of the Materials needed and an estimate of the amount of Time that the Activity will take. Following this introduction is a step-by-step Procedure outline and a set of Questions and Conclusions to facilitate student understanding, encourage constructive thinking, and advance the drawing of scientific conclusions.

Each Student section concludes with additional activities for students in What Can I Do?

The Teachers' Guide contains What Is Happening?, a more thorough version of the background information given to students. The section How Do We Know This? explains techniques or research methods geologists currently use to generate knowledge related to the Activity. This is followed by possible student Preconceptions, which can be used to initiate classroom discussions. Next comes a summary of What Students Need to Understand. Then Time Management discusses the estimated amount of time the Activity will take. Preparation and Procedure describes the setup for the Activity. Extended Learning challenges students to extend their study of each topic. Interdisciplinary Study relates the science in each Activity to other disciplines, such as language arts, history, and social sciences. Connections links geology to a similar process or concept in astronomy, meteorology, or physical oceanography. The final portion of each Teachers' Guide includes possibilities for Differentiated Learning, Answers to Student Questions, and suggestions for Assessment.

Although the scientific method often has been presented as a "cookbook" recipe—state the problem, gather information, form a hypothesis, perform experiments, record and analyze data, and state conclusions—students should be made aware that the scientific method provides an approach to understanding the world around us, an approach that is rarely so straightforward. For instance, many factors can influence experimental outcomes, measurement precision, and the reliability of results. Such variables must be taken into consideration throughout the course of an investigation.

As students work through the Activities in this volume, make them aware that experimental outcomes can vary and that repetition of trials is important for developing an accurate picture of concepts they are studying. By repeating experimental procedures, students can learn to distinguish between significant and insignificant variations in outcomes. Regardless of how carefully they conduct an experiment, they can never entirely eliminate error. As a matter of course, students should be encouraged to look for ways to eliminate sources of error. However, they also must be

National Science Teachers Association

made aware of the inherent variation possible in all experimentation.

Finally, controlling variables is important in maintaining the integrity of an experiment. Misleading results and incorrect conclusions often can be traced to experimentation where important variables were not rigorously controlled. Teachers should encourage students to identify experimental controls and consider the relationships between the variables under study and the factors held under control.

Key Concepts

The Activities in this book are organized within the context of the unifying geological theory of plate tectonics, which encompasses the following four key concepts:

Key Concept I: Geological patterns and lithospheric plates
Key Concept II: Movement of plates
Key Concept III: Geological phenomena and plate tectonics
Key Concept IV: Rocks and minerals

Key Concept I deals with the fact that Earth's surface, the lithosphere, is comprised of individual lithospheric plates. Key Concept II is that the plates move or "ride" atop the solid but plastic asthenosphere. Key Concept III is concerned with the fact that many geological events and features occurring on Earth's surface, such as earthquakes, volcanic eruptions, volcanoes, and mountain ranges, are directly related to plate tectonic activity. Key Concept IV has to do with the rocks and minerals that comprise such features, which are produced over time by complex, cyclical geological processes.

Project Earth Science: Geology and the National Science Education Standards

An organizational matrix for the Activities in *Project Earth Science: Geology, Revised 2nd Edition,* appears on pages xvi–xvii. The categories listed along the *x*-axis of the matrix, listed below, correspond to the categories of performing and understanding scientific activity identified as appropriate by the National Research Council's (NRC's) 1996 *National Science Education Standards.*

Subject and Content: Specifies the topic covered by an Activity.

Scientific Inquiry: Identifies the "process of science" (i.e., scientific reasoning, critical thinking, conducting investigations, formulating hypotheses) employed by an Activity.

Unifying Concepts: Links an Activity's specific subject topic with "the big picture" of scientific ideas (i.e., how data collection techniques inform interpretation and analysis).

Technology: Establishes a connection between the natural and designed worlds.

Personal/Social Perspectives: Locates the specific geology topic covered by an Activity within a framework that relates directly to students' lives.

Historical Context: Portrays scientific endeavor as an ongoing human enterprise by linking an Activity's topic with the evolution of its underlying principle.

Project Earth Science: Geology hopes to address the need for making science— in this case, geology—something students do, not something that is done to students. The standards organizational matrix on the following pages provides a tool to assist teachers in realizing this goal.

Safety in the Classroom Practices

The teaching and learning of science today through hands-on, process, and inquiry-based activities make classroom and laboratory experiences effective. Addressing potential safety issues is critical to securing this success. Although total safety cannot be guaranteed, teachers can make science safer by adopting, implementing, and enforcing legal standards and best professional practices in the science classroom and laboratory. Safety in the Classroom Practices includes both basic safety practices and resources specific to the Project Earth Science series. It is designed to help teachers and students become aware of relevant standards and practices that will help make activities safer.

1. When working with glassware, wires, projectiles, or other solid hazards, students should use appropriate personal protective equipment, including safety glasses or goggles, gloves, and aprons.

2. When working with hazardous liquids, indirectly vented chemical splash goggles, gloves, and aprons must be used.

3. Always review Material Safety Data Sheets (MSDSs) with students relative to safety precautions when working with hazardous chemicals.

4. When dealing with hazardous chemicals, an eyewash station within 10-seconds access is required because of the possibility of a splash accident in the eyes. If there is potential for a body splash, an emergency shower is required with 10-seconds access.

5. Make sure appropriate laboratory ventilation is used when working with hazardous vapors or fumes.

6. When heating liquids other than water, use only heat-resistant glassware (Pyrex- or Kimax-type equipment). Remember that glass labware is never to be placed directly on heating surfaces. Also remember that hot containers are potential hazards. Water may be heated in glassware, but teapots or other types of pans also may be used.

7. When heating liquids on electrical equipment such as hot plates, use ground-fault-protected circuits (GFI).

8. Always remind students of heat and burn hazards when working with heat sources such as hot plates for melting wax, heating water, and more. Remember that it takes time for the hot plate and the objects heated on the hot plate to cool.

9. Use caution in working with scissors, plastic knives, pocket pencil sharpeners, rocks, or other sharp objects—cut or puncture hazards.

10. If a relatively harmless liquid (e.g., water, dilute chemical) is spilled on the floor, always wipe it up immediately to prevent slip and fall hazards. However, if a spilled liquid (e.g., concentrated acid) is causing, or has the potential to produce, toxic fumes, the classroom or lab must be vacated and appropriate emergency authorities called immediately. Teachers must know in advance what to do in this type of emergency.

11. Never consume food or drink that has been either brought into or used in the laboratory.

12. Teachers should always model appropriate techniques before requiring students to cut, puncture, or dissect, and so on.

13. Wash hands with soap and water after doing activities dealing with hazardous chemicals.

14. Use caution when working with hot water—it can burn skin.

15. Use caution when working with flammables—keep away from ignition or spark sources.

16. Markers can have volatile organic compounds (VOCs) that can irritate the eyes, nose, and throat. Use in well-ventilated areas, or use only low VOC markers.

17. Lighted bulbs can get hot and burn skin. Handle with care.

18. Make sure that all food is disposed of properly so that it does not attract rodents and insects in the lab or classroom.

19. Work with care when placing boards on the floor—they can be a trip and fall hazard.

20. When using a vise, be careful not to place fingers in the vise—a pinch hazard. It can break or damage skin.

For additional safety regulations and best professional practices, go to NSTA: Safety in the Science Classroom: *www.nsta.org/pdfs/SafetyInTheScience Classroom.pdf*

NSTA Safety Portal: *www.nsta.org/ portals/safety.aspx*

Standards Organizational Matrix

Activity	Subject Matter and Content	Scientific Inquiry	Unifying Concepts and Processes
Activity 1 GeoPatterns	Global earthquake distribution	Analyzing data	Explaining nature's spatial patterns
Activity 2 Volcanoes and Plates	Where volcanoes form	Plotting and analyzing data	Using a theory to explain data
Activity 3 Volcanoes and Hot Spots	Chains of volcanoes	Modeling to understand trends	Explaining data and predicting
Activity 4 All Cracked Up	Earth's layers, models	Modeling, visualizing	Representing data with a model
Activity 5 Seafloor Spreading	Divergent plate boundaries, ocean floor patterns	Modeling	Modeling to explicate a process
Activity 6 Mapping the Seafloor	Seafloor and ocean depths	Measuring and graphing data	Collecting data strategically
Activity 7 Rocks Tell a Story	Characterizing rocks	Observing, describing	Inferring processes of change
Activity 8 The Rock Cycle	Rock cycle: formation and change	Modeling change	Change within open systems
Activity 9 Solid or Liquid?	Properties of rock in the asthenosphere	Experimenting	Change and rate of applied stress
Activity 10 Edible Plate Tectonics	Plate tectonics: interaction	Modeling, visualizing	Influence of physical properties on change
Activity 11 Convection	Heat transfer within Earth's mantle	Experimenting	Density differences and heat transfer
Activity 12 A Voyage Through Time	Breakup of Pangaea	Modeling, predicting	Evolution of landmasses
Activity 13 Magma and Volcanoes	Volcanic eruption	Modeling	Modeling to illustrate a process
Activity 14 Shake It Up	Earthquakes' effects on structures	Experimenting	Rapid energy transfer
Activity 15 Study Your Sandwich	Deforming rocks	Visualizing in 3-D	Analyzing models of rock structures

National Science Teachers Association

Technology	Personal/Social Perspectives	Historical Context	Key Concept
	Natural hazards	Evidence supporting a new paradigm	I, III
	Natural hazards	Evidence supporting a new paradigm	I, III
	Natural hazards	Evidence supporting a new paradigm	I, II, III
		Changing knowledge of Earth's interior	I, II
Adapting technology for science	Teamwork	Evolving theories	I, II, III
Method of measurement	Group decision of priorities	Historical methods of science	I, III
	Scientific perspective of deep time	Inferring history from rocks	III, IV
	Natural resources	Changing understanding of rock origins	III, IV
			II
		Evolving theories	I, II
Convection in technology		Evolving theories	I, II
Animation		History of Earth	I, II, III
	Cultural interpretation of volcanic events		I, III
Design of structures	Natural hazards	Analyzing historical earthquakes	I, III
		Chronology of rock formation and deformation	I, III, IV

Activities at a Glance

Activity	Pages	Subject and Content	Objective	Materials
Activity 1 GeoPatterns	1–15	Global earthquake distribution	Study earthquake distribution around the world and look for patterns of earthquake distribution.	Each student or group will need: all five panels of the strip map, scissors, glue (or clear tape), map of the ocean floor, colored pencils (optional), atlas, indirectly vented chemical splash goggles (if glue is used)
Activity 2 Volcanoes and Plates	17–29	Where volcanoes form	Investigate the relationship between volcanic activity and plate boundaries, and also explore how the kind of rock that is formed at volcanoes depends on the type of plate boundary.	Each student or group will need: colored pencils
Activity 3 Volcanoes and Hot Spots	31–39	Chains of volcanoes	Study volcanoes formed over hot spots, and investigate how plate movement is related to a pattern of volcanic island formation.	Each group will need: a box with clear sides, such as a plastic shoe box or an aquarium, if done as a demonstration; a small dropping bottle with a narrow neck; red food coloring; hot tap water; cold tap water; a Styrofoam "tectonic" plate; gloves and aprons
Activity 4 All Cracked Up	41–52	Earth's layers, models	Use models to understand some of Earth's interior features and evaluate the realism of various models.	For your demonstration: several hard-boiled eggs, preferably brown or dyed; one small kitchen knife (or cut eggs in half at home and wrap tightly to keep moist and shell in place); narrow- and broad-tipped markers For each student group: at least three other objects to serve as Earth models
Activity 5 Seafloor Spreading	55–63	Divergent plate boundaries, ocean floor patterns	Construct a paper model to illustrate why seafloor is newest or youngest at mid-ocean ridges, and is relatively old at and near trenches.	Each group will need: one copy of the seafloor spreading model; scissors; tape; orange-, yellow-, green-, and blue-colored pencils or crayons
Activity 6 Mapping the Seafloor	65–74	Seafloor and ocean depths	Map a simulated seafloor and create a profile of it. Practice teamwork and learn about possible effects of limited data and financial limitations on projects.	Each group of four or more will need: masking tape, permanent marker, graph paper and pencil, data sheets, meter stick The class will need: objects in container to represent seafloor; a large trash can or bucket, kiddie pool, or aquarium with sides covered; hardware cloth or other wire screen to cover water container; water-soluble paint, food coloring, or ink; water; strings long enough to reach bottom, with weights on ends

Time	Vocabulary	Key Concepts	Margin Features
45 minutes	Earthquake	I, III	Safety Alert!, What Can I Do?, Fast Fact, Connections, Resources
50 minutes	Lithosphere, Lithospheric plates, Lava, Igneous rock, Convergent boundary, Divergent boundary, Mid-ocean ridge, Transform boundary	I, III	What Can I Do?, Fast Fact, Connections, Resources
30 minutes	Hot spot, Seamount	I, II, III	Fast Fact, Safety Alert!, What Can I Do?, Connections, Resources
30 minutes	Crust, Plates, Mantle, Asthenosphere, Core	I, II	Safety Alert!, Fast Fact, Connections
50 minutes or less	Plate tectonics, Seafloor spreading, Trenches	I, II, III	Fast Fact, What Can I Do?, Connections
50 minutes	Sounding lines, Terrain, Topography	I, III	Fast Fact, Safety Alert!, What Can I Do?, Connections, Resources

Activity	Pages	Subject and Content	Objective	Materials
Activity 7 Rocks Tell a Story	77–84	Characterizing rocks	Observe characteristics of rock specimens and learn their significance.	Rock-sample set containing gabbro and basalt, shale and slate, granite and gneiss, sandstone and conglomerate, limestone and marble
Activity 8 The Rock Cycle	87–96	Rock cycle: formation and change	Investigate processes that form and alter rocks, and see how rocks change over time.	Each student will need: indirectly vented chemical splash goggles, a lab apron, a pocket pencil sharpener, scrap paper Each lab group will need: eight wax crayons, tongs, two pieces of lumber about 2.5 × 12.5 × 20 cm, hot plate, aluminum foil, four envelopes, newspaper, vise (optional)
Activity 9 Solid or Liquid?	99–108	Properties of rock in the asthenosphere	Investigate and observe how a substance can, under certain conditions, behave like a solid and, under other conditions, behave like a liquid.	**Part 1**—Data tables for all: **BLM 9.1** **Part 2**—Each group will need: Silly Putty, hammer, data tables for all: **BLM 9.2**, board, safety glasses for all, lab aprons **Part 3**—Each person will need: Mystery Substance X, towels for cleanup
Activity 10 Edible Plate Tectonics	111–119	Plate tectonics: interaction	Investigate how plates move on Earth's surface, and observe how some geologic features form as a result of this movement.	Each student will need: one Milky Way bar or similar type of product, towels for cleanup
Activity 11 Convection	121–132	Heat transfer within Earth's mantle	Investigate and observe how material moves within a convection cell, and consider how your observations might pertain to Earth's interior.	Each group will need: indirectly vented chemical splash goggles, aprons, and gloves for each student; room-temperature water; hot water (about 70°C); towels for water spills; food coloring in small containers; basin or sink for used water; plastic pan, pipette or medicine dropper; four foam cups; one cup lid; two sheets of white paper; data sheets for each student
Activity 12 A Voyage Through Time	135–146	Breakup of Pangaea	Model the breakup of the supercontinent Pangaea and the subsequent movement of continents.	Each student will need: a copy of the three map sheets, colored pencils or crayons (red, orange, yellow, green, blue, purple, tan), scissors, a current world map showing terrain such as mountains and seafloor (this could be on display only)

Time	Vocabulary	Key Concepts	Margin Features
50 minutes	Igneous, Sedimentary, Metamorphic	III, IV	Fast Fact, Safety Alert!, What Can I Do?, Connections
Approximately 150 minutes	Igneous rock, Weathering, Erosion, Sediment, Sedimentary rock, Metamorphic rock, Rock cycle	III, IV	Fast Fact, Safety Alert!, What Can I Do?, Connections
50 minutes or less	Glaciers	II	Safety Alert!, Fast Fact, What Can I Do?, Connections
15 minutes		I, II	Safety Alert!, Fast Fact, Connections
50 minutes	Convection, Experiment, Density	I, II	Safety Alert!, What Can I Do?, Fast Fact, Connections, Resources
50 minutes	Supercontinent	I, II, III	Fast Fact, What Can I Do?, Connections, Resources

Activity	Pages	Subject and Content	Objective	Materials
Activity 13 Magma and Volcanoes	149-156	Volcanic eruption	Create a model of a volcano with magma that rises to Earth's surface.	For each volcano model, students will require: two wax crayons, 25 cm of string, beaker (50–100 mL), scissors, paper cup (300 mL), plaster of paris (100–150 mL), hot plate, wire gauze, spoon, pan to boil water, water, tongs, indirectly vented chemical splash goggles, aprons, and gloves
Activity 14 Shake It Up	159–171	Earthquakes' effects on structures	Compare how well various construction designs withstand the effects of an earthquake.	Each group will need: two books (same size), one shoe box lid or tray, 20 sugar cubes, pencil or crayon, ruler, Student Worksheet
Activity 15 Study Your Sandwich	173–186	Deforming rocks	Investigate core sampling techniques geologists use to collect information about rock formations and their relative ages, and geologic structures.	Each group will need: one slice white bread, one slice whole wheat bread, one slice dark rye bread, two tablespoons jelly, two tablespoons soy—not peanut or almond—butter mixed with raisins, two paper plates, plastic knife, measuring spoon, clear plastic straws

Time	Vocabulary	Key Concepts	Margin Features
100 minutes	Tephra, Magma, Viscous	I, III	Fast Fact, Safety Alert!, What Can I Do?, Connections
50 minutes		I, III	Safety Alert!, What Can I Do?, Fast Fact, Connections, Resources
50 minutes	Sedimentary rock, Rock formation, Core sampling	I, III, IV	Safety Alert!, Fast Fact, What Can I Do?, Connections

Activity 1 Planner

Activity 1 Summary

Students explore patterns of where earthquakes occur. They build a paper globe already printed with earthquake epicenters and add recent earthquake data. Questions direct them to think about patterns as to where earthquakes occur and relationships with seafloor topography.

Activity	Subject and Content	Objective	Materials
GeoPatterns	Global earthquake distribution	Study earthquake distribution around the world and look for patterns of earthquake distribution.	Each student or group will need: all five panels of the strip map, scissors, glue (or clear tape), map of the ocean floor, colored pencils (optional), atlas, indirectly vented chemical splash goggles (if glue is used)

Time	Vocabulary	Key Concepts	Margin Features
45 minutes	Earthquake	I: Geological patterns and lithospheric plates III: Geological phenomena and plate tectonics	Safety Alert!, What Can I Do?, Fast Fact, Connections, Resources

Scientific Inquiry	Unifying Concepts and Processes	Personal/Social Perspectives	Historical Context
Analyzing data	Explaining nature's spatial patterns	Natural hazards	Evidence supporting a new paradigm

GeoPatterns
Global Earthquake Distribution

Background

One of the things scientists do is look for patterns in nature. Geologists look for patterns so they can answer questions about how Earth formed, how it has changed over time, and how it is likely to change in the future. Why are certain types of fossils almost always found in the same kind of rock? Why do mountains often occur in groups called ranges or belts? Why are volcanoes found in only a few places on Earth? Why do **earthquakes** occur more often in some places than in others? Explaining patterns like these is one of the goals of scientific research.

Earthquakes in the United States occur often in California and Alaska, but not very often in Iowa and Nebraska. Why are earthquakes more common in California than Nebraska? Do earthquakes occur randomly, or are there patterns to their distribution? Does where earthquakes occur shed light on why they occur? What causes earthquakes? What determines where an earthquake will occur? Geologists and geophysicists have studied these questions for many decades. A long-term goal of geologists is to predict when and where earthquakes will occur to prevent death, injuries, and damage to property.

In this Activity, you will look for patterns—or the absence of patterns—in the distribution of earthquakes around the world.

Vocabulary

Earthquake: When the ground shakes or trembles suddenly. These events occur naturally when rocks break beneath Earth's surface, when rocks move against each other in a fracture zone called a "fault," when molten rock suddenly rises in the crust (in a volcano, for instance), or even when a landslide occurs.

Objective

Study earthquake distribution around the world and look for patterns of earthquake distribution.

Topic: earthquakes
Go to: *www.scilinks.org*
Code: PSCG001

Procedure

Procedure for Making Map

1. Your teacher will give you five strip map panels (**BLMs 1–5**). Cut the panels out along their outside edges.

2. Lay the panels face up on your table, aligning them as shown in **Figure 1.1**. Glue (or tape) the panels together along the tab lines, but at this point *do not connect* panel 5 to panel 1. Now you have a map of the world that also can be assembled into a type of globe.

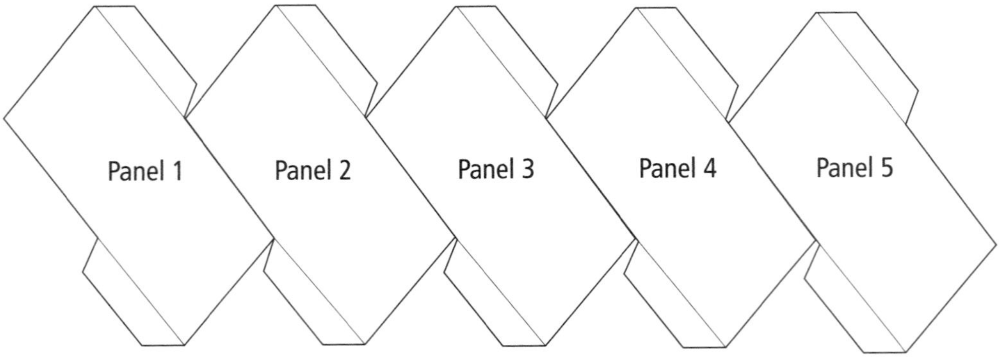

Figure 1.1
Arrangement of strip map panels 1–5 to make world map

| Panel 1 | Panel 2 | Panel 3 | Panel 4 | Panel 5 |

Materials

Each student or group will need
- all five panels of the strip map
- scissors
- glue (or clear tape)
- map of the ocean floor
- colored pencils (optional)
- atlas
- indirectly vented chemical splash goggles (if glue is used)

Time

45 minutes

SAFETY ALERT

1. Indirectly vented chemical splash goggles are required when using liquid glues.

2. Wash hands with soap and water upon completing the lab.

3. Your map shows thousands of dots. Each dot marks the location on the surface directly above where an earthquake originated (its epicenter). Look closely at the distribution of these dots over Earth's surface.

4. Your teacher may suggest that you color certain regions of the map. It is easiest to color your panels at this point, before you transform them into a globe.

5. Your teacher may ask you to use an atlas to add to the epicenter data by adding marks for each earthquake listed in **Table 1.1**.

Procedure for Making Globe From Map

6. Fold each of the panels along the straight lines printed on the map and along the tab lines. (This will make forming the globe shape easier.)

7. Join panels 5 and 1 by gluing or taping together their tabs. Finish your globe by folding panels inward along the creases and gluing or taping connecting panels together.

8. Once you are finished, examine your globe closely. Locate the various continents and ocean basins. Also notice the thousands of dots, each representing the epicenter of an earthquake. Look closely at the distribution of these dots over Earth's surface.

9. Use your globe and other resources in your classroom to answer the questions below. When you have completed this Activity, your teacher will either tell you that you may take your globe home, or that you should keep it at school for possible additional uses with other Activities.

Questions and Conclusions

1. What do you observe about the location of earthquake epicenters on your globe? Are these distributed randomly or in patterns around the world?
2. Does the earthquake data from **Table 1.1** add to or detract from any patterns you observed?
3. Do certain features appear in a pattern, or does randomness seem to be the rule on the seafloor? Give an example to support your answer.
4. Compare the distribution of earthquakes on your globe and the distribution of features on the seafloor. Do you think there is a connection between these different phenomena? Why or why not?
5. What else would you like to know about earthquakes?

What Can I Do?

1. Prepare for an earthquake by teaching your family how to respond during an earthquake. Search for "USGS Earthquake Preparedness" at *http://earthquake.usgs. gov/prepare/*.

2. If you feel an earthquake, report your observations to the U.S. Geological Survey to help geologists determine the extent of damage and the earthquake's intensity. You will be participating in scientific research. Search for "Did You Feel It?" at *http://earthquake.usgs.gov/ earthquakes/dyfi/*.

Fast Fact

Some cell phones and laptops can be used to measure earthquakes. They have built-in devices to prevent damage if dropped. With download-able software, the devices can also record ground tremors or earthquakes (and heartbeats, too).

Activity 1

Table 1.1: Recent Earthquakes, Locations, and Magnitudes— Earthquakes Magnitude 7.0 and Greater in 2010 and 2009

	Year	Month	Day	Latitude	Longitude	Magnitude	Region
1.	2010	09	03	43.4 S	172.0 E	7.0	South Island of New Zealand
2.	2010	08	12	1.3 S	77.3 W	7.1	Ecuador
3.	2010	08	10	17.6 S	168.0 E	7.3	Vanuatu, South Pacific
4.	2010	08	04	5.8 S	150.8 E	7.0	New Britain region, P.N.G.
5.	2010	07	23	6.8 N	123.3 E	7.4	Mindanao, Philippines
6.	2010	07	23	6.5 N	123.5 E	7.6	Mindanao, Philippines
7.	2010	07	23	6.7 N	123.4 E	7.3	Mindanao, Philippines
8.	2010	07	18	5.9 S	150.6 E	7.3	New Britain region, P.N.G.
9.	2010	06	16	2.2 S	136.5 E	7.0	North Coast Papua, Indonesia
10.	2010	06	12	7.8 N	91.9 E	7.5	Nicobar Islands, India region
11.	2010	05	27	13.7 S	166.6 E	7.1	Vanuatu, South Pacific
12.	2010	05	09	3.8 N	96.0 E	7.2	Northern Sumatra, Indonesia
13.	2010	04	06	2.4 N	97.0 E	7.8	Northern Sumatra, Indonesia
14.	2010	04	04	32.3 N	115.3 W	7.2	Baja California, Mexico
15.	2010	02	27	36.1 S	72.9 W	8.8	Offshore Bio-Bio, Chile
16.	2010	02	26	25.9 N	128.4 E	7.0	Ryukyu Islands, Japan
17.	2010	01	12	18.4 N	72.6 W	7.0	Haiti region
18.	2010	01	03	8.8 S	157.3 E	7.1	Solomon Islands
1.	2009	11	09	17.2 S	178.4 E	7.3	Fiji
2.	2009	10	07	13.1 S	166.5 E	7.4	Vanuatu, South Pacific
3.	2009	10	07	12.5 S	166.4 E	7.8	Santa Cruz Islands
4.	2009	10	07	13.1 S	166.3 E	7.7	Vanuatu, South Pacific
5.	2009	09	30	0.7 S	99.9 E	7.5	Southern Sumatra, Indonesia
6.	2009	09	29	15.5 S	172.1 W	8.1	Samoa Islands region
7.	2009	09	02	7.8 S	107.3 E	7.0	Java, Indonesia
8.	2009	08	10	14.1 N	92.9 E	7.5	Andaman Islands, India region
9.	2009	08	09	33.2 N	137.9 E	7.1	Near south coast of Honshu, Japan
10.	2009	07	15	45.8 S	166.6 E	7.8	West Coast South Island, New Zealand
11.	2009	05	28	16.7 N	86.2 W	7.3	Offshore Honduras
12.	2009	03	19	23.0 S	174.7 W	7.6	Tonga region
13.	2009	02	18	27.4 S	176.3 W	7.0	Kermadec Islands region
14.	2009	02	11	3.9 N	126.4 E	7.2	Kepulauan Talaud, Indonesia
15.	2009	01	15	46.9 N	155.2 E	7.4	East of Kuril Islands
16.	2009	01	03	0.7 S	133.3 E	7.4	North Coast of Papua, Indonesia
17.	2009	01	03	0.4 S	132.9 E	7.7	North Coast of Papua, Indonesia

Source: Data from U.S. Geological Survey Earthquakes Hazards Program: *http://earthquake.usgs.gov/earthquakes/eqarchives/year/*

Glue to panel 2

Glue to panel 5

Glue to panel 5

1

Glue to panel 3

Glue to panel 1

Glue to panel 1

2

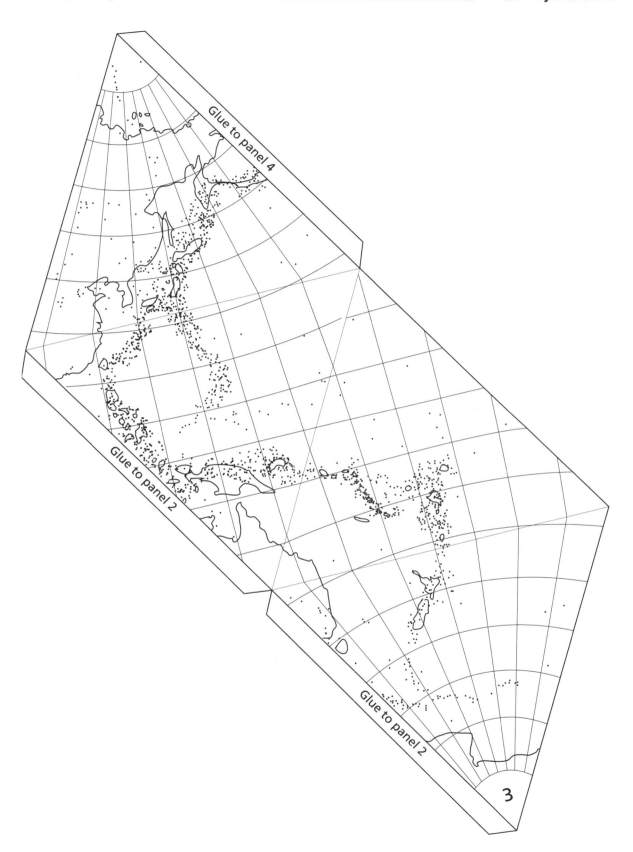

Glue to panel 4

Glue to panel 2

Glue to panel 2

3

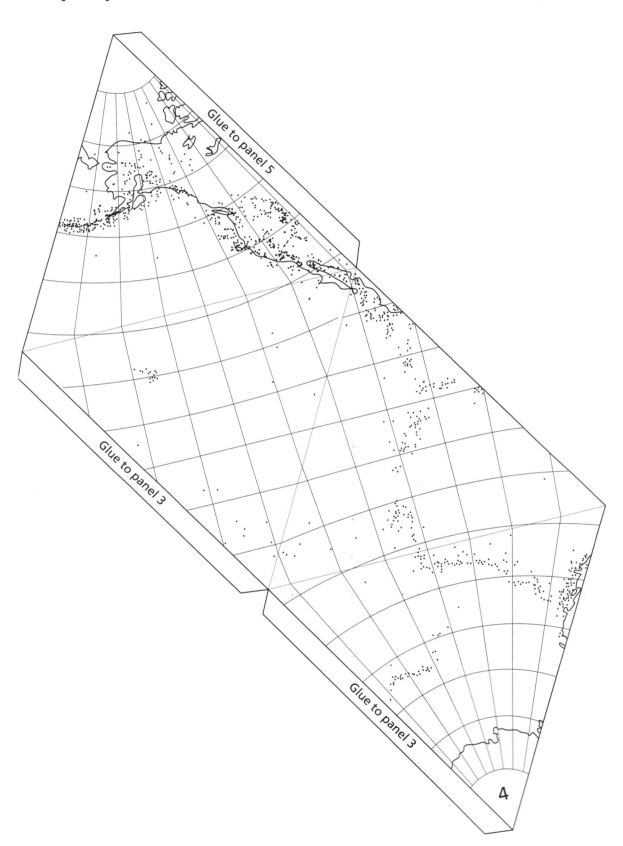

Glue to panel 5

Glue to panel 3

Glue to panel 3

4

Glue to panel 1

Glue to panel 4

Glue to panel 4

5

Teachers' Guide to Activity 1

GeoPatterns
Global Earthquake Distribution

What Is Happening?

Students need experience with pattern recognition and pattern explanation. They must also learn to distinguish between significant and insignificant patterns in what they observe. In this Activity, students look for patterns in earthquake distribution and begin building an understanding of plate tectonics. This project is open-ended; students must decide for themselves whether the patterns they identify have significance.

When rock in the outer part of Earth suddenly breaks or shifts position, energy is released and this causes shaking of the ground that is associated with earthquakes. Data on earthquake distribution provide evidence that most of these events occur in relatively narrow zones distributed around the world. These zones are now known to be the boundaries between the lithospheric plates that make up the outer part of Earth. (However, do not tell students this yet because they will learn about plates and plate boundaries in Activity 2. Let them discover the plate boundaries.) These plates move independently at Earth's surface. Plates may collide or pull apart, or one plate may slide past another. Most earthquakes occur where a plate is moving against another plate.

Studying the distribution of earthquakes gives geologists a good map of plate boundaries. Many geologic features, such as ocean trenches and ridges, some volcanoes, and certain types of mountain ranges, occur along plate boundaries, too. Trenches form where two plates come together and one plate slides beneath the other; volcanoes may form at this type of boundary. Mid-ocean ridges are composed of chains of volcanoes that form at a plate boundary where two plates move apart. Mountain ranges are created if continents collide where two plates move toward each other.

Objective
Study earthquake distribution around the world and look for patterns of earthquake distribution.

Key Concepts
I: Geological patterns and lithospheric plates
III: Geological phenomena and plate tectonics

Materials
Each student or group will need
- all five panels of the strip map
- scissors
- glue (or clear tape)
- map of the ocean floor
- colored pencils (optional)
- atlas
- indirectly vented chemical splash goggles (if glue is used)

Time
45 minutes

How Do We Know This?

Some earthquakes occur in areas where there are no people. How do we know the locations of these earthquake epicenters?

A worldwide distribution of monitoring stations equipped with seismographs makes it possible to locate the epicenters and sometimes the focal points of earthquakes, even many quakes that are felt by few or even no people. To accomplish this, an earthquake must be recorded by at least three seismograph stations; then it becomes a simple geometry problem to locate where the earthquake occurred.

Encourage students to think about the patterns they observe in earthquake distribution. In Activity 2, they will look at volcanoes and be able to see that many of them are located in the same places where earthquakes are common.

Although students spend only a short time looking for patterns in earthquake distribution, remind them that geologists have spent decades collecting earthquake data and piecing it together. Help students appreciate the work that went into the data they are analyzing. Recognizing patterns in such data has been crucial in developing the scientific theory of plate tectonics, one of the most basic unifying theories of science.

Preconceptions

Ask students, "What is something you know about earthquakes?" Or, "What do you think you know about where earthquakes occur?"

- Earthquakes are extremely rare events.
- Earthquakes occur randomly, not in discernible patterns.
- Earthquakes occur only where there are volcanoes.
- Earthquakes occur only close to oceans and at edges of continents.
- Volcanic eruptions are the cause of all earthquakes.
- All earthquakes and volcanic eruptions occur at or near plate boundaries.

What Students Need to Understand

- World earthquake distribution is not random.
- The occurrence of patterns in nature—such as earthquake distribution—leads scientists to look for explanations.
- Earthquakes and many geologic features—such as trenches, mid-ocean ridges, and mountains—tend to cluster along plate boundaries. The distribution of these events and features also can be used to map these boundaries.

Time Management

Construction of the globe requires approximately 15–20 minutes. The time required for student investigation and problem solving will vary depending on whether students work individually or in small groups.

This Activity can also be extended out of class. The central components can be completed in one class period.

Preparation and Procedure

To best display worldwide patterns of distribution, data need to be plotted on a flat map or on a globe. For this Activity, we use five panels that join together to form a somewhat unusual-looking world map, but one that can be folded and glued to form an approximation of a globe. This "globe" has 20 faces, each an equilateral triangle, and approaches the shape of a sphere; this geometric form is an *icosahedron*. When copying the map panels for student use, you may wish to use heavy-grade paper, such as card stock, to increase durability. (Note: Coloring and gluing the maps into a globe could take more time than you wish to consume in the classroom; if so, coloring and gluing could be omitted, or done by students as optional or even required homework.)

An attractive color icosahedron globe that shows elevations of land and seafloor can be downloaded and purchased from the National Geophysical Data Center (National Oceanic and Atmospheric Administration; NOAA). The website for online ordering and to download the globe (additional materials and information also are available) is *www.ngdc.noaa.gov/mgg/fliers/04mgg02. html*. Search for "NOAA Icosahedron Surface of Earth."

You will need to have on display a map showing the seafloor of all the oceans. If students are to plot data from **Table 1.1** on their map/globe, have at least one world atlas available in your classroom or access to the internet. Because earthquake and volcanic activity overlap considerably, you could augment this Activity by presenting maps showing the distribution of active volcanoes on Earth. (Note that in Activity 2, volcanoes are specifically considered.) Earthquake data could be supplemented from recent almanacs; the U.S. Geological Survey maps more than a century of earthquakes online at *http://earthquake.usgs.gov/ earthquakes/world/seismicity/index.php*. Search for "USGS World Seismicity Index." The reference books in the Resources section at the back of the book also contain data on volcanic activity.

It is possible that you may want students to make use of their map/globe for future activities. If so, tell students if they are to keep the map/globe at school, or if they can take it home.

Alternative Preparation

Another way to do this Activity is to use Google Earth or comparable software on computers. Google Earth will allow students to explore the data by zooming into areas of interest and learn about individual earthquakes by clicking on them. It can also enable students to overlay data for volcanoes in Activity 2.

Computers will need to have Google Earth installed. To do this, search for "Google Earth" at *www.google.com/earth/index.html*. Download the version that works for your computer and install it.

You also will need earthquake data in the format that Google Earth uses, KML files. For this data, search for "USGS Google Earth/KML files" at *http://earthquake.usgs.gov/earthquakes/eqarchives/epic/kml/*. Then choose "Earthquake Catalogs." Select a year or years to download. You can save a file and tell students how to gain access to it, or teach students to download and open the file themselves.

SAFETY ALERT

1. Indirectly vented chemical splash goggles are required when using liquid glues.

2. Use appropriate ventilation to remove vapors (if glue is used).

3. Wash hands with soap and water upon completing the lab.

Extended Learning

- Earthquakes and volcanoes do not always occur along plate edges. To appreciate this, students could seek information on two specific cases: the 1811 and 1812 earthquakes in New Madrid, Missouri, and the 1886 earthquake in Charleston, South Carolina.
- Have students investigate what happened at these locations, and how geologists explain earthquake activity far from plate boundaries.
- Students also could learn about the impact of particular earthquakes on selected communities in the United States and other countries. What are all of the harmful things that might happen during and immediately after an earthquake? What are some specific examples?
- Students could explore the science of earthquake prediction, including its methods and limitations. Why has prediction of earthquake location, timing, and intensity not been very successful thus far?
- Have students investigate the differences between the Richter and Mercalli Intensity scales, and learn why each is used to describe earthquake activity. (These measurement scales are described in Reading 3: Earthquakes.)

Interdisciplinary Study

Patterns can be found from many observations. For example, there are or may be patterns in building locations, room arrangements in buildings, places where specific plants and trees grow, musical arrangements, features in paintings and drawings, movement of planets in our solar system, and markings on paper or cloth. Each of these patterns may exist for a specific reason, and understanding the reason may provide information of use to us.

- Have students investigate patterns that they can observe. Ask them to share their findings with the class.
- Have students research the musical tone(s) at which Earth rings during earthquakes.
- Have students investigate how geologists work with historians and archeologists to use artifacts and documents to learn about earthquakes that occurred before our modern seismic network existed. Students could use the earthquakes from 1886 Charleston, 1811–1812 New Madrid, 1906 San Francisco, 1755 Lisbon, Portugal, or 1700 Cascadia.

Differentiated Learning

For students who completed this Activity quickly, invite them to explore significant earthquakes using an internet-based Geographic Information System (GIS). NOAA provides a GIS on natural hazards such as earthquakes, volcanoes, and tsunamis. Search for "NGDC Hazards ArcIMS viewer" at *http://map.ngdc.noaa.gov/website/seg/hazards/viewer.htm.*

Connections

Tsunamis are potentially large ocean waves caused by the sudden displacement of water—by an earthquake lurching the ocean floor up or down or a landslide changing the ocean floor. Have students investigate the relationship between earthquakes and tsunamis or other facets of tsunamis. Search for "NOAA Tsunami" at *www.tsunami.noaa.gov/.*

This GIS has more capabilities than Google Earth does. Once students choose the earthquake layer in the Layers menu, by selecting the Information tool in the toolbar and clicking on an epicenter, they can learn details about the earthquakes. As well, by selecting the Query tool on the same toolbar, they can select all earthquakes that meet the criteria they specify.

Answers to Student Questions

1. Most earthquakes occur in well-defined zones near the boundaries of continents and in mid-ocean. (These locations mark plate boundaries, but students will learn this in Activity 2). If earthquakes occurred randomly around the world, they would not be found primarily in these regions. (About 5% of earthquakes do not occur at or close to plate boundaries.)

2. Answers may vary depending on how accurately students plot earthquake location information from **Table 1.1**. Most of the new data points will plot in the vicinity of points already on students' map or globe.

3. Students should identify patterns and be encouraged to consider the connections between patterns. Encourage students to suggest as many plausible hypotheses as possible. Ask them how these hypotheses could be tested.

4. Students should notice the relationships among mid-ocean ridges, oceanic trenches, and earthquake activity. Again, encourage students to suggest as many plausible hypotheses as possible. Ask them how these hypotheses can be tested. If concepts related to plate tectonics do not arise in their discussions, suggest some concepts and ask students for their reactions to them.

5. Answers will vary. Some students might not have any further questions about earthquakes. However, if they do, acknowledge their questions and use them as a springboard for discussions and investigations.

Assessment

- You can assess prior student knowledge by asking students what they think they know about earthquakes or where they occur (see Preconceptions).
  To assess what students learn by doing this Activity, you could watch and listen to their conversation as they plot recent earthquakes on the globes, as they look for patterns, and as they answer the questions. You also might monitor their accuracy in plotting these recent earthquakes. If students work on this Activity in small groups, their pooled answers should reflect their discussion.

- At the end of the lesson, ask students what they now know about earthquakes or where they occur to see how their responses have changed.

- For formal summative assessment, you can grade the Answers to Student Questions.

Resources

http://earthquake.usgs.gov/prepare/

http://earthquake.usgs.gov/earthquakes/dyfi/

www.ngdc.noaa.gov/mgg/fliers/04mgg02.html

http://earthquake.usgs.gov/earthquakes/world/seismicity/index.php

www.google.com/earth/index.html

http://earthquake.usgs.gov/earthquakes/eqarchives/epic/kml/

www.tsunami.noaa.gov/

http://map.ngdc.noaa.gov/website/seg/hazards/viewer.htm

Activity 2 Planner

Activity 2 Summary

Students compare locations of volcanoes to the types of rocks erupted and tie this in to the motions of lithospheric plates. They map rocks by their main chemical components. Students then discern plate boundaries from their maps plus other sources and relate rock types to types of plate boundaries.

Activity	Subject and Content	Objective	Materials
Volcanoes and Plates	Where volcanoes form	Investigate the relationship between volcanic activity and plate boundaries, and also explore how the kind of rock that is formed at volcanoes depends on the type of plate boundary.	Each student or group will need: colored pencils

Time	Vocabulary	Key Concepts	Margin Features
50 minutes	Lithosphere, Lithospheric plates, Lava, Igneous rock, Convergent boundary, Divergent boundary, Mid-ocean ridge, Transform boundary	I: Geological patterns and lithospheric plates III: Geological phenomena and plate tectonics	What Can I Do?, Fast Fact, Connections, Resources

Scientific Inquiry	Unifying Concepts and Processes	Personal/Social Perspectives	Historical Context
Plotting and analyzing data	Using a theory to explain data	Natural hazards	Evidence supporting a new paradigm

Volcanoes and Plates

Volcanic Activity and Plate Boundaries

Background

The outer part of Earth is water, soil, and rock. The term used to describe outer, solid Earth is **lithosphere**, or **lithospheric plates**. These plates, about 100 km thick, are composed almost entirely of solid rock. Plates move a few centimeters per year.

Volcanoes are hills or mountains formed from molten rock. Molten rock sometimes flows from a fracture in a lithospheric plate onto Earth's surface. This **lava** cools and solidifies to become **igneous rock**, or molten rock solidifies just below the surface and erupts from the volcano as ash and perhaps larger solid rock particles. The accumulation on Earth's surface of the products of once-molten rock can cause volcanoes to build to high elevations.

Some of the plates move together, some move apart, and still others slide past each other. The area where two plates meet when they move together is a **convergent boundary** (**Figure 2.1**). The zone where plates meet and one plate goes beneath the other is often thousands of kilometers long, and volcanoes may form above the plate that moves down into Earth. The convergent boundary in **Figure 2.1** is the type where both converging plate edges have oceans above them.

Vocabulary

Lithosphere: The solid and rigid rock outer layer of Earth. It includes the crust and the very upper part of the mantle.

Lithospheric plates: Sections of the lithosphere that move very slowly as stiff or rigid pieces over long periods of time.

Lava: Molten rock that has erupted onto Earth's surface; also the rock that forms when that molten rock cools and then hardens.

Igneous rocks: Rocks that form when molten rock cools and hardens.

Convergent boundary: Where two plates move toward each other.

Objective

Investigate the relationship between volcanic activity and plate boundaries, and also explore how the kind of rock that is formed at volcanoes depends on the type of plate boundary.

Activity 2

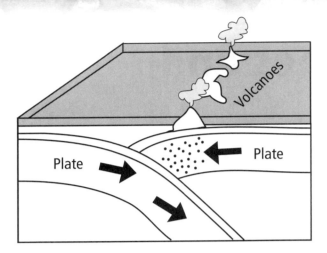

Figure 2.1
Convergent plate boundary—ocean on each plate

Another example of a convergent boundary occurs where one plate edge has an ocean on it, but there is a continent at or near the edge of the other plate. **Figure 2.2** shows this boundary.

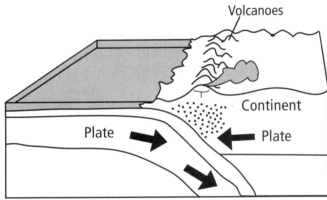

Figure 2.2
Convergent plate boundary—continent at edge of one plate

The boundary where two plates move away from each other is a **divergent boundary (Figure 2.3)**. **Mid-ocean ridges** of igneous rock typically form at a divergent boundary. These ridges are chains of volcanic mountains, most of which are below the surface of the ocean.

Vocabulary

Divergent boundary:
Where two plates move away from each other.

Mid-ocean ridge:
A high ridge in ocean basins where two lithospheric plates move away from each other or separate as molten rock rises between them. This is a divergent zone.

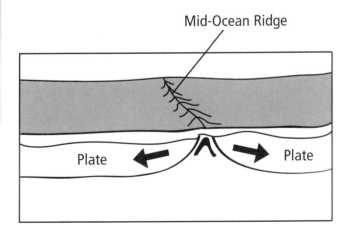

Figure 2.3
Divergent plate boundary

18

The boundary where two plates move and slide past each other is a **transform boundary** (**Figure 2.4**). The San Andreas Fault in California is a well-known example of a transform boundary or fault.

Vocabulary

Transform boundary: Boundary or fault where two lithospheric plates slide or move in opposite directions alongside or past each other.

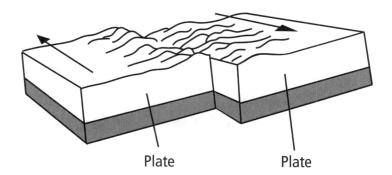

Plate   Plate

Figure 2.4
Transform plate boundary

Of the three types of plate boundaries, volcanoes are associated most often with convergent and divergent boundaries. Because convergent and divergent plate boundaries are so different—the former has plates moving toward each other and the latter has plates moving away from each other—the volcanoes that occur in each area form in different ways and have different characteristics. Volcanic rocks found in the two zones also differ. Andesite is dark grey rock, and rhyolite is light grey or pink rock; these rocks are found where plates converge. Basalt is black rock found where plates diverge. Color differences result from different amounts of iron and other constituents in the rock.

Volcanoes also occur far away from plate boundaries over hot spots. These volcanoes will be investigated in Activity 3.

Topic: volcanoes
Go to: www.scilinks.org
Code: PSCG019

Procedure

In this Activity, you will plot the locations of volcanoes using a different-colored pencil for each kind of rock associated with it. From your finished map and other sources, you will consider whether plate boundaries occur at the locations you have plotted. If you think that they do, you will try to determine the type of boundary.

1. Using the longitude and latitude coordinates in **Table 2.1**, plot all volcanoes on the World Grid Map (**BLM 2.1**). Note that **Table 2.1** shows only a small number of the world's active volcanoes.

2. **Table 2.1** indicates the percentage of several substances found in igneous rock at each volcano. These substances are silicon dioxide (SiO_2), aluminum oxide (Al_2O_3), and compounds of iron oxide ($FeO + Fe_2O_3$). Variations in the amounts of these substances produce different kinds of igneous rocks. The kind found at each volcano is listed in **Table 2.1**. Use a different-colored pencil or a different symbol to indicate the rock associated with each volcano as follows:

Materials

Each student or group will need

• colored pencils

Time

50 minutes

Activity 2

What Can I Do?

Learn which volcanoes are currently active in the United States and Pacific Ocean and contribute your own report should you see any ashfall. The U.S. Geological Survey's Volcano Hazards Program gives real-time information from volcano observatories. Search for "USGS Volcano Hazards" at *http://volcanoes. usgs.gov/*. If you see new volcanic ash, report it to the Alaska Volcano Observatory—the staff of the observatory wants you to let them know. Search for "AVO ashreport" at *www.avo.alaska.edu/ ashreport.php*. You can even collect a sample for them.

Fast Fact

When you think of volcanoes, you probably think of the western United States, where Mount St. Helens and other active volcanoes are located. The East Coast has its share of volcanoes, too, but they are ancient and have not erupted for millions of years. Although erosion long ago removed the actual volcanic mountains, deposits from these volcanoes are found in Georgia, South and North Carolina, Virginia, and states to the northeast, plus eastern Canada. In addition, there are volcanic deposits in Ireland, Scotland, and Norway of similar age and chemistry. All of these volcanic deposits were part of a single mountain range that was later split into two parts when the Atlantic Ocean formed.

- andesite—red or A
- rhyolite—blue or R
- basalt—green or B

3. Sketch lines where you think plate boundaries might occur (the relatively small amount of data you are using may make it difficult to do this accurately). On what basis did you determine your location of plate boundaries?
4. Write "divergent" where your data indicate two plates are moving apart. Write "convergent" where your data indicate two plates are moving together.

Questions and Conclusions

1. Based on what you have learned in this Activity, describe the relationship between volcanoes and plate boundaries.
2. What kind(s) of volcanic rock is (are) generally found at divergent plate boundaries? What kind(s) of volcanic rock is (are) generally found at convergent plate boundaries?
3. Compare your sketch of plate boundaries to the World Map with Plate Boundaries (**BLM 2.2**). How does your map showing volcano locations compare to those on the World Map with Plate Boundaries?
4. Volcanic rocks often can be classified based on color, as follows:
   - rhyolite—light grey, pink
   - andesite—dark grey
   - basalt—black

   The color of volcanic rocks is partly related to the proportion of silicon dioxide they contain. Which of the rocks listed in **Table 2.1** tend to have the highest proportion of silicon dioxide (SiO_2)? The next highest? The lowest?
5. Volcanic rocks with a high silicon dioxide content are likely to have explosive histories. Using **Table 2.1**, which are the three volcanoes that are or were most likely to be explosive?
6. Geologists found ancient rocks composed of andesite and rhyolite distributed over a narrow zone or belt several hundred kilometers long. These rocks probably formed at an ancient plate boundary, but the boundary no longer exists. What type of boundary was it most likely to have been?

Table 2.1: Location of Volcanoes and Composition of Magma

Volcano	Location		Magma Composition			Rock Type
	Latitude	Longitude	SiO_2	Al_2O_3	$FeO+Fe_2O_3$	
Pacific U.S.						
1. Lassen, CA	40° N	121° W	57.3	18.3	6.2	Andesite
2. Crater Lake, OR	43° N	122° W	55.1	18.0	7.1	Andesite
3. Mt. Rainier, WA	47° N	122° W	62.2	17.1	5.1	Andesite
4. Mt. Baker, WA	49° N	122° W	57.4	16.6	8.1	Andesite
U.S. Interior						
5. Yellowstone Park, WY	45° N	111° W	75.5	13.3	1.9	Rhyolite
6. Craters of the Moon, ID	43° N	114° W	53.5	14.0	15.2	Andesite
7. San Francisco Peaks, AZ	35° N	112° W	61.2	17.0	5.7	Andesite
Central America/West Indies						
8. Paricutin, Mexico	19° N	102° W	55.1	19.0	7.3	Andesite
9. Popocatepetl, Mexico	19° N	98° W	62.5	16.6	4.9	Andesite
10. Mt. Pelee, Martinique	15° N	61° W	65.0	17.8	4.5	Andesite
11. Santa Maria, Guatemala	15° N	92° W	59.4	19.9	5.9	Andesite
12. Mt. Misery, St. Kitts	17° N	63° W	59.8	18.3	7.3	Andesite
South America						
13. Cotopaxi, Ecuador	1° S	78° W	56.2	15.3	9.7	Andesite
14. Misti, Peru	16° S	71° W	60.1	19.0	5.0	Andesite
Alaska & Aleutian Islands						
15. Katmai, Alaska	58° N	155° W	76.9	12.2	1.4	Rhyolite
16. Adak, Aleutians	52° N	177° W	60.0	17.0	6.9	Andesite
17. Umnak Island, Aleutians	53° N	169° W	52.5	15.1	12.8	Andesite
18. Kamchatka, Russia	57° N	160° E	60.6	16.4	7.9	Andesite
Japan						
19. Mt. Fuji, Honshu	35° N	139° E	49.8	20.6	11.2	Basalt
20. Izu-Hakone, Honshu	35° N	139° E	53.8	14.8	13.0	Andesite
East Indies						
21. Mayon, Philippines	13° N	124° E	53.1	20.0	8.2	Andesite
22. Krakatoa, Java & Sumatra	6° S	105° E	67.3	15.6	4.3	Rhyolite
23. Karkar, New Guinea	5° S	146° E	60.1	16.4	9.6	Andesite
Central Pacific						
24. Mauna Loa, Hawaii	19° N	156° W	49.6	13.2	11.9	Basalt
25. Galapagos Islands	1° S	91° W	48.4	15.4	11.8	Basalt
26. Mariana Islands	16° N	145° E	51.2	17.3	10.9	Basalt
South Pacific						
27. Aukland, New Zealand	38° S	176° E	49.3	15.6	11.9	Basalt
28. Tahiti	18° S	149° W	44.3	14.3	12.4	Basalt
29. Samoa	13° S	172° W	48.4	13.3	12.3	Basalt
North Atlantic						
30. Surtsey, Iceland	63° N	20° W	50.8	13.6	12.5	Basalt
31. Mid-Ocean Ridge	60° N	18° W	48.2	16.5	11.7	Basalt
Africa						
32. Kilimanjaro, Tanzania	3° S	37° E	45.6	10.3	12.6	Basalt

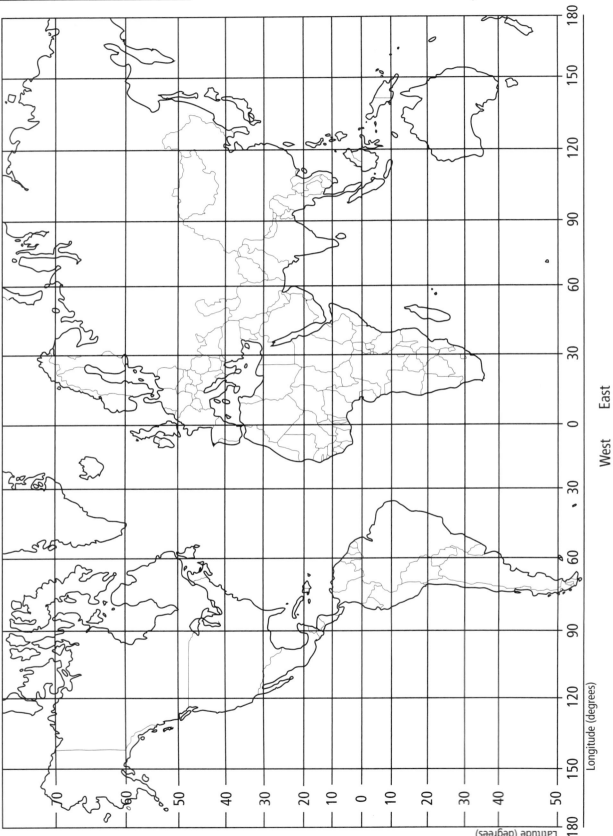

Longitude (degrees)

West   East

Latitude (degrees)

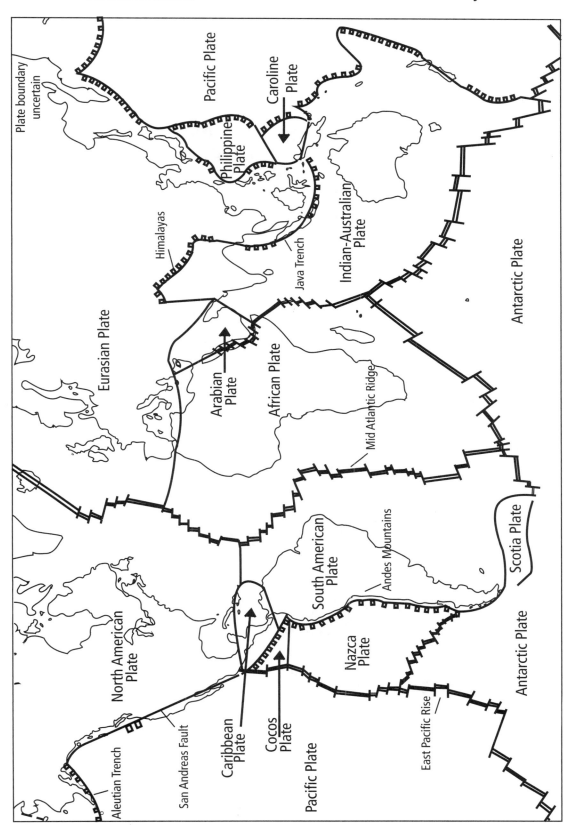

Volcanoes and Plates
Volcanic Activity and Plate Boundaries

What Is Happening?

Plate boundaries are recognized by the occurrence of relatively high levels of volcanic and seismic (earthquake) activity. It was after an extensive study of the patterns of both volcanic and earthquake activity that scientists began to piece together the theory of plate tectonics. (See the Preparation and Procedure section for suggestions on how to introduce this topic to students.)

Further study of volcanoes has shown a relationship between a specific type of plate boundary and the volcanoes that occur there. The kind of volcanic rock present at a given location depends on whether the plate boundary is divergent or convergent. Volcanic rocks at the surface thus tell geologists much about processes occurring at depths within Earth. Generally, basaltic (black igneous) rock is produced at divergent boundaries as molten rock rises to the surface and solidifies. At convergent boundaries, where one plate sinks below another, basalt from the sinking plate is remelted, often with the addition of some overlying sediments and water, to form andesite, a dark grey rock, or rhyolite, a lighter grey or pink rock. Andesite and rhyolite are found at the surface above convergent boundaries, while basalt is found at the surface above divergent boundaries.

In this Activity, students will match volcanoes with rock types on a world map. Once plotted, the information will be used to deduce the types of plate boundaries occurring at various geographic locations.

A few words about the language of plate tectonics are appropriate: The geographic areas where plates converge, diverge, or slide past one another are huge, usually covering thousands of kilometers. The word *margin* often is used

Objective

Investigate the relationship between volcanic activity and plate boundaries, and also explore how the kind of rock that is formed at volcanoes depends on the type of plate boundary.

Key Concepts

I: Geological patterns and lithospheric plates
III: Geological phenomena and plate tectonics

Materials

Each student or group will need

• colored pencils

Time

50 minutes

How Do We Know This?

How do we know that there are places (subduction zones) where one plate goes beneath another plate?

Typically, volcanoes form above the down-going plate, and earthquakes occur within the down-going plate. With sufficient monitoring stations, it is possible to determine where earthquakes occur within Earth, and thus the pattern of earthquake focal points indicates that the plate is being subducted. The various focal points (or foci) are deeper farther from the edge of the overriding plate.

to describe plate boundaries, as in "divergent or convergent margin." The word *zone* sometimes is used for the location where one plate sinks beneath another plate at a convergent boundary—as in *subduction zone*. However, to lessen the possibility for confusion among middle school students, it seems best to use "boundary" to describe where adjacent plates touch or abut.

Preconceptions

Ask students, "What can you tell me about lithospheric plate boundaries?" Or, "What do you understand about where volcanoes occur?"

- Boundaries between plates cannot be determined.
- The sinking of one plate below another plate means that Earth is gradually becoming smaller.
- The formation of volcanoes where plates move away from each other causes Earth to become larger.
- Volcanoes occur only on islands.
- Plates are found only under oceans.
- All earthquakes and volcanic eruptions occur at or near plate boundaries.

What Students Need to Understand

- Plate boundaries are recognized by the frequent occurrence of volcanoes (and earthquakes).
- Different kinds of rock are associated with volcanoes located at different types of plate boundaries.
- The kind of volcanic rock found in a given area can help determine what type of plate boundary—convergent or divergent—occurs there now (or occurred in the distant past).

Time Management

This Activity can be completed in about 50 minutes.

Preparation and Procedure

At the very beginning of this lesson, students will benefit from seeing maps with numerous volcanoes, and maps with numerous earthquake epicenters. (If you have done Activity 1: GeoPatterns, students will already be familiar with where earthquake epicenters occur.) Sources of maps include the following:

- Discovering Plate Boundaries website. Search for "Discovering Plate Boundaries" at *http://terra.rice.edu/plateboundary/downloads.html* and then choose the Downloads button from the menu. These maps (Seismology and Topography/Bathymetry) will allow students to overlay a map with volcanoes with a map of earthquakes. You will need to print the Seismology map on paper and the Topography/Bathymetry map on transparencies.

- Smithsonian's Volcanoes of the World website. Search for "Global Volcanism Program, Find a Volcano by Region" at *www.volcano.si.edu/world/find_regions.cfm*.
- If you can use and display Google Earth, you can show earthquake and volcano data simultaneously. For earthquake data, search for "USGS Google Earth/KML files," and then choose "Earthquake Catalogs" at *http://earthquake.usgs.gov/earthquakes/eqarchives/epic/kml/*. Pick a year or years for the data you want to use.
- For volcanoes, search for "Global Volcanism Program Google Earth Placemarks" at *www.volcano.si.edu/world/globallists.cfm?listpage=googleearth*. Select the "Download Holocene Volcanoes Placemark" button.

Allow students to compare where volcanoes and earthquakes occur, and to discuss them in the context of lithospheric plate boundaries. Then have them follow the Procedure and answer the Questions to refine their understanding of the relationship between plate boundaries and kinds of volcanism.

If you have samples of basalt, rhyolite, and andesite, let students examine them during the lesson.

Extended Learning

- Ask students to find information about volcanic explosions and the disasters they have caused.
- Materials from volcanoes (rocks, gases) are used in many ways; have students investigate these uses.
- Have students try to determine why many different kinds of rocks can form from molten rock.
- Have students create models or diagrams of different types of plate boundaries and volcanic eruptions.
- Have students investigate possible relationships between volcanic eruptions and earthquakes.

Interdisciplinary Study

- A *syntu* is a type of poem that originated in Japan. Its five-line form is governed by a simple set of rules:

    Line 1 - One word only
    Line 2 - An observation about line 1, using only one sense (sight, touch, etc.)
    Line 3 - A feeling, thought, or evaluation about line 1
    Line 4 - An observation about line 1 (using a different sense than line 2)
    Line 5 - A one-word meaning for line 1

Syntus are typically written about nature. Ask students to compose their own syntus. Have students illustrate their syntus and, if possible, display them in your classroom. For more on syntus, have students go to *www.gov.mb.ca/ conservation/parks/popular_parks/eastern/whiteshell_falcon.html* and search for "Syntu volcano mountain."

- Have students investigate legends and myths about ancient cities or civilizations that disappeared due to volcanic explosions (e.g., Pompeii and Santorini). Are these stories true? Partly true? How might students tell what is true and what is not?

Differentiated Learning

- For students who struggle with imagining the world in three dimensions, the globes from Activity 1 can be used for this exercise. Someone will need to label the latitude and longitude on the globes to help with plotting points for this Activity.

- For mathematically and scientifically inclined students, graphing the chemistry of the rocks (**Table 2.1**) provides a real example of the way scientists apply mathematics. Graphing SiO_2 versus $FeO + Fe_2O_3$ or $SiO_2 + Al_2O_3$ versus $FeO + Fe_2O_3$ reveals the inverse relationship between the chemical constituents. It extends and quantifies question 4. As well, these are graphs that geologists actually make and use.

- For students who finish this Activity early, encourage them to explore volcanoes using an internet-based Geographic Information System (GIS). The National Oceanic and Atmospheric Administration (NOAA) provides a GIS on natural hazards such as volcanoes, earthquakes, and tsunamis. Search for "NGDC Hazards ArcIMS viewer" at *http://map.ngdc.noaa.gov/website/seg/ hazards/viewer.htm*

Once students choose the volcano layer in the menu on the right, by selecting the Information tool in the menu on the left and clicking on an epicenter, they will learn details about the event. By selecting the Query tool on the same menu, they can select all events that meet the criteria they specify.

Answers to Student Questions

1. Volcanoes occur most frequently on Earth where plate boundaries are located.

2. Basalt. Andesite and rhyolite.

3. Student answers may vary. It is important at this stage to have students compare in order to understand the relationship between volcanoes and plate boundaries. Because students plotted data for only a small number of volcanoes, it is not possible for their map to give them a complete picture of global volcanic activity.

4. Rhyolite, andesite, then basalt.

5. Ancient volcano in Yellowstone Park, Katmai in Alaska, Krakatoa (or Krakatua) in East Indies.

6. The compositions are consistent with a convergent boundary.

Assessment

- You can assess prior student knowledge by asking the questions included in the Preconceptions. To assess what students learn by doing this Activity, watch and listen to their conversation as they plot volcanoes on the map and as they answer the questions. Monitor their accuracy in plotting the points.

- You can also ask the questions in the Preconceptions section again at the end of the lesson to see how students' responses have changed.

- If you have been using Google Earth, students can check their own work by comparing their decisions about kinds of boundaries against the U.S. Geological Survey's map. Search for "KML Earth's Tectonic Plates." You will then have the choice between opening and saving the file.

- For formal summative assessment, you can grade answers to questions and require each student to plot some points on a map to ensure they all can use latitude and longitude correctly.

Resources

http://volcanoes.usgs.gov/

www.avo.alaska.edu/ashreport.php

http://terra.rice.edu/plateboundary/downloads.html

www.volcano.si.edu/world/find_regions.cfm

http://earthquake.usgs.gov/earthquakes/eqarchives/epic/kml/

www.volcano.si.edu/world/globallists.cfm?listpage=googleearth

www.gov.mb.ca/conservation/parks/popular_parks/eastern/whiteshell_falcon.html

http://map.ngdc.noaa.gov/website/seg/hazards/viewer.htm

Activity 3 Planner

Activity 3 Summary

Students relate plate movement to trails of volcanoes by modeling a hot spot with hot colored water rising under a floating Styrofoam plate. Questions guide students to connecting their model to Hawaiian volcanoes and the Emperor Seamounts.

Activity	Subject and Content	Objective	Materials
Volcanoes and Hot Spots	Chains of volcanoes	Study volcanoes formed over hot spots, and investigate how plate movement is related to a pattern of volcanic island formation.	Each group will need: a box with clear sides, such as a plastic shoe box or an aquarium, if done as a demonstration; a small dropping bottle with a narrow neck; red food coloring; hot tap water; cold tap water; a Styrofoam "tectonic" plate; gloves and aprons

Time	Vocabulary	Key Concepts	Margin Features
30 minutes	Hot spot, Seamount	I: Geological patterns and lithospheric plates II: Movement of plates III: Geological phenomena and plate tectonics	Fast Fact, Safety Alert!, What Can I Do?, Connections, Resources

Scientific Inquiry	Unifying Concepts and Processes	Personal/Social Perspectives	Historical Context
Modeling to understand trends	Explaining data and predicting	Natural hazards	Evidence supporting a new paradigm

Volcanoes and Hot Spots

Formation of Hawaiian Islands

Background

Most of Earth's volcanoes form along a boundary where plates converge or diverge. But, volcanoes also can form a long distance from plate boundaries. These volcanoes are caused by **hot spots**—concentrations of heat directly beneath a plate. A hot spot produces molten rock, which works its way upward through the overlying plate where it may form a volcano (**Figure 3.1**). Both the Hawaiian Islands and the Emperor **Seamounts** in the Pacific Ocean are chains of active and extinct volcanic islands and underwater volcanoes that formed over a hot spot.

Vocabulary

Hot spot: Where heat is concentrated in a relatively small area beneath a lithospheric plate causing melting and volcanism.

Seamount: A volcanic peak that is below sea level.

Fast Fact

Yellowstone National Park has a hot spot underneath it that supplies the heat for Old Faithful and other geysers and hot springs.

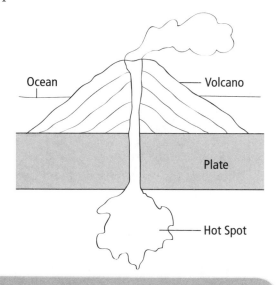

Ocean

Volcano

Plate

Hot Spot

Figure 3.1
Volcano forming above a hot spot that is below the plate

Objective

Study volcanoes formed over hot spots, and investigate how plate movement is related to a pattern of volcanic island formation.

Activity 3

In this Activity, you will simulate the creation of a volcano over a hot spot and investigate how chains of volcanoes form.

Look at the map of the Pacific Ocean below (**Figure 3.2**) and locate the Hawaiian Islands and the Emperor Seamounts. Do you see a pattern?

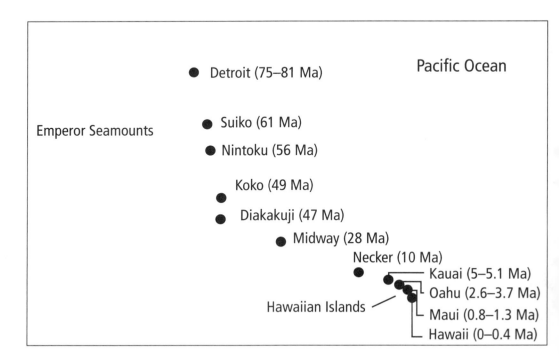

Figure 3.2
Part of the Pacific Ocean with some of the Hawaiian Islands and Emperor Seamounts. The numbers are ages (Ma), in millions of years, of rocks that make up the island or seamount.

Materials

Each group will need

- a box with clear sides, such as a plastic shoe box or an aquarium, if done as a demonstration
- a small dropping bottle with a narrow neck
- red food coloring
- hot tap water
- cold tap water
- a Styrofoam "tectonic plate"
- gloves and aprons

Time

30 minutes

Procedure

To perform this Activity, the class will be divided into groups.

1. Get a tray of materials from your teacher.
2. Fill the shoe box (or other box that will hold water) about two-thirds full with cold tap water.
3. Add hot tap water to the dropping bottle. Then add a few drops of red food coloring to the bottle.
4. Carefully place the uncapped dropping bottle in the center of the shoe box. Make sure that the cold water covers the top of the bottle. DO NOT tilt the bottle when placing it in the cold water.
5. Place a Styrofoam "plate" on the surface of the water so that one end is directly over the bottle (**Figure 3.3**).

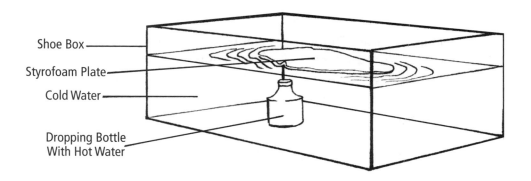

Shoe Box ———

Styrofoam Plate ———

Cold Water ———

Dropping Bottle
With Hot Water

Figure 3.3
Experimental setup for
Activity 3

6. Observe and consider what happens to the hot and cold water. Note where the hot, colored water contacts the "plate." Sometimes an air bubble can become trapped in the mouth of the bottle, blocking flow of the hot water. If this occurs, use a pencil, a straw, or a straightened paper clip to dislodge the bubble.

7. Next, simulate plate motion by gently moving the Styrofoam so that a new area of it is directly over the dropping bottle. Do this very gently so you do not disturb the water in the shoe box. Just touch the top surface of the Styrofoam carefully with one finger. Observe where the hot water now contacts the "plate."

8. Repeat step 7 until you run out of room in the box. Observe the pattern created if volcanoes had formed above the plume of rising water.

9. Once you have made your observations, empty the water from both the shoe box and the dropping bottle. Clean your equipment and work area.

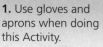

SAFETY ALERT

1. Use gloves and aprons when doing this Activity.

2. Wash hands with soap and water upon completing the lab.

Questions and Conclusions

1. What happened to the hot water in the dropping bottle?

2. What happened to the cold water in the shoe box?

3. Why does hot water (and molten rock) tend to rise?

4. Geologists believe that hot spots remain nearly stationary below lithospheric plates. What happens to an active volcano when plate movement causes the volcano to move beyond the hot spot?

5. Look at **Figure 3.4**. In which direction is the plate probably moving? Draw an arrow on the plate to indicate the direction of plate motion.

6. Where is the next volcano in **Figure 3.4** most likely to form? Mark the location with an X.

7. Look again at the map of the Pacific Ocean (**Figure 3.2**). What pattern do you observe when you look at the Hawaiian Islands and the Emperor Seamounts?

Activity 3

What Can I Do?

View Hawaiian volcanoes through the perspective of the U.S. Geological Survey's Hawaiian Volcano Observatory. Search for "HVO webcam page" at *http://volcanoes.usgs.gov/hvo/cams/*.

8. The youngest volcano in the Hawaiian Islands is at the southeastern end of the chain. What does this fact tell you about the direction of movement of the Pacific Plate?

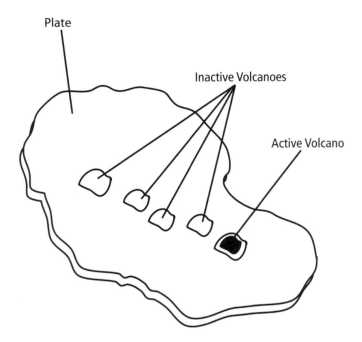

Figure 3.4
Chain of volcanoes on a moving plate above a hot spot

Volcanoes and Hot Spots
Formation of Hawaiian Islands

What Is Happening?

As a plate moves over a stationary hot spot, molten rock (magma) may periodically rise to Earth's surface, sometimes creating a volcano. As the plate continues to move over thousands and millions of years, one volcano moves off the hot spot and a new volcano forms directly over the hot spot (**Figure 3.4**). Where this process continues over time, a chain of volcanoes and volcanic islands may form. Sometimes the volcanoes that form do not rise above sea level.

The Hawaiian Islands and Emperor Seamounts are a well-known example of a volcanic chain formed above a hot spot that had a plate move over it. Names of Hawaiian volcanoes and the islands on which they occur are listed in **Table 3.1**. Also listed are the distance of each volcano from Kilauea Volcano on (the Big Island of) Hawaii, and the age of the rocks that make up the volcanoes. A quick look at the table shows an obvious trend in ages.

How Do We Know This?

How do we know that hot spots exist, and if they exist, how do we recognize their locations?

Hot spots are concentrations of high heat within and immediately below Earth's crust. We know that such concentrations of heat exist because they are responsible for melting rock and producing new igneous rocks and volcanoes over long periods of time.

Hot spots are under Hawaii, Iceland, and Yellowstone, and at least 50 other locations around the world. The heat that creates hot spots comes from deep within Earth, perhaps as deep as the mantle-core boundary.

Objective
Study volcanoes formed over hot spots, and investigate how plate movement is related to a pattern of volcanic island formation.

Key Concepts
I: Geological patterns and lithospheric plates
II: Movement of plates
III: Geological phenomena and plate tectonics

Materials
Each group will need
- a box with clear sides, such as a plastic shoe box or an aquarium, if done as a demonstration
- a small dropping bottle with a narrow neck
- red food coloring
- hot tap water
- cold tap water
- a Styrofoam "tectonic plate"
- gloves and aprons

Time
30 minutes

Table 3.1: Hawaiian Island Volcanoes, Distance From Kilauea Volcano, and Age of the Volcanic Rocks

Volcano and Island	Distance (km) From Kilauea on Island of Hawaii (Big Island)	Approximate Age (Million Years)
Loihi Volcano (submarine) near Island of Hawaii	30 km (to southeast)	0
Kilauea Volcano on Island of Hawaii	0 km	0–0.4
Mauna Kea Volcano on Island of Hawaii	54 km (to northwest)	0.4
Haleakala Volcano on east Maui Island	182 km (to northwest)	0.8
Kahoolawe Volcano and Island (southwest of Maui Island)	185 km (to northwest)	1.0
Kahalawai Volcano on west Maui Island	221 km (to northwest)	1.3
Lanai Volcano on Lanai Island	226 km (to northwest)	1.3
East Molokai Volcano on Molokai Island	256 km (to northwest)	1.8
West Molokai Volcano on Molokai Island	280 km (to northwest)	1.9
Koolau Volcano on Oahu Island	339 km (to northwest)	2.6
Waianae Volcano on Oahu Island	374 km (to northwest)	3.7
Kauai Volcano on Kauai Island	519 km (to northwest)	5.1

Source: Data from Hawaiian Center for Volcanology: *www.soest.hawaii.edu/GG/HCV/haw_formation.html*

Magma rises through the solid rock that makes up a plate because magma is less dense. The density of a substance is directly related to its temperature. Since hot water is less dense than cold water, it rises through cold water. In this Activity, the dropping bottle filled with hot water represents a hot spot below a plate; a piece of Styrofoam represents the plate. The hot water in the dropping bottle rises to the bottom of the Styrofoam "plate." If this were a real hot spot below a real plate, rock would melt at this location, and a volcano could form directly above. As the plate moves, a new part of it migrates directly over the hot spot and a new volcano begins to form. The old volcano becomes inactive. As the plate continues to move, a chain of inactive volcanoes is formed. There is one active volcano at the end of the chain. The pattern produced by the Hawaiian Islands and the Emperor Seamounts provides convincing evidence of plate motion.

To help visualize this process, WGBH's Teachers' Domain has a short video animation, "Plate Tectonics: The Hawai'ian Archipelago," that can be downloaded at no cost. If you wish to show this to students, wait until after they do the Activity—the Activity will have more impact this way. Search for "WGBH Hawaiian Archipelago" at *www.teachersdomain.org/resource/ess05.sci.ess. earthsys.hawaii/*.

Preconceptions

Ask students, "What do you know about where volcanoes erupt?" When or if they say "along plate boundaries," ask students if they can think of exceptions.

- Volcanic eruptions cannot occur far from the boundaries of plates.
- Hot spots occur only at plate boundaries and that is where they form volcanoes.
- Plates move too slowly for their movement to be measured.
- Plates have nothing to do with Earth's surface.
- Molten or solid rock within the Earth cannot rise toward or to Earth's surface.
- Volcanoes serve no useful purposes.

What Students Need to Understand

- Molten rock (magma) rises because it is less dense than surrounding rock, just as hot water rises through cold water.
- Not all volcanoes occur at plate boundaries.
- Volcanoes that are a long way from plate boundaries usually formed above an essentially stationary hot spot.
- A chain of volcanoes can form above a hot spot as the result of movement of the plate.
- The formation of a chain of volcanoes above a hot spot requires many millions of years.

Time Management

This Activity can be completed in approximately 30 minutes.

Preparation and Procedure

Before beginning the Activity, cut the "tectonic plate" out of thin Styrofoam like that used for packaging meat. Each plate should fit within the width of the box. It should be long enough to allow room for several volcanoes to develop and short enough to allow movement from one end of the box to the other.

Extended Learning

- How does an extinct volcano differ from an active volcano? Students could investigate eruptions of volcanoes that were thought by many to be extinct.
- Students could obtain information about other hot spots and their effects. (The hot spot under Yellowstone National Park might be a good one to investigate.)
- Satellite (e.g., GPS) data now can provide specific information about how fast and in what direction individual plates are moving. Ask students to learn about GPS, and have them design an experiment to determine how fast the plate on which they live is moving.
- In a few places close beneath Earth's surface, there is, at least periodically, a small amount of molten rock. Much of this material reaches Earth's surface where it cools and solidifies. But, some molten rock does not reach the surface. Have students investigate, or at least speculate, why some molten rock stays beneath Earth's surface where it, too, eventually becomes solid.

Interdisciplinary Study

- The Hawaiian Island chain generally is considered one of Earth's most beautiful locations. What is beauty? Ask students to give their explanation or definition of beauty.
- Have students write a description of the most beautiful thing they have ever seen. Are beautiful things always valuable because they are beautiful?
- Have students use data from **Table 3.1** to determine how fast the plate on which the Hawaiian Islands are located has moved over the past 5 million years. (The answer is about 10 cm/year.) At this rate, how long would it take the plate to move 1 km? 1 mi.?
- Recent DNA analyses suggest that many Polynesians, including Samoans, Tahitians, and Hawaiians, are genetically linked to people from parts of Southeast Asia. Ask students to learn the basics of DNA analysis. Then have them speculate and discuss how it might have been possible over a thousand years ago for people to move very long distances across the Pacific Ocean.

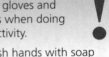

38

Differentiated Learning

As an optional assignment, students might plot the information in **Table 3.1** on graph paper (i.e., distance of sample from the Big Island of Hawaii versus age). The graph that is obtained does not show a perfect correlation (e.g., a straight line through all data points). Ask students why a line through the data points is not straight. (Answers will vary, but possible good ones include measurement errors, limited samples [a specific island may have formed over a period of time that is not adequately indicated by the available age information], speed of plate might have changed, or hot spot might have moved.)

Answers to Student Questions

1. Hot water rose from the dropping bottle toward the bottom of the Styrofoam "plate."
2. Cold water flowed into the dropping bottle and formed a layer at the bottom of the bottle as hot water flowed out.
3. Hot water and molten rock are both less dense than their surrounding materials. Less dense materials rise through more dense materials.
4. The active volcano becomes inactive and eventually extinct.
5. The plate is moving to the upper left (or northwest).
6. The X drawn by students should be to the right and perhaps a bit below the lowermost symbol (active volcano).
7. The Hawaiian Islands and Emperor Seamounts form a continuous chain of volcanoes across the Pacific Ocean. The volcanoes are generally oriented from northwest to southeast, but there is a distinct bend in the middle of the chain. That bend suggests the direction of plate motion has changed over time.
8. Recent Pacific plate movement has been to the northwest.

Assessment

- You can assess prior student knowledge by asking the questions included in the Preconceptions section.
- Conduct formative assessment by circulating as students do this Activity.
- You can also ask the questions in the Preconceptions section again at the end of the lesson to see how students' responses have changed.
- For formal summative assessment, you can grade answers to questions.

Connections

Have students compare and contrast the movement of ocean currents and air masses to the movement of hot molten rock.

Resources

www.soest.hawaii.edu/GG/HCV/haw_formation.html

www.teachersdomain.org/resource/ess05.sci.ess.earthsys.hawaii/

http://volcanoes.usgs.gov/hvo/cams/

Activity 4 Planner

Activity 4 Summary

Students analyze a hard-boiled egg as a model for Earth's interior structure. They then scrutinize and evaluate other objects as models for Earth.

Activity	Subject and Content	Objective	Materials
All Cracked Up	Earth's layers, models	Use models to understand some of Earth's interior features and evaluate the realism of various models.	For your demonstration: several hard-boiled eggs, preferably brown or dyed; one small kitchen knife (or cut eggs in half at home and wrap tightly to keep moist and shell in place); narrow and broad-tipped markers For each student group: at least three other objects to serve as Earth models

Time	Vocabulary	Key Concepts	Margin Features
30 minutes	Crust, Plates, Mantle, Asthenosphere, Core	I: Geological patterns and lithospheric plates II: Movement of plates	Safety Alert!, Fast Fact, Connections

Scientific Inquiry	Unifying Concepts and Processes	Historical Context
Modeling, visualizing	Representing data with a model	Changing knowledge of Earth's interior

All Cracked Up
Model of Earth's Layers

Background

In this Activity, you will learn more about the structure or layering of Earth. In addition, you will look at things that could be used to represent or model Earth's interior.

Models

For most people, it is difficult to think about really large or really small objects. In both cases, their size makes it difficult or impossible to see features or details that you might like to be able to observe. Planets are too big and atoms are too small to be easily studied. To solve this problem, people sometimes build scale models, like shrinking a planet down to the size of a basketball or blowing an atom up to the size of a baseball. Examples of other things sometimes represented by scale models are buildings, airplanes, cars, and animals. Scale models can make objects easier to study, and they also make it easier to learn about patterns found in nature.

Good models often emphasize only some parts of an object. A model car, for example, may show just its shape and appearance but not how the engine works. A classroom globe usually shows national boundaries but not what kind of rocks make up Earth's surface. Different scale models serve different purposes. Geologists sometimes build scale models to study Earth. In this Activity, you will examine several models of Earth as you learn more about Earth's interior.

SCI LINKS
THE WORLD'S A CLICK AWAY

Topic: Earth's interior
Go to: *www.scilinks.org*
Code: PSCG041

Objective
Use models to understand some of Earth's interior features and evaluate the realism of various models.

Activity 4

Vocabulary

Crust: Earth's outermost compositional layer, made of solid rock.

Plates: Pieces of the lithosphere, the solid, rigid rock outer layer of Earth. It includes the crust and part of the mantle.

Mantle: The layer below the crust and above the core. It is made of solid rock that is somewhat different in composition than the crust.

Asthenosphere: The upper part of the mantle that is solid yet flows slowly.

Core: Earth's innermost division, made of mostly metals, especially iron and nickel.

Earth's Structure

The name of the solid outer layer of Earth can seem confusing because sometimes **crust** is used, and sometimes **plate** or plates. But, the layers called crust and plates are not the exact same thing. Plates include all of the crust plus the upper part of the **mantle** layer below the crust. **Figure 4.1** is a simplified sketch of the outer part of Earth showing how the crust and mantle relate, and also how the crust and plates relate. It also shows the **asthenosphere**, the layer below the plate. The asthenosphere is part of the upper mantle.

Geologists often use crust, mantle, and **core** when talking about Earth's interior, especially if they are interested in what makes up the layers—the compositional differences between the layers. For example, rock samples from the crust usually have a different composition than rocks from the mantle, and thus they are different kinds of rocks. (Earth's core starts about 2,900 km below Earth's surface, and is not shown in **Figure 4.1**.)

In the 1960s, geologists realized that continents have moved and are still moving (*continental drift*). But, the movement was not that "simple." More evidence showed it was not just continents that moved. Instead, all of Earth's crust moved, as well as a significant amount of rock under the crust. This solid and also brittle rock is what we call lithosphere or plates. The plates cover all of Earth—land areas and oceanic areas. Because the plates are everywhere, and because interactions between moving plates have been so important in changing Earth, geologists often refer to the upper layer of Earth as lithosphere or plates (even though *crust* is still a useful term). Plates are rock that is

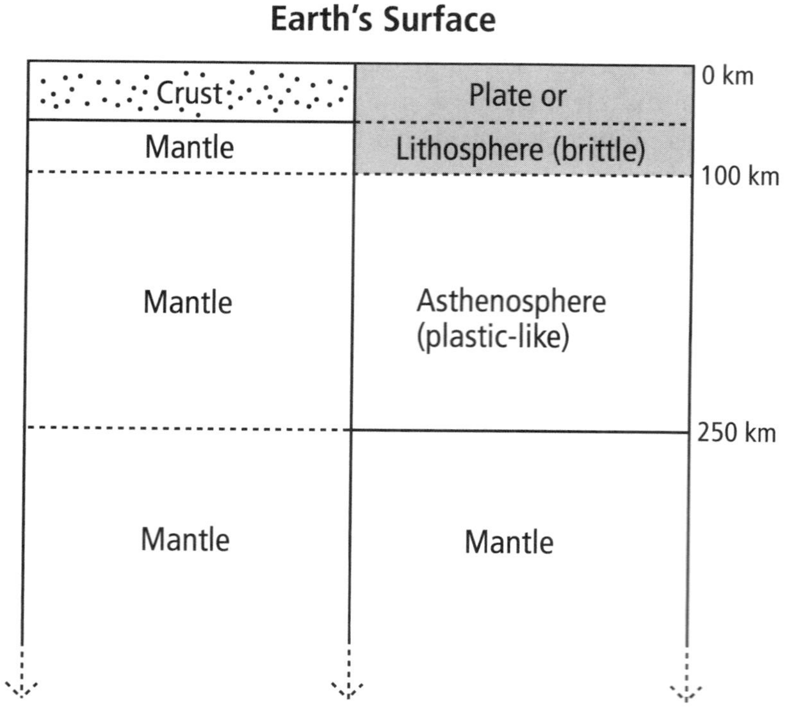

Earth's Surface

Figure 4.1
Outer Earth's layers and spatial relationships between compositional layers (crust and mantle) and layers with different physical properties (lithosphere—or plates—and asthenosphere). Distances are below Earth's surface.

relatively cold, solid, and brittle that moves on top of the asthenosphere, a layer of rock that is hot, solid, but relatively soft (**Figure 4.1**).

Beneath the mantle is the outer core and inner core. The hot molten (liquid) outer core apparently is composed mostly of metals, primarily iron and nickel. The inner core is believed to be solid and, like the outer core, composed primarily of iron and nickel.

From Earth's surface to its center, Earth materials become denser and hotter, and pressures increase. Because of the very high temperatures, you might think that everything would be molten. However, the very high pressures make it difficult or impossible for most materials to melt in the interior of Earth.

Procedure

1. Your teacher will do a short demonstration using an egg as a model of Earth (**Figure 4.2**). During the demonstration, make notes in **BLM 4.1** about the strengths and weaknesses of using an egg as an Earth model. Initially, look for representations of crust, mantle, and core. After you have done this, see if you can also use the egg to represent the lithosphere (plates), asthenosphere, mantle (the part below the asthenosphere), and core (outer and inner, if possible).

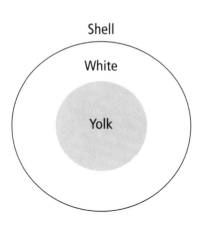

Shell

White

Yolk

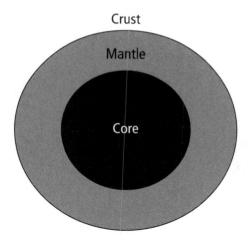

Crust

Mantle

Core

2. Your teacher will supply several different objects to serve as models for Earth. In **BLM 4.1**, write the name or type of object after Model A, B, C, and D. Based on your understanding of Earth, determine each model's strengths and weaknesses. Write your evaluations on **BLM 4.1**.

Materials

For your demonstration, you will need

- several hard-boiled eggs, preferably brown or dyed
- one small kitchen knife (If having a knife is forbidden at school, cut eggs in half at home and wrap them tightly to keep them moist and the shell in place.)
- narrow and broad-tipped markers

Each student group will need

- at least three other objects to serve as Earth models

Time

30 minutes

Figure 4.2
Comparison of major compositional layers in egg and Earth

SAFETY ALERT

1. Never eat food used in the lab Activity or bring any other food or drink in to the lab.

2. Wash hands with soap and water upon completing the lab.

Activity 4

Fast Fact

The Earth is not really a sphere. The radius to the equator is 3,678 km. The radius to the poles is 3,657 km. Thus, the Earth is almost round but is a bit flattened because of its spin.

Questions and Conclusions

1. How does the structure of a hard-boiled egg compare to the crust, mantle, and core structure of Earth? What do the egg's layers represent? What might the cracks represent?

2. How do Earth's layers compare in composition and properties with the egg's layers?

3. Can an egg be used as a satisfactory model for Earth's lithosphere (plates) and asthenosphere, plus the rest of the mantle, and the core? How? (Hint: Look very carefully under the shell—could the membrane there represent the asthenosphere?)

4. Overall, is the cracked egg a useful model for Earth? Why or why not?

5. Unlike the eggshell sections, Earth's plates move relative to one another. A plate may move away from another plate, or it may move toward it. Earthquakes often result from interactions between plates. Predict what other consequences might result from plate motion.

6. Why do we use scale models when studying geology?

7. Of the several possible nonegg models of Earth, which do you feel is most appropriate? Why?

8. Of the several possible nonegg models of Earth, which do you feel is least appropriate? Why?

Models	Strengths	Weaknesses
1. Egg Model		
2. Model A: _____		
3. Model B: _____		
4. Model C: _____		
5. Model D: _____		

All Cracked Up
Model of Earth's Layers

What Is Happening?

Scale models represent objects in manageable sizes. Students need to appreciate how models are used in scientific research and elsewhere. They also must learn how to evaluate models for strengths and weaknesses. This Activity presents several different Earth models and encourages their close examination and evaluation.

The crust, mantle, and core layers of Earth are defined by their different compositions. The lithosphere (plates) and asthenosphere layers are defined by their properties. These two layers are both almost entirely solid rock layers: the lithosphere is cold, rigid, and brittle, and the asthenosphere is hot, soft, and plastic-like. (Activities 9 and 10 explore these properties.) The lithosphere consists of the crust and the uppermost portion of the mantle. Lithosphere is broken into a series of plates that move independently of one another. Although slow in human terms—plates usually move at rates of only a few centimeters each year—this motion can be substantial over thousands and millions of years. Interactions of lithospheric plates can cause earthquakes and volcanoes. They also can result in the creation of mountain ranges on land, mid-ocean ridges, and ocean trenches. **Table 4.1** provides details about Earth's interior. There may be more information in **Table 4.1** than you would want to give to students, but some of it might be of use to them.

Objective

Use models to understand some of Earth's interior features and evaluate the realism of various models.

Key Concepts

I. Geological patterns and lithospheric plates
II: Movement of plates

Materials

For your demonstration, you will need

- several hard-boiled eggs, preferably brown or dyed
- one small kitchen knife (If having a knife is forbidden at school, cut eggs in half at home and wrap them tightly to keep them moist and the shell in place.)
- narrow and broad-tipped markers

Each student group will need

- at least three other objects to serve as Earth models

Time

30 minutes

How Do We Know This?

How do we know that Earth's interior consists of three regions of different composition: crust, mantle, and core?

Some earthquake or seismic waves travel though Earth's interior. When these waves encounter material of different composition and different properties, portions of the waves are reflected back to Earth's surface. By knowing the length of time it took for the waves to travel back to the surface, and the velocity of the waves, it is possible to calculate the depths within Earth where there is a change in material. This is how these boundaries were determined.

Table 4.1: Earth's Interior and Earth's Layers

Earth's Interior	
Characteristics	Layered structure Average density for Earth: ~5.5 g/cm³ (water = 1 g/cm³) Radius of Earth: ~6,400 km (4,000 mi.) Circumference of Earth: ~40,000 km (25,000 mi.) Temperature and pressure increase toward Earth's center
Sources of Information About Earth's Interior	Samples (mines—but only go ~3 km deep; drilling—maximum only ~12 km deep; volcanic eruptions—from as deep as ~200 km)
	Information about deeper Earth from (1) earthquake (seismic) waves; (2) meteorites

Earth's Layers	
Layers With Different Compositions: Crust, Mantle, Core	**Crust:** Solid: Minerals and rocks (igneous, sedimentary, metamorphic) Thickness: ~8–50 km Density ~2.8 g/cm³ (average)
	Mantle: Solid (mostly); similar to stony meteorites Thickness: ~2,900 km Density ~4.5 g/cm³ (average)
	Core: Outer is liquid; inner is solid; composition similar to iron meteorites Thickness—Outer: ~2,300 km; Inner: ~1,200 km (radius) Density up to ~13 g/cm³
Outer Earth Layers With Different Physical Properties: Lithosphere, Asthenosphere	**Lithosphere (or plates)—includes all of the crust and the uppermost mantle** Thickness: ~100 km (average) Solid, cold, relatively brittle or rigid rock
	Asthenosphere—part of mantle Depth of 100–250 km Solid rock (mostly), but hot, plastic-like and able to flow very slowly

Preconceptions

Ask students if they have ever made models and, if so, what kinds? Did they ever think about whether a model they made was a good representation of the real thing? In what ways? In what ways did it fall short? In what ways did it disappoint them?

- All of Earth's plates are a very long distance from us.
- Everywhere on Earth there is a molten layer of rock close to the surface.
- Earth is completely solid.
- Earth's plates are arranged like a stack of dishes.
- Except for its rocky crust, Earth is molten.
- Plates are far below Earth's surface.
- The center or core of Earth is hollow.
- Earth's crust and plates are the exact same things.

What Students Need to Understand

- Earth's interior has several layers, differing in their chemical and physical properties.
- Earth's outer layer—the lithosphere—is broken into pieces called plates.
- Earth's plates move independently of one another. Their movements and interactions produce geologic features and events.
- Models are useful, but they have both strengths and weaknesses.

Time Management

This Activity can be completed in approximately 30 minutes.

Preparation and Procedure

This Activity is in two parts:

1. You will lead a demonstration using an egg as an Earth model.
2. Students will examine and assess additional models of Earth for strengths and weaknesses.

Demonstration

1. Show students a plain hard-boiled egg. Ask them what would happen if you tapped the egg on a hard surface. Discuss with students the characteristics of materials that are brittle.
2. Gently tap the egg on a hard surface until cracks are produced. Using the narrow tip of a permanent marker, outline enough of the cracks so that there are about 8–12 large "plates" and roughly 6–8 smaller ones. (Do not worry

SAFETY ALERT

1. Never eat food used in the lab Activity or bring any other food or drink in to the lab.

2. Wash hands with soap and water upon completing the lab.

about cracking the egg in too many places. You probably will end up with more cracks than intended; just don't mark all of them!)

3. Discuss with students how the egg's cracked shell might provide a useful model for Earth's surface. Introduce or remind students of the concept of Earth's plates or lithosphere.

4. Using a sharp, wet knife, cut the egg in half so you have a circular section through the yolk. If the knife blade is wet, the egg is less likely to stick to the blade. Also, have another uncracked hard-boiled egg available in case the first one falls apart while cutting. One half of the cut egg will model Earth's cross-section. (Note what would happen if you were to cut the egg lengthwise: the shape of the cut surface would not be circular; you could do this and point out to students that this would result in a poorer model.)

5. Make a large dot in the center of the yolk with the broad tip of your marker. The dot will represent Earth's inner core. The shell can represent Earth's crust. (Note: Initially focus class discussion on crust, mantle, and core—we will discuss lithosphere and asthenosphere very shortly.) The egg white represents the mantle. The outer part of the yolk represents the outer core and the colored dot in the yolk's center represents the inner core.

   After students have considered crust, mantle, and core, ask if closer study of the egg might make it possible to find something to represent lithosphere and asthenosphere, as well as the rest of the mantle and the core. The shell could be lithosphere, the membrane under the shell could represent the asthenosphere, and the egg white and yolk could represent the (rest of) the mantle and the core, respectively. Eggs have another possible layer (although a very thin one)—the shell color of a brown egg, or eggs could be dyed.

6. Ask students to identify the strengths and weaknesses of the cracked egg model and record them in **BLM 4.1**. Be sure they understand that one major weakness of the model is the fact that Earth's plates move independently and interact with other plates, causing earthquakes and volcanoes.

Students Examine and Assess Models

For the second part of this Activity, students examine models of Earth for strengths and weaknesses. You might want to have students do this Activity in groups. Give students three or four possible models. They do not all need to be approximately spherical (but if not spherical, students should note that this is a weakness of using the object as a model). You also could give students a flat (two-dimensional) diagram of Earth's interior (but, again, they should recognize this limitation). Cut the objects in half before class, or provide things that you can easily and quickly cut just before giving them to students. Possibilities might include a Styrofoam ball, an apple or orange or other fruit or vegetable, balls made of clay, chocolate cream eggs, or a tennis ball that has been opened.

Extended Learning

Loss of details on models much smaller that the actual objects is sometimes difficult to understand. Students may have difficulty appreciating how reductions in scale can "flatten" mountains and valleys, and make all but the largest lakes and rivers disappear on a perfectly scaled globe that shows details of Earth's surface. For example, even though Mount Everest has an elevation of about 8,850 m, if you try to accurately represent the height of this mountain on a globe with a diameter about 0.3 m, the top of Everest would be only 0.02 cm above the globe's sea level. This is about the width of a period on a normal printed page; thus Mount Everest would disappear at that scale!

- Have students construct their own scale models of Earth's crust or lithosphere in cross-section using clay or other materials. Encourage students to be creative (but accurate) in their model design. Have them pay particular attention to what happens to certain topographical features when different scales are used. They could compare and contrast their findings with pictures of the topographical features with which they have been working.

- To give students a better understanding of how relatively insignificant changes over a short time can amount to something significant over long periods of geologic time, have students calculate the consequences of 1 cm of movement per year for 1 million years, 10 million years, and so on.

Interdisciplinary Study

- Have students investigate the use of models in fields other than geology. It is likely that many students will have made or used models of cars, planes, dinosaurs, ships, houses (e.g., dollhouses), and so on. Topographic maps are models of landscapes. Models of the solar system are used to demonstrate planetary motions. Atoms are so small that models are needed to understand their properties and behavior.

- Computer modeling and simulations are now widespread. Students might explore these applications.

- In this Activity, we have talked about an Earth that is nearly spherical. Five hundred years ago, many people thought Earth was flat. What observations many years ago led people to recognize the actual shape of Earth?

- Ask students to locate descriptions of Earth that developed in other cultures and in other historical periods.

Differentiated Learning

For students who are abstract thinkers, ask them to describe generally what makes a model valid or useful. Does a model need to be a physical model, for instance? Is a map a model? A sketch? A concept map? An algebraic equation?

Connections

Have students research the structure of other planetary bodies and propose or even build models of them.

Answers to Student Questions

1. From outside to inside, the different compositional layers are as follows:
   Shell = crust
   Egg white = mantle
   Egg yolk (outer) = outer core
   Center of egg yolk (dot) = inner core
   Students also could reply:
   Pigments on the outer surface = soil, oceans
   Cracks represent the boundaries between plates.

2. Answers will vary. Possible answers include the following: all of the egg is solid; none is molten or hot; none of the egg is metal or rock.

3. An egg can be used as a satisfactory model, but it is not perfect. For example, the membrane is (relatively) much too thin. Answers should include some of the following points: The outer portion of both Earth and the egg are solid and brittle, while the underlying layer is solid but not brittle; the cooked egg is solid, and most of Earth is solid; the cross-sectional shapes are similar; of course, the materials that make up Earth and the egg are very different.

4. The cracked egg is a useful model for Earth, but quite a few things do not "fit." Answers will vary, but they should include the fact that both Earth and the egg are made up of layers with different characteristics. The cracked shell is reasonably analogous to lithospheric plates. On the other hand, the egg's elongate shape is not a good representation of Earth.

5. Possible consequences that might result from plate motion include mountain ranges, volcanoes, and rift valleys.

6. While student answers will vary, they should be aware that models are used in many instances to study subjects where the real thing cannot easily be studied. Models can significantly enhance learning, but they also have important limitations.

7. Correct answers will vary, depending on the possible models that students were given.

8. Correct answers will vary, depending on the possible models that students were given.

Assessment

- You can monitor and guide students' conversations while they work with models.
- For formal summative assessment, you could provide another model students have not yet seen. Ask them to evaluate its utility as a model for Earth and explain their reasoning.
- You could also grade students' answers to the questions.

Activity 5 Planner

Activity 5 Summary

Students make and use a paper model to understand seafloor spreading. By doing so, they explore patterns of rock ages and rock magnetism parallel to mid-ocean ridges.

Activity	Subject and Content	Objective	Materials
Seafloor Spreading	Divergent plate boundaries, ocean floor patterns	Construct a paper model to illustrate why seafloor is newest or youngest at mid-ocean ridges, and is relatively old at and near trenches.	Each group will need: one copy of the seafloor spreading model; scissors; tape; orange-, yellow-, green-, and blue-colored pencils or crayons

Time	Vocabulary	Key Concepts	Margin Features
50 minutes or less	Plate tectonics, Seafloor spreading, Trenches	I: Geological patterns and lithospheric plates II: Movement of plates III: Geological phenomena and plate tectonics	Fast Fact, What Can I Do?, Connections

Scientific Inquiry	Unifying Concepts and Processes	Technology	Personal/Social Perspectives	Historical Context
Modeling	Modeling to explicate a process	Adapting technology for science	Teamwork	Evolving theories

Seafloor Spreading
Divergent Plate Boundaries

Activity **5**

Background

About 50 years ago, geologists and oceanographers discovered that there are both age and magnetic patterns in the seafloor. This provided more evidence that plates both exist and move. It resulted in the development of the theory of **plate tectonics**, which describes the motions of plates and the interactions between them that occur at plate boundaries.

The new discoveries established that new seafloor rock has continually been forming over millions of years at mid-ocean ridges, which wind throughout all of Earth's oceans. Molten rock, called magma, rises toward the seafloor from inside Earth. It cools as it rises, and some of it solidifies before it reaches the surface. Some molten rock spills out into the surface, solidifying and forming volcanoes at the mid-ocean ridges. This new rock is pulled apart at mid-ocean ridges, forming two rock masses that slowly move away from each other in opposite directions. In other words, the seafloor "spreads" very slowly away from the ridges. Geologists refer to this process as **seafloor spreading**.

In other areas of seafloor, there are long, narrow **trenches** where the ocean is extremely deep—the deepest is 10,911 m. In contrast to the youngest or newest seafloor rock found at mid-ocean ridges, the oldest rock is found at or close to trenches. The oldest seafloor rock is "only" about 180 million years old. Many continental rocks are much older than this; the oldest continental rock is over 4 billion years old. These age differences or patterns are an important part of the plate tectonics story.

Vocabulary

Plate tectonics: Geologists' understanding of the way rigid plates of the outer solid Earth move and interact.

Seafloor spreading: Molten rock rises from below mid-ocean ridges, cools, and solidifies (crystallizes) into new seafloor rock. This new rock splits into two portions that move as the plates move away from each other.

Trenches: Deep linear areas of the ocean where a plate made of relatively old seafloor rock sinks into the asthenosphere.

Topic: seafloor spreading
Go to: *www.scilinks.org*
Code: PSCG055

Objective

Construct a paper model to illustrate why seafloor is newest or youngest at mid-ocean ridges, and is relatively old at and near trenches.

Activity 5

Fast Fact

Four billion years is also 4,000,000,000 years, 4,000 million years, or 4.0×10^9 years.

Materials

Each group will need
- one copy of the seafloor spreading model
- scissors
- tape
- orange-, yellow-, green-, and blue-colored pencils or crayons

Time

50 minutes or less

As rocks at the mid-ocean ridges crystallize, some minerals containing iron line up with Earth's magnetic field. They point to the magnetic poles, just as compass needles do. These minerals capture the orientation of Earth's magnetic field at the time of their formation. However, Earth's magnetic field changes over time. The strength varies, the poles wander, and they switch north for south and back again—their polarity reverses like flipping a bar magnet 180°. The record of polarity reversals is frozen in oceanic rocks from the mid-ocean ridges to the trenches as the seafloor spreads.

In this Activity, you will construct a paper model to investigate patterns that exist in the rocks or plates that make up the seafloor at mid-ocean ridges.

Procedure

1. Locate **BLM 5.1**, the seafloor spreading model pattern. Make three cuts the length of the page or sheet so that you end up with two strips, each labeled orange-yellow-green-blue. Then, cut along the dashed lines of the left side of **BLM 5.1** (marked Slit A, Slit B, and Slit C) to make the three slits.
2. Color the areas indicated on the two strips with crayons or colored pencils.
3. Tape together the orange ends of the strips with the colored sides facing each other (**Figure 5.1**).

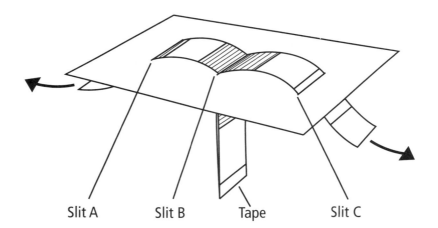

Figure 5.1
How to assemble BLM 5.1 and use as seafloor spreading model

4. Thread the taped end (orange) of the two strips through slit B of the sheet with the three slits. Pull one blue end down through slit A and the other through slit C (**Figure 5.1**). Be sure to have the colored sides of the strips facing up.
5. Pull the strips through slits A and C so that the same color on each strip emerges at the same time from slit B. (The colors that you see on one strip should be a mirror image of what you see on the other strip—this is the pattern you are looking for.)

Questions and Conclusions

1. How does what is happening at slit B correspond to what happens where the seafloor is spreading and moving in opposite directions? What feature occurs at the corresponding location on the seafloor?

2. What features on the seafloor are comparable to slits A and C? What is happening at slits A and C?

3. If you were to sample and date the rocks along the colored strip starting at slit B and moving toward slit A, what change, if any, would you see in the age of the rocks?

4. If you were to sample and date the rocks along the colored strip starting at slit B and moving toward slit C, what change, if any, would you see in the age of the rocks?

5. In this model, what do the strips represent? What do the colors represent?

6. New seafloor rock is continually being formed at mid-ocean ridges, and old seafloor rock is continually being removed from Earth's surface at ocean trenches. Rock on continents also is continually formed but is not removed. How then, would the age of the oldest rocks on the continents compare with the age of the oldest rocks on the seafloor?

7. What are the strengths and weaknesses of this model as a demonstration of seafloor spreading?

8. Look at the map showing Earth's plates and the direction of their motion in **Figure 5.2**. Is the Atlantic Ocean growing or shrinking? Explain. The Pacific Ocean is staying about the same size. Why?

Fast Fact

Iceland straddles a mid-ocean ridge where the seafloor spreads slowly—about 2.5 cm per year in the North Atlantic. As the seafloor spreads, so does the island. That means that an Icelander will see his or her country expand by about 2 m during the average lifespan of 82 years.

What Can I Do?

Scientists measure tectonic plate motions now with Global Positioning System (GPS) units. You could learn to use a GPS unit and set up a GPS trail for a friend to follow. You could learn how GPS works, design an experiment to use it to measure plate motion, and then research how scientists make the measurements.

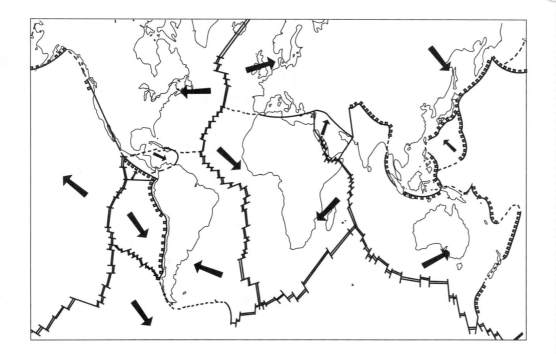

Figure 5.2
World map showing plates and continents and direction of plate movement

Slit A

Orange | Orange

Yellow | Yellow

Slit B

Green | Green

Slit C

Blue | **Blue**

Seafloor Spreading
Divergent Plate Boundaries

What Is Happening?

The formation of new seafloor occurs at the boundary between two plates that are moving away from each other. As the plates diverge, molten rock from beneath the surface moves upward between them. The molten rock solidifies below and at the surface along mid-ocean ridges, is split, and then is pulled apart by the motion of the plates. New rock continues to be formed at the ridge, while the older rock moves away from the ridge on either side. (Reading 1: Plate Tectonics provides an explanation of this concept.) Some students might think that the divergent plate motion would produce huge gaps between plates, but this is prevented by the continuing injection of magma.

Seafloor spreading results in nearly symmetrical patterns of rock of different ages on both sides of mid-ocean ridges, or spreading centers. The oldest rocks are furthest from the ridge on either side, and the youngest rocks are at the ridge (**Figure 5.3**).

Objective

Construct a paper model to illustrate why seafloor is newest or youngest at mid-ocean ridges, and is relatively old at and near trenches.

Key Concepts

I: Geological patterns and lithospheric plates
II: Movement of plates
III: Geological phenomena and plate tectonics

Materials

Each group will need

- one copy of the seafloor spreading model
- scissors
- tape
- orange-, yellow-, green-, and blue-colored pencils or crayons

Time

50 minutes or less

How Do We Know This?

How do we know there are places on the seafloor where new rock material is steadily being added to Earth's plates?

Mid-ocean ridges and their volcanic activity indicate locations of seafloor spreading, but the most convincing evidence comes from the magnetic patterns preserved in rocks on both sides of mid-ocean ridges, as well as the ages of these rocks (youngest at the ridges, progressively older outward in both directions).

Figure 5.3
Formation of new rock at mid-ocean ridge. In part 1, new igneous rock forms at A; at a later time, as shown in part 2, seafloor spreading has split A and moved some of A to the left and some to the right of the ridge, and new rock (B) forms at the ridge; still later, A has moved farther, B has split and moved, and C is forming at the ridge. Spreading has the effect of a conveyor belt moving rock material away from the ridge in both directions. As shown in part 3, the rock on one side of the ridge is essentially a mirror image of the rock on the other side.

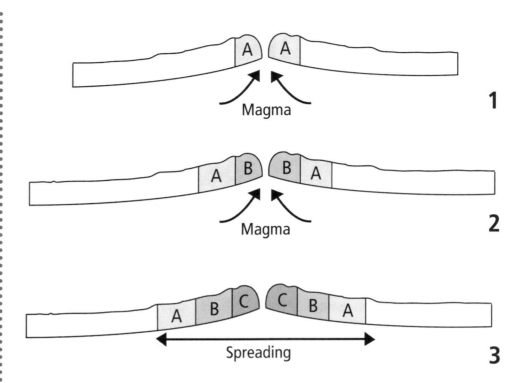

Elsewhere on the seafloor, at plate boundaries where one plate sinks beneath another, older rocks go down into trenches and again become part of the asthenosphere. The oldest seafloor rocks are only about 180 million years old because of this cycle of rock creation and rock removal. By contrast, the oldest continental rocks (which are less dense than seafloor and therefore usually do not go down into trenches) are about 4 billion years old.

Minerals that contain iron are magnetic. They can behave in a similar way to compass needles. When new igneous rock forms at mid-ocean ridges, its magnetic minerals "point" to where magnetic north is at that time, and that record is preserved in the rock. We know from studying seafloor rocks that some of them show that the position of magnetic north when they formed was in about the same place as it is today—these rocks are said to have normal magnetic polarity. However, other rocks record magnetic north as being where magnetic south is today. This means the magnetic north and south poles must have reversed or flipped positions! Over the past 10 million years, this happened 40 to 50 times at irregular intervals.

Evidence of magnetic reversals preserved in seafloor rocks shows a pattern that mimics the pattern shown by ages of seafloor (**Figure 5.3**). Imagine that rock A in part 1 of **Figure 5.3** represents rock that formed at a time of normal magnetic polarity; the minerals indicate that magnetic north at that time was about where magnetic north is today. As time passes, seafloor spreading splits rock A, and the split rock moves away from the ridge in both directions (part 2). If a magnetic reversal took place after rock A formed, new rock B (part 2) would form with reversed polarity. Eventually, plate movement would carry rock B away from the ridge, and another reversal would cause normal polarity rocks to again form at the ridge. Additional reversals and plate movement produce identical "magnetic stripes" on both sides of the mid-ocean ridge, with the stripes representing alternating normal and reversed polarity, repeated again and again. Discovery of this pattern in seafloor rocks did much to show people how seafloor spreading and plate tectonics "work."

Preconceptions

Ask students to describe or draw what they imagine a divergent plate boundary to look like—a mid-ocean ridge. What happens there? What would they see there?

- All rock that makes up the seafloor is of the same age.
- Where plates move apart, a huge gap forms between them.
- A plate can never split into smaller plates.
- Earthquakes are the cause of all volcanic eruptions and volcanoes.
- If new igneous rock is added to the edge of a plate, that plate must be getting larger.
- Mountains always form quickly.

What Students Need to Understand

- New seafloor is continually created at mid-ocean ridges. This is where two plates are moving away from each other. (Huge gaps do not form between plates because of continued formation of new igneous rock.)
- The youngest seafloor rock is found at mid-ocean ridges. Progressively older rock is located farther away from the ridges on either side.
- Seafloor spreads apart at mid-ocean ridges, creating symmetrical patterns of rock on either side.
- Old seafloor rock is eventually removed from Earth's surface at trenches, where one plate slides beneath another.
- Seafloor rock is recycled—it is created at mid-ocean ridges and removed at trenches.
- Continental rock normally is not recycled into Earth's interior; consequently, the oldest continental rock is much older than the oldest seafloor rock.

Time Management

Students can do this Activity in about 50 minutes or less.

Preparation and Procedure

Ask students the questions in the Preconceptions section. Make sure that all students have experience with magnetic compasses. Otherwise, this Activity requires no special preparation.

Extended Learning

- Have students study a detailed map of the seafloor and locate mid-ocean ridges and trenches.
- Suggest that students look for information about why plates do not get larger as the result of rock material being added at mid-ocean ridges.
- See if students seem to understand density. If they do understand, ask students why the relatively low density of continental rocks helps keep those rocks at Earth's surface instead of going down into Earth as seafloor does at trenches.
- Have students investigate why earthquakes often occur at mid-ocean ridges.
- Students could seek information on the source(s) of the heat that melts rock, which causes volcanoes at mid-ocean ridges.
- Ask students how a magnetic compass works. How might they make use of a compass?

Interdisciplinary Study

- Greek philosopher Heraclitus said, "Nothing endures but change." Discuss with students whether they think change is constant.
- Do students think change occurs in things besides nature?
- Have students discuss things in their lives or surroundings that have changed. Perhaps you or designated students could make a list of things that students say have changed. Types of change that could be mentioned include evolution of living organisms, modifications of human cultures and societies, and development of individuals and technologies.
- Have students select a topic on change. Ask them to write a short essay, focusing on these issues: Is change good or bad? How long does it take for significant change to occur? How can we recognize that change has taken place?

Differentiated Learning

- Ensure that all students can differentiate the colors on the bands, and change the colors if necessary.

• Have students who finish quickly or are curious explore the effects of Earth's magnetic field, and consider what might happen should a reversal take place. (Although there have been no reversals during recorded history, there is no evidence that such an event would be significantly harmful to humans or other forms of life.) Students could, for instance, investigate organisms like honey bees and migratory birds in terms of how they may be affected by Earth's magnetic field.

Answers to Student Questions

1. New "rock" (paper strip) is being added to seafloor. The formation of new seafloor occurs, as does a mid-ocean ridge.
2. Ocean trenches are comparable to slits A and C. The old seafloor is sinking into Earth's interior at slits A and C.
3. The age of the rocks would increase.
4. The age of the rocks would increase.
5. The strips represent the plates that make up the seafloor. The colors represent rocks of different age (or different magnetic patterns).
6. The oldest continental rocks would be older than the oldest rocks on the seafloor.
7. Answers will vary, but encourage students to evaluate as many aspects of this model as possible.
8. The Atlantic Ocean is growing as a result of seafloor being added along the mid-ocean ridge that runs its length. The Pacific Ocean is neither growing nor shrinking; trenches located near South America, Alaska, and eastern Asia are continually removing seafloor as new seafloor is being added along the Pacific's mid-ocean ridges.

Assessment

• You can assess prior student knowledge by asking the questions included in the Preconceptions section.
• At the end of the Activity, ask students to revise the writing or sketch they did in the Preconceptions section.
• You can also ask students to show you their model and explain to you what it represents.
• For more formal assessment, you can grade the questions or ask students on a quiz where the youngest rocks in the ocean are and why they are located there, or where the oldest rocks are and why they are located there.

Connections

Magnetism was critical to understanding seafloor spreading. Earth's magnetic field is also critical for protecting Earth from cosmic radiation. We could not live without our magnetosphere. Have students investigate magnetic fields on other planets.

Activity 6 Summary

Students measure seafloor topography using sounding lines in a model ocean. As a team, they plan their strategy to stretch limited funding for maximum results, conduct their research, analyze their results, and repeat the process when you give additional funding.

Activity	Subject and Content	Objective	Materials
Mapping the Seafloor	Seafloor and ocean depths	Map a simulated seafloor and create a profile of it. Practice teamwork and learn about possible effects of limited data and financial limitations on projects.	Each group of four or more will need: masking tape, permanent marker, graph paper and pencil, data sheets, meter stick The class will need: objects in container to represent seafloor; a large trash can or bucket, kiddie pool, or aquarium with sides covered; hardware cloth or other wire screen to cover water container; water-soluble paint, food coloring, or ink; water; strings long enough to reach bottom, with weights on ends

Time	Vocabulary	Key Concepts	Margin Features
50 minutes	Sounding lines, Terrain, Topography	I: Geological patterns and lithospheric plates III: Geological phenomena and plate tectonics	Fast Fact, Safety Alert!, What Can I Do?, Connections, Resources

Scientific Inquiry	Unifying Concepts and Processes	Technology	Personal/Social Perspectives	Historical Context
Measuring and graphing data	Collecting data strategically	Method of measurement	Group decision of priorities	Historical methods of science

Mapping the Seafloor

Background

To study something, it is usually necessary to know or find out what it looks like and what its major features are. But, until about the 1950s, we had very little information about the appearance of the seafloor. Were there hills and mountains? Were there valleys? If so, where were they? Most of our knowledge about the depth of the ocean had come from investigators tying a weight to a rope, dropping it over the side of a ship or boat until the weight hit bottom, and measuring the length of rope dropped overboard. By using these **sounding lines** in many different places, it was possible to piece together a partial picture of the appearance of the seafloor. However, this process was slow and oceans were so large that much of seafloor was still unexplored in the middle of the 20th century. Fortunately, in the 1950s the development of techniques using sound waves (sonar) to survey seafloor made it possible to construct detailed maps. These maps showed that the **terrain** or **topography** of the seafloor is at least as varied as that of land: seafloor does have mountains, valleys, ridges, volcanoes, and many other features.

In this Activity, you will experiment with the old but still useful technique of using sounding lines to make seafloor maps. As is done often in science and in other fields, you will work in teams. You should observe that the number of measurements or the amount of data that you collect will have a huge effect on the success of a project, as can the cost of gathering that information.

Vocabulary

Sounding lines: Ropes with weights at the ends that sailors or oceanographers lower until the weight touches bottom and the line goes slack.

Terrain: The features that make the shape of the land (or seafloor).

Topography: The shape of the land (or seafloor).

Topic: bathymetry
Go to: *www.scilinks.org*
Code: PSCG065

Fast Fact

In 1960, Jacques Piccard and Lt. Don Walsh dove the *Trieste* into the Challenger Deep of the Marianas Trench, 36,000 ft. below sea level—and found fish living there. That is the deepest anyone has ever been in the ocean.

Objective

Map a simulated seafloor and create a profile of it. Practice teamwork and learn about possible effects of limited data and financial limitations on projects.

Activity 6

Materials

Each group of four or more will need

- masking tape
- permanent marker
- graph paper and pencil
- data sheets
- meter stick

The class will need

- objects in container to represent seafloor
- a large trash can or bucket, kiddie pool, or aquarium with sides covered
- hardware cloth or other wire screen to cover the water container
- water-soluble paint, food coloring, or ink
- water
- strings long enough to reach bottom, with weights on the ends

Time

50 minutes

The theory of plate tectonics was developed primarily from information obtained from the seafloor. By studying seafloor topography and rock that makes up the seafloor, geologists learned much about how Earth's surface has changed over time.

Procedure

To perform this Activity, the class will be divided into groups of four or more students. Each group could take a vessel name like *HMS Beagle*, *Kon-Tiki*, *RV Calypso*, *MS Explorer*, *USS Cape Johnson*, *Nautilus*, *R/V Atlantis*, or *Alvin*.

1. Assign the following roles to group members: sounder, measurer, recorder, and grapher.
2. Decide as a team the best way to get the most accurate picture of the features on the bottom of your container using only the number of measurements your team can afford (specified by your teacher). (Note: Why limit the number of measurements? In the "real world," this type of investigation would cost a lot of money; budgets would be limited, and therefore only a certain number of measurements would be possible.)
3. When it is your turn to do soundings, select a row of openings in a straight line across the screen or wire mesh. Place a strip of masking tape along the top of the screen next to the row you have selected. Use the permanent marker to number the openings along the tape beginning at one side and crossing to the other.
4. The sounder begins the mapping process by lowering the weighted string through one of the selected openings into the bucket until he or she feels the weight hit the bottom.
5. The measurer then takes hold of the string where it emerges through the screen (**Figure 6.1**). Next, the measurer removes the string from the bucket

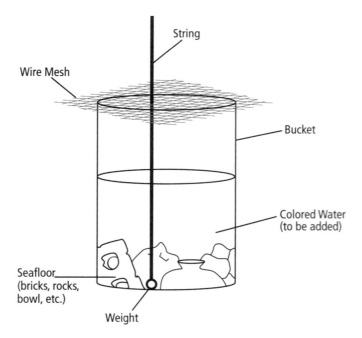

Figure 6.1
Container with simulated seafloor on bottom, covered by water, with wire screen on top of container. Measure from the screen to the hidden object.

and obtains the depth by measuring the distance in centimeters along the string from the point where it is held to the bottom of the weight. (For an actual sounding in the ocean, depth would be measured from sea level; using the screen as the reference surface makes this Activity a bit easier to do.)

6. The measurer reports this reading to the recorder, who writes the depth and the location of the measurement on the data sheet (**BLM 6.1**).

7. This procedure is repeated for all the points you have already selected along your line on the screen. Once your team has made its measurements, the grapher plots the readings on graph paper (from the teacher) and connects the points to create a profile of the bottom. Graph paper should already be labeled with depth on the *y*- or vertical axis—0 cm at the top—and numbers for measurement locations on the *x*- or horizontal axis (think of quadrant IV in a coordinate plane).

8. Look closely at your profile. Do you think that one or a few additional measurements will give your group a much better profile? If you can afford additional measurements (determined by your teacher), decide where it would be best to make them. Obtain these measurements using the procedure outlined above and add the data to your initial profile. Did your profile change? If it changed, were the changes large ones?

9. After the profiles from all groups are complete, display them so all students can see them.

10. Either remove the water from your container or, if the simulated seafloor is in one piece, remove it from the container. Compare your group's profile to the actual "seafloor" to see how accurate it is. Also, look at the profiles made by other groups. Did some groups make more accurate profiles than others? Less accurate profiles? Why do you think this happened?

Questions and Conclusions

1. How does your profile compare to the simulated seafloor?
2. Did the accuracy of your group's profile change after you plotted additional measurements?
3. If you were to repeat this Activity, could you improve your sounding technique to get a more accurate profile? What would you do?
4. In this Activity, you have profiled the bottom of a well-defined enclosed area. Given the varying conditions on the open sea, what complications could you face if you tried to map the real seafloor using this technique?

SAFETY ALERT

2. Be careful to wipe up any spilled water on the floor quickly—slip and fall hazard.

3. Wash hands with soap and water upon completing the lab.

What Can I Do?

1. If you want to build a simple submarine, search for "NOAA Build Underwater Robot" at *http://oceanservice.noaa. gov/education/yos/activities/ buildunderwaterrobot. pdf*. Or search for "MIT Sea Perch" and follow the link "Build" at *http://seaperch. mit.edu/*. Work with an adult if you build and operate either of these vehicles.

2. To learn about careers in oceanography, search for "SeaGrant Marine Careers" at *www.marinecareers.net*.

Group Name:		
Sounding Number	**Location**	**Depth (centimeters)**

Mapping the Seafloor

What Is Happening?

For many years, people believed the seafloor to be an immense expanse of flat, uninteresting terrain. In the 1950s, one of the most significant features on Earth's surface was discovered—the mid-ocean ridges. This series of mountain ranges extends for more than 65,000 km throughout all the major ocean basins. Mid-ocean ridges and deep ocean trenches have provided crucial pieces of evidence supporting the theory of plate tectonics.

Special techniques are used to map or profile seafloor features. In addition to sonar soundings to measure water depth, seismic-wave reflection techniques show the thickness of sediment overlying the solid rock of the plates. Satellite measurements of the ocean surface coupled with gravity data now provide maps of ocean floor where none existed before. These reveal objects such as seamounts but are not accurate enough to detect all navigational hazards. The satellite altimetry measurements are refined by shipboard measurements.

The completeness of a seafloor profile still depends upon the number, accuracy, and location of the measurements taken. These are limited by time and cost considerations. This Activity demonstrates an early method of mapping the seafloor. It also demonstrates the logistics of teamwork and the effects of time and cost limitations on projects.

How Do We Know This?

How do we know how deep the ocean is and what the seafloor looks like?

Until about World War II, sounding lines were used to measure the depth of the ocean—this is essentially what is done in this Activity. Beginning in the 1930s and 1940s, reflections of sound from the ocean floor were used to determine depth of water. These sonar techniques made it possible to construct extremely accurate maps of the seafloor.

Objective

Map a simulated seafloor and create a profile of it. Practice teamwork and learn about possible effects of limited data and financial limitations on projects.

Key Concepts

I: Geological patterns and lithospheric plates
III: Geological phenomena and plate tectonics

Materials

Each group of four or more will need

- masking tape
- permanent marker
- graph paper and pencil
- data sheets
- meter stick

The class will need

- objects in container to represent seafloor
- a large trash can or bucket, kiddie pool, or aquarium with sides covered
- hardware cloth or other wire screen to cover the water container
- water-soluble paint, food coloring, or ink
- water
- strings long enough to reach bottom, with weights on the ends

Time

50 minutes

Preconceptions

To engage students in the idea of exploring unknown territory, ask them about books, movies, or television shows that they know with this theme. Then ask them, "How would you explore the ocean floor? How would you have done that a century ago? What do you think you would have found?"

- The seafloor is essentially flat.
- We do not have any way of knowing what the seafloor looks like.
- The Mid-Atlantic Ridge formed as a result of collision between two plates.
- Changes to the appearance of Earth's surface are always very rapid.
- Changes to the appearance of Earth's surface are always very slow.
- The shape of an ocean basin or continent can never change.

What Students Need to Understand

- Observations of the geologic features of the seafloor have led to improved knowledge about processes occurring beneath Earth's surface, especially those that are part of the theory of plate tectonics.
- Accurate techniques are needed to obtain useful data, such as the measurements needed to "map" or profile the seafloor.
- Big and complex projects such as seafloor mapping often require teamwork and are affected by limitations on time, money, and resources.

Time Management

This Activity can be completed in 50 minutes.

Preparation

Prior to the Activity, label sheets of graph paper for use by the grapher in each team. The vertical scale needs to show depth in centimeters, beginning with zero (the surface) at the top of the axis, going down to a depth that is a few centimeters more than the distance from the screen to the lowest part of your simulated ocean. The horizontal scale needs to show the maximum possible number of measurement locations (i.e., if there are 30 openings across the widest part of the container, then the horizontal scale should go from 1 to 30).

Place nonfloating objects in the bottom of a trash can, bucket, kiddie pool, or other large water container to simulate seafloor. Make the seafloor sufficiently complicated so that a few measurements are unlikely to provide an accurate profile. Anything that does not float will work. Things that can be removed whole from the water and shown to students at the end of the Activity are best. It is a good idea to arrange objects in such a way that enthusiastic sounding will not knock them over or cause them to move.

If objects are stacked, it works best if they have flat surfaces and are stacked on these surfaces—this helps prevent their moving while measurements are taking place. Try to mimic the ocean floor by having a ridge, trench, or seamount.

Fill the container with water, and color the water so that the objects are hidden from view. Water-soluble finger paint works well. Food coloring and ink also may work, but be careful not to get these coloring agents on skin and clothes.

Cover the container with a piece of hardware cloth or wire screen with large openings, and fasten it to the container so that it will not move. Having at least 20 openings across the container works well (**Figure 6.1**). Distribute string and other materials to the groups.

Alternative Preparation

An alternative to using buckets or trash cans is to use lab sinks. Simply place the simulated ocean floor on the bottom of the sink, plug the drain, fill the sink, and color the water. Place the screen on the counter over the sink, use tape so the screen will not move, and have students proceed as directed. This alternative makes it easy to drain the water to study the simulated seafloor; then the sink can be refilled prior to the next class. It also is possible to use a garbage can and peg board or other board with large holes, rather than a smaller container and wire mesh. The larger container allows for more measurements, and the board provides regular holes for sampling while impeding students' view of the bottom. Eliminating water altogether might reduce the mess involved. If this is an activity that you will do multiple times, it might be worth making permanent "seafloors" that could be quickly inserted into containers. For example, these could be made of blocks of wood fastened together to give an irregular surface, plus a brick or two to keep the wood from floating to the surface.

Procedure

Begin the Activity by dividing the class into groups of four or more. Assign each group a vessel name, or let them make up their own names. Assign or instruct each group to select its own sounder, measurer, recorder, and grapher.

Tell each group they can afford five measurements from which they must graph the profile of the seafloor. Students must decide where, in a straight line across the screen, to take measurements in order to try to get the best profile. (Students will be making a "transect.") Even spacing of measurements over the entire distance generally works best—but do not tell students this. Point out that in gathering data, limitations on time and money almost always make it impossible to achieve the ideal. In this Activity, "ideal" would be at least one measurement per opening, or continuous measurements over the entire profile.

To help convey the importance of planning and consequences of financial limitations on projects, you could distribute play money to each group that they would use to "pay" for obtaining data: For example, you could give each group

> **SAFETY ALERT**
>
> **1.** Use caution when handling wire screen material—it can have sharp wire edges, which can cut skin
>
> **2.** Be careful to wipe up any spilled water on the floor quickly—slip and fall hazard.
>
> **3.** Wash hands with soap and water upon completing the lab.

$10,000, and tell them that each measurement will cost $1,000. However, they cannot use all the money for measurements because some of it must be used to pay for other costs of the project (e.g., ship operation, salaries, food, transportation).

While one group is making its soundings, the other groups should be (1) planning their missions, and (2) working on something related. For example, they could investigate the vessel they have chosen for a name. Each vessel is or was involved in ocean exploration. Or, they could do one of the activities in Extended Learning or Interdisciplinary Study.

When the groups have completed their profiles, collect the profiles and present them to the class for review. Point out that once some information is available, it can be used to help determine what to do next, such as identifying where to take additional measurements. Tell the groups that they have received additional funding (e.g., $3,000 or $4,000) so they can now afford a few more measurements. Return the profiles to each group and let them decide where to take additional measurements.

After students have modified their profiles, remove the simulated seafloors (or the water) from the container and display them along with each profile. Point out any instances in which too few measurements, or measurements not distributed over the width of the screen, have resulted in an inaccurate or incomplete profile. If flat surfaces were used in this Activity, remind students that the seafloor is actually more varied than the flat surfaces may suggest.

Extended Learning

- Study topographic maps and profiles of actual seafloor, and note major geologic features and dramatic depth changes.
- Have students compare mountains on the seafloor and mountains on land. Are the biggest mountains on land or in oceans? How is the height of a mountain normally measured? Where are the longest mountain ranges?
- Build a scale model of a section of actual seafloor with significant features such as trenches and mid-ocean ridges.
- What is sonar, and how is it used to map seafloor?
- Have students plan an expedition to map an unexplored part of seafloor: they could make a list of important and necessary things that need to be done before, during, and after the trip.
- Have students explore the ocean in Google Earth. There is a layer called Ocean Expeditions under the Ocean layer. Google Earth is free and down-loadable. Search for "Google Earth" at *www.google.com/earth/index.html*.

Interdisciplinary Study

- Have students investigate author and humorist Samuel L. Clemens (1835–1910), who is better known as Mark Twain. The name *Mark Twain* supposedly came from the expression "by the mark, twain," which referred to a river water depth of two fathoms. Why is Twain an important author? What were his books about? What is a "fathom," and in what ways is this word sometimes used today?

- Have students study use of sonar by animals: Bats, whales, and porpoises are among animals that have "built-in" sonar. How do they use this unusual ability?

- Sampling is a technique employed in a variety of endeavors. It is an especially important tool in American politics in the form of public opinion polls. Have students identify similarities and differences between sampling techniques used to map seafloor and those used by pollsters.

- Successful large-scale undertakings require linking effective management skills with effective knowledge. The human genome project is a nationwide undertaking to identify and map the genes that control all aspects of human life. Have students investigate management strategies that biologists are employing in this investigation.

Differentiated Learning

Ask students to take this concrete Activity a step further by doing the following:

- Learn about the history of the discovery of seafloor spreading, particularly the roles of Marie Tharp and Harry Hess.
- Learn about analogous modern exploration. (See Connections.)

Answers to Student Questions

1. Answers will vary, but the profile may not include enough detail to show all the features of the seafloor.
2. Answers may vary, but the seafloor profile probably became more accurate and may now include features not disclosed by the first profile.
3. Some possible responses are to take more measurements, be more accurate in taking and recording measurements, and choose different locations for taking measurements.
4. Some possible answers are ocean currents, winds, reefs, drifting of ship, marine life, extreme depth, navigational hazards, rope breaking, and interruptions such as foul weather and rough seas.

Connections

Measuring a surface that is hard to reach and difficult to see is still a problem. Venus has a thick atmosphere that is opaque, yet we know its topography includes volcanoes. Have students learn about how we explore Venus.

Resources

http://oceanservice.noaa.gov/ education/yos/activities/build-underwaterrobot.pdf

http://seaperch.mit.edu/

www.marinecareers.net

www.google.com/earth/index. html

Assessment

- This Activity has built-in assessment—the "reveal" when you expose the forms at the bottom of the water container.
- You can discuss the answers to the questions, particularly questions 3 and 4.
- For formal assessment, you can grade students' work, including their graphs.

Activity 7 Planner

Activity 7 Summary

Students observe and compare pairs of related rocks and learn about the conditions in which they formed.

Activity	Subject and Content	Objective	Materials
Rocks Tell a Story	Characterizing rocks	Observe characteristics of rock specimens and learn their significance.	Rock-sample set containing gabbro and basalt, shale and slate, granite and gneiss, sandstone and conglomerate, limestone and marble

Time	Vocabulary	Key Concepts	Margin Features
50 minutes	Igneous, Sedimentary, Metamorphic	III: Geological phenomena and plate tectonics IV: Rocks and minerals	Fast Fact, Safety Alert!, What Can I Do?, Connections

Scientific Inquiry	Unifying Concepts and Processes	Personal/Social Perspectives	Historical Context
Observing, describing	Inferring processes of change	Scientific perspective of deep time	Inferring history from rocks

Rocks Tell a Story

Rock Characteristics and Environmental Clues

Background

Identifying rocks can be difficult, even for geologists. Proper rock identification depends on the quality of the specimen and on the clarity of its significant characteristics. If a rock has decomposed or weathered, anyone can find it hard to recognize minerals and determine what rock it is—or what it used to be. It is usually easy to tell when rocks and minerals have been weathered—they may crumble when handled and their surfaces may be dirty or covered with what appear to be brownish stains. Typically, geologists examining a weathered rock will break it with a hammer to expose a fresh or unweathered surface. The characteristics of rocks provide clues about the environmental conditions under which they formed (**Figure 7.1**). Geologists use that information to reconstruct an area's geologic history. This Activity will give you an opportunity to study various rock samples, and to suggest probable reasons why certain rocks have specific characteristics.

Throughout this Activity, it is important to remember that most rocks are mixtures of different minerals. The specific minerals and their relative concentrations—how much of each mineral appears in the rock—are responsible for some of the rock's characteristics, including color, density, and texture.

Keep in mind the three major rock types—**igneous, sedimentary**, and **metamorphic**. In general, specimens of the

Vocabulary

Igneous: Rocks that harden from cooled molten rock.

Sedimentary: Rocks that formed from fragments of other rocks or fossils, or that crystallized from salts dissolved in water.

Metamorphic: Rock that has been changed by heat, pressure, or fluids.

Fast Fact

The oldest mineral found on Earth is a zircon that is 4.4 billion (4.4×10^9) years old. This zircon is in a metamorphosed conglomerate in Australia. The conglomerate formed 3 billion years ago.

Topic: rocks
Go to: *www.scilinks.org*
Code: PSCG077

Objective

Observe characteristics of rock specimens and learn their significance.

Activity 7

Figure 7.1
A rock about to tell its story

Once upon a time...

Materials

- Rock-sample set containing:
1. Gabbro and 2. Basalt
3. Shale and 4. Slate
5. Granite and 6. Gneiss
7. Sandstone and
8. Conglomerate
9. Limestone and
10. Marble

Time

50 minutes

SAFETY ALERT

Wash hands with soap and water upon completing the lab.

What Can I Do?

If you are interested in rocks and the stories they tell, you can learn to identify minerals, fossils, and textures in rocks. They provide the clues that will help you decipher a rock's history. To do this, look at books from the library, join a rock and mineral club, or go to a science or nature museum. Recognize, however, that minerals, fossils, and rocks in museum collections are often especially fine or rare examples; this is why they are in a museum.

same kind of rock (for example, the igneous rock granite or the sedimentary rock sandstone) will have similar characteristics, such as texture (mineral grain size), color, and density. However, variations in characteristics may exist between individual specimens. A rock's characteristics can tell geologists about its composition, and about the conditions under which it formed.

Procedure

1. From the information provided in the rock-sample set, complete the first two columns of the table in **BLM 7.1**.

2. For each rock, record your observations of the specimen in the table in **BLM 7.1**. Pay particular attention to the specimen's color, density, texture, and other characteristics that may provide clues as to the rock's geologic history.

3. Now compare specimens 1 and 2. These two rocks are related in some way. How are they similar? How are they different? Compare rocks 3 and 4, rocks 5 and 6, rocks 7 and 8, and rocks 9 and 10 in the same way. Record the rock names and your observations in the table in **BLM 7.2**.

4. For each pair of rocks, suggest reasons for the similarities and differences you recorded in the tables. Write down your thoughts, and be prepared to share your ideas as part of a class discussion.

5. The rocks in each pair are related in some way. What story can you create to explain their relationship? Be prepared to share your story with the class, either in writing or orally.

BLM 7.1: Name, Type, and Characteristics of Rock Samples

Date_____

Activity 7: Rocks Tell a Story

No.	Name	Type	Characteristics
1			
2			
3			
4			
5			
6			
7			
8			
9			
10			

Rock Pair	Differences	Similarities
Samples 1 and 2		
Samples 3 and 4		
Samples 5 and 6		
Samples 7 and 8		
Samples 9 and 10		

Rocks Tell a Story
Rock Characteristics and Environmental Clues

What Is Happening?

This Activity relies on a student's ability to make accurate observations. The most important question for students to think about is: What might the characteristics of a particular rock tell us about the conditions under which the rock was formed and about the composition of the rock?

In this Activity, it is important to de-emphasize classification and naming of rocks. Instead, students should focus on the characteristics of an individual specimen. Accordingly, each student or group of students should be provided with a rock-sample set that clearly displays the names of the rocks, along with their classification within the three major rock types: igneous, sedimentary, and metamorphic.

The factors that go into determining a rock's characteristics can be complex. This Activity is only an introduction to how rocks can be used to determine geologic history.

How Do We Know This?

How do we know about environmental conditions that existed long ago? Fortunately, rocks have formed during almost all parts of Earth's history, and the composition and characteristics of those rocks often tell us a great deal about the conditions that existed at the time and place where the rock formed. For example, a limestone that contains corals and fossils of other organisms associated with reefs almost certainly formed in a warm and shallow ocean. Therefore, if we know where the rock came from and its age, we know something quite specific about Earth's environment at a certain time and place. Rocks of other compositions and characteristics could indicate desert environments, or possibly a time of glaciation.

Objective
Observe characteristics of rock specimens and learn their significance.

Key Concepts
III: Geological phenomena and plate tectonics
IV: Rocks and minerals

Materials
- Rock-sample set containing
1. Gabbro and 2. Basalt
3. Shale and 4. Slate
5. Granite and 6. Gneiss
7. Sandstone and
8. Conglomerate
9. Limestone and
10. Marble

Time
50 minutes

Preconceptions

Ask students, "What do you know or think you understand about different kinds of rocks and how they formed?"

- Granite, an igneous rock with a large or coarse grain size, forms only at Earth's surface.
- Sand grains at a beach always have been there.
- Fossils in a sedimentary rock indicate that some organisms once lived in the rock.
- All rocks have the same density.
- The breaking of a large rock into small pieces is all that is necessary to create new rocks.
- Igneous rocks always have mineral grains of the same size.

What Students Need to Understand

- A rock's type (igneous, sedimentary, or metamorphic) provides information about the conditions that existed where and when the rock formed.
- Mineral grain size and shape may provide details about events that led to the formation of a specific rock (e.g., rapid or slow cooling of magma, transportation history of sediments).
- The color of a rock and its mineral composition provide clues about the chemical composition of a rock.
- Two rocks of the same composition can have quite different appearances. The differences indicate that the two rocks did not form in exactly the same way, meaning they have different geologic histories.

Time Management

This Activity can be performed in 50 minutes.

SAFETY ALERT
Wash hands with soap and water upon completing the lab.

Preparation and Procedure

No special preparations are required for this Activity. Rock-sample sets may be purchased from Earth science or geological supply companies (see Resources).

Once students have completed and recorded their observations, ask them to suggest reasons for the similarities and differences they observed between the rocks in each pair of samples. Initiate class discussion by encouraging responses. Allow students to suggest different reasons to explain the similarities and differences they observed. As discussion proceeds, use the following information to assist students in evaluating their ideas.

#1 & #2. Gabbro and Basalt: Both are igneous rocks of essentially the same composition that formed from molten material. The relatively large mineral grains in gabbro indicate slow underground cooling. Basalt contains very tiny mineral grains, indicating fast cooling. Some basalts have cavities formed by trapped gas bubbles. Both rocks typically are found in oceanic crust (parts of plates below oceans). (In Activity 2, students learn this for themselves when they map volcanic rocks of different compositions, including basalt.)

#3 & #4. Shale and Slate: Shale is a sedimentary rock, and is one of the parents of the metamorphic rock slate. Both may have similar colors. The density and hardness of the slate indicate that the shale from which it formed was subjected to intense pressure. The pressure caused tiny mineral grains to line up parallel. Slate usually breaks along those parallel grains, resulting in flat smooth surfaces.

#5 & #6. Granite and Gneiss: Granite is an igneous rock, and is one of the parents of the metamorphic rock gneiss. Large mineral grains within granite and gneiss indicate slow cooling. The mineral grains within gneiss may be deformed due to pressures that helped create the rock. Within gneiss, distorted layering that is further evidence of deformation may be visible, but small samples can make it difficult to see this layering. Gneiss and granite may have the same composition and therefore be about the same color; or composition and color may differ.

#7 & #8. Sandstone and Conglomerate: Both are sedimentary rocks formed from fragments of rocks (or mineral grains, or fossils) that were cemented together. Fragment size is much smaller in sandstone, suggesting a long distance of transportation for these grains. Sandstone may form in coastal regions from sand transported from far inland, while conglomerate might form in a river channel from fragments that traveled only a short distance.

#9 & #10. Limestone and Marble: Limestone is a sedimentary rock, and is the parent rock of the metamorphic rock marble. Limestone usually is relatively soft. Marine fossils are often visible within limestone, indicating formation in warm oceans. Metamorphism usually destroys fossils when limestone is converted to marble. Marble's higher density indicates it was subjected to intense pressures. Marble sometimes has visible interlocking grains due to their growth during metamorphism.

Extended Learning

- Have students investigate other rocks, focusing on the characteristics that seem to indicate something about their geologic history.
- If possible, have students collect local rocks, especially if those that are available show different characteristics (for example, rocks of different color or mineral grain size, rocks of different density, or rocks that break into different shapes).
- Using local rocks, and rocks collected on trips, have students make (or add to) a rock collection for their classroom. All samples should be identified as to location, and, if possible, rock type plus name (e.g., Morrison, Colorado; Sedimentary, Sandstone).

- Many banks, courthouses, libraries, and other buildings, especially older ones, have attractive and sometimes unusual rock in lobbies and on facades. Have students visit some of these buildings to observe and record characteristics of these rocks. (Caution students not to scratch these rocks or try to obtain samples.)

Interdisciplinary Study

- Storytelling has been an important component of human culture for many centuries, especially before the age of widespread literacy. Ancient people sometimes created rock art as part of their storytelling. Petroglyphs (drawings carved on the surface of rocks) may have had religious significance, or they recorded other information important to people in that society. Have students obtain information about petroglyphs, and the stories that some of them apparently "tell."

- Stories were passed orally from generation to generation to perpetuate traditions and cultural identity, and to provide a record of that society. How has the art and practice of storytelling changed over time?

- Have students interview older Americans, such as grandparents or neighbors, to ask about their experiences with storytelling (either the telling of stories, or the hearing of them, or both).

- Ask students to share with the class a story passed along to them by an older relative or friend.

Differentiated Learning

To help students focus on the textures of rocks, particularly the relationships among mineral grains, fossils, or rock fragments, ask students to draw a small part of it at a 1:1 scale. For students who are easily distracted, a way to do this is to cut a circle the size of a coin out of a 3" × 5" card or sheet of paper. Have students lay the card on top of the rock sample and sketch what they see through the hole on the card on the same piece of paper, right next to the hole.

Assessment

Try a performance-based assessment—give students a pair of samples and ask them to compare and contrast the samples. The samples can be the same rock types used in this Activity, but different samples of the rocks. For instance, you can use granite and gneiss samples, but different samples than students have seen. Ask students to tell you what they think about the origins of the rock.

Connections

We can hold lunar and Martian rocks in our hands. The Martian ones are unusual meteorites found on Earth. We also know about some Martian rocks from analyses done on Mars by robotic Martian rovers. Have students learn about how geologists know that the meteorites are Martian and how pieces of Mars got to Earth. Students might also investigate how the rovers *Spirit* and *Opportunity* conducted their analyses on Mars.

Activity 8 Planner

Activity 8 Summary

Students explore the rock cycle with a physical model made from colored crayon shavings. They form the shavings into layers, compress them, and ultimately melt them, replicating pathways a rock can take in the rock cycle.

Activity	Subject and Content	Objective	Materials
The Rock Cycle	Rock cycle: formation and change	Investigate processes that form and alter rocks, and see how rocks change over time.	Each student will need: indirectly vented chemical splash goggles, a lab apron, a pocket pencil sharpener, scrap paper Each lab group will need: eight wax crayons, tongs, two pieces of lumber about 2.5 × 12.5 × 20 cm, hot plate, aluminum foil, four envelopes, newspaper, vise (optional)

Time	Vocabulary	Key Concepts	Margin Features
Approximately 150 minutes	Igneous rock, Weathering, Erosion, Sediment, Sedimentary rock, Metamorphic rock, Rock cycle	III: Geological phenomena and plate tectonics IV: Rocks and minerals	Fast Fact, Safety Alert!, What Can I Do?, Connections

Scientific Inquiry	Unifying Concepts and Processes	Personal/Social Perspectives	Historical Context
Modeling change	Change within open systems	Natural resources	Changing understanding of rock origins

The Rock Cycle
Rock Formation and Change

Background

Earth is over four *billion* years old (or 4,000,000,000 years—writing all the zeros often makes the immensity of the number more obvious). By comparison, the oldest people in the world live to be about 100 years old. How many hundreds does it take to make a million? A billion? Most of Earth's changes occur very slowly, and people do not readily perceive them. But, Earth has evolved and changed dramatically over the past 4 billion years, and it will continue to do so.

A single rock could provide an example of how slowly most geological changes occur on Earth. If you picked up a rock and kept it for the rest of your life, you would probably notice that it changes little, if at all. Yet, rocks can and do change; it often just takes quite a long time. Many factors cause rocks to change, but what is important to understand is that change *does* occur. This Activity will give you an opportunity to investigate how rocks can change over time.

Here is one example of how rocks could change: Deep within Earth, rocks can encounter temperatures high enough to make them melt. As the melted (molten) rock cools, it solidifies and is a new rock. This new rock is **igneous rock**. **Weathering** causes rocks to break down into smaller pieces, and some, or perhaps all, of the rock may dissolve. **Erosion** causes rock fragments to be transported to other places, mainly by wind and water. As rock fragments are deposited in a particular place, they form layers of **sediment**. As the layers build up, their combined weight causes the lowest layers to compact. The tiny spaces between rock fragments fill with

Objective

Investigate processes that form and alter rocks, and see how rocks change over time.

Vocabulary

Igneous rocks: Rocks that form when molten rock cools and hardens.

Weathering: Processes that break down rocks chemically and physically.

Erosion: Processes that move and transport rocks, rock fragments, and substances dissolved from the rock.

Sediment: Loose fragments of rocks, plant, or animal material that can accumulate, be buried, and become sedimentary rock.

Fast Fact

The Mississippi River carries 230 million tons of sediment into the Gulf of Mexico every year. That is about the weight of 170,400,000 Honda Civics. This sediment comes from rock that has eroded from an area that stretches from the eastern Rocky Mountains to the western Appalachians. This sediment is destined to become sedimentary rock.

Activity 8

Vocabulary

Sedimentary rock: Rock that forms by compression (and sometimes cementation) of fragments of other rocks, plants, or animal remains, or that has crystallized from salts dissolved in water.

Metamorphic rock: Rock that has changed because of heat, pressure, or fluids.

Rock cycle: All the processes of rocks forming, breaking down, reforming, and changing, taken together.

Materials

Each student will need

- indirectly vented chemical splash goggles
- a lab apron
- a pocket pencil sharpener
- scrap paper

Each lab group will need

- eight wax crayons
- tongs
- two pieces of lumber about 2.5 × 12.5 × 20 cm
- hot plate
- aluminum foil
- four envelopes
- newspaper
- vise (optional)

Time

Approximately 150 minutes

natural cementing agents that act like a kind of glue, or the mineral grains in the rock grow and interlock. This forms a different type of rock—**sedimentary rock**. In some locations on Earth, tectonic plates move toward one another and collide in a convergence zone. These collisions create enormous pressures that can transform both igneous and sedimentary rock into **metamorphic rock**. Collision of plates can even bury rocks deeply enough so that they melt.

Any type of rock can be transformed or recycled into another type of rock. This may happen repeatedly, or a specific rock could remain essentially unchanged for millions and even billions of years. The group of processes that changes rocks from one type into another type is called the **rock cycle**.

Procedure

It is a good idea to make notes for your own use about what happens when you do any type of experiment. These notes may help you answer questions; they also may help if you need to redo the experiment.

Part 1

1. Cover all tabletops with newspaper. Cover the hot plate surface with aluminum foil.

2. If necessary, trade crayons with another group or groups so that each group has four different colors.

3. Shave the crayons with the pocket pencil sharpener over a piece of the scrap paper. Keep all the shavings of each color in a separate pile. Examine the shavings and make a note about your observations. If the shavings must be stored overnight, place each pile in a separate envelope. What part of the rock cycle is the shaving of crayons? Hint: Crayons represent rocks.

Part 2

4. Fold a 30-cm-square piece of aluminum foil in half to form a rectangle. Place one color of crayon "rock" fragments in the middle of the folded aluminum foil. Spread the shavings into a square layer approximately 1 cm thick.

5. Carefully spread another color of "rock" shavings on top of the first layer, forming a second layer. Do this with each remaining color so there is a four-layer stack of crayon rock fragments in the middle of the foil rectangle (**Figure 8.1**). What part of the rock cycle does this step represent?

6. Carefully fold each side of the aluminum foil over the stack of "rock" fragments, allowing for a 1 cm gap between the edge of the shavings and where the foil folds.

7. Place the foil package between two boards. Put the boards-plus-foil package on the floor or on a lab bench. Apply moderate pressure by pressing the boards together with your hands. What part of the rock cycle does this step represent?

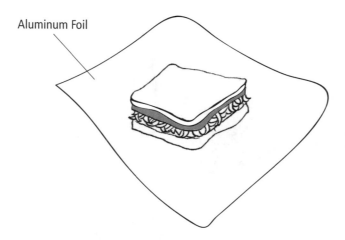

Aluminum Foil

Figure 8.1
Four-layer "sandwich" made from shavings of crayons of different color

8. Remove the foil package from between the two boards, and then carefully open it. Record your observations. Gently lift the sandwiched "rock" material out of the package with both your hands, placing your fingers underneath and your thumbs close together on top. Now break the sandwich into two pieces. Observe and record any changes that occurred to the sandwich. Dump any loose fragments onto a piece of scrap paper and save them. Put the two parts of the broken sandwich back together, place them into the foil, and refold the package.

Part 3

9. Place the foil package back between the two boards and apply as much pressure as you can. A vise works best, but you can apply enough pressure by putting the boards-plus-sandwich on the floor and simply standing on the top board. What part of the rock cycle does this step represent?

10. Open the foil package and reexamine the newly formed "rock." Break the "rock" into several pieces and record your observations.

Part 4

11. Fold a 30-cm-square piece of aluminum foil in half and fashion it into a melting bowl large enough to contain the "rock" that you made from crayons.

12. Place the "rock" into the bowl, along with any fragments that resulted from breaking the sandwich.

13. Make sure the hot plate is completely covered with aluminum foil; then turn it to medium temperature. Place the foil melting bowl on top of the hot plate and melt the rock fragments (**Figure 8.2**). Be careful to melt them slowly enough to keep the wax from spattering. Stop the melting before everything completely melts into a single color.

SCILINKS®
THE WORLD'S A CLICK AWAY

Topic: rock cycle
Go to: *www.scilinks.org*
Code: PSCG089

Activity 8

Figure 8.2
Melting the rock fragments
in the foil melting bowl

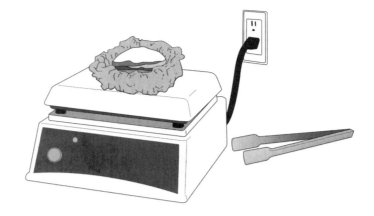

14. Turn the hot plate off. Choose one person to use the tongs to carefully remove the bowl from the hot plate. Set it aside to cool for about 10 min. What part of the rock cycle does this step represent?

15. Once the melted crayon has thoroughly cooled, remove it from the bowl. Break the cooled crayon so that you can see its interior, and think about how this material could relate to the rock cycle. Finally, record your observations.

Questions and Conclusions

1. Name and describe the process by which rocks decompose and become sediments. In what stage of this Activity did this occur?

2. Explain how a sedimentary rock becomes a metamorphic rock.

3. Briefly explain how the four parts (1–4) of the Procedure for this Activity relate to the rock cycle. What are the strengths and weaknesses of this Activity as a model for how the rock cycle works?

4. How likely is it that you will see what was simulated in this Activity within your lifetime? What is the only rock you are likely to have an opportunity to see forming? Explain your answers.

What Can I Do?

Turn off lights, avoid excess use of heating and air conditioning, unplug chargers when they are idle, and generally reduce your electricity use. In 2005, 49.6% of the electricity used in the United States came from burning coal, a sedimentary rock that contains sulfur. Sulfur becomes sulfur dioxide when coal burns, and, in the atmosphere, it combines with water to make sulfuric acid. Sulfuric acid chemically weathers rocks and adversely affects organisms in lakes and rivers. If you have ever examined limestone or marble grave markers, sculptures, or buildings, you have probably seen the effects—blurred lettering and etched surfaces. In 2005, 10,400,000 tons of sulfur dioxide (SO_2) escaped into the atmosphere from electricity generation.

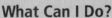

90

The Rock Cycle
Rock Formation and Change

What Is Happening?

Earth is constantly changing, yet people are unable to perceive most of Earth's changes because they occur over such long periods of time. Many students may think that a rock is always a rock, and have no idea that a rock they pick up today has not always appeared the way they see it. Rocks can and do change over time, and this Activity is designed to illustrate some of those changes. Conceptually, geologic change over a vast expanse of time can be difficult for students to comprehend. This Activity focuses on the main components of the rock cycle (**Figure 8.3**), and enables students to investigate that cycle by using a physical model to simulate tectonic forces.

There are three primary rock types: igneous, sedimentary, and metamorphic. Igneous rock is formed when magma cools at or beneath Earth's surface. Much sedimentary rock forms as a result of the compaction of layer upon layer of deposits of sediment. Both igneous and sedimentary rock can be changed by high temperature or pressure into metamorphic rock.

All three rock types are subject to weathering and erosion. Weathering occurs both chemically and mechanically. Chemical weathering involves the change of one mineral into another. Mechanical weathering involves the physical breakup of minerals and rocks. Erosion means weathering coupled with transportation

How Do We Know This?

How do we know that one kind of rock can change into another kind of rock?

Rocks can be observed in intermediate stages of transition. For example, granite, an igneous rock, may be exposed to air and moisture at Earth's surface, causing the granite to slowly decompose (weather). As a result of weathering, all of the mineral grains in granite except quartz could be dissolved or changed into tiny clay particles, and these weathering products could be washed away by streams. Quartz is relatively unchanged and, eventually, all that is left of the granite could be a layer of quartz sand. These quartz grains could then be cemented together by minerals deposited from water. The result would be a new rock—a sedimentary quartz sandstone—which could then be metamorphosed into a quartzite or even remelted.

Objective

Investigate processes that form and alter rocks, and see how rocks change over time.

Key Concepts

III: Geological phenomena and plate tectonics
IV: Rocks and minerals

Materials

Each student will need

- indirectly vented chemical splash goggles
- a lab apron
- a pocket pencil sharpener
- scrap paper

Each lab group will need

- eight wax crayons
- tongs
- two pieces of lumber about 2.5 × 12.5 × 20 cm
- hot plate
- aluminum foil
- four envelopes
- newspaper
- vise (optional)

Time

Approximately 150 minutes

of rock and mineral fragments, such as by rivers. Weathering, erosion, and deposition play important roles in the formation of sedimentary rock because they result in sedimentary layers that are deposited on top of one another.

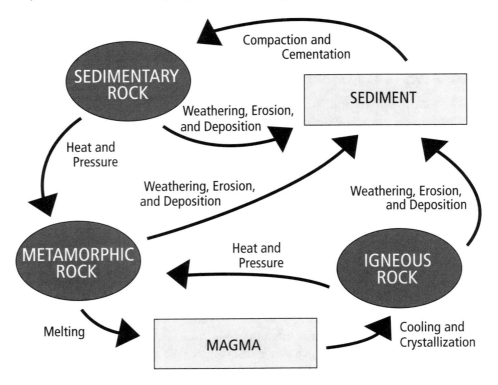

Figure 8.3
The rock cycle. Rock types plus magma and sediment are in capital letters. Processes that alter rocks or sediments are in capital and lower case. Arrows indicate how one type of rock material may change as geological conditions change. These changes need not occur, or could take many millions of years to happen.

Below Earth's surface, rocks may change due to high temperatures and pressures to become metamorphic rock. These conditions are often associated with converging plate boundaries. Any rock can be metamorphosed, even metamorphic rock. Metamorphic rock can be lifted to Earth's surface, where it is subject to weathering and erosion and may become sediments, or it could stay within Earth, become hotter, and possibly become magma. This magma eventually would cool and form igneous rock.

The rock cycle can be fairly complex. Nonetheless, the basic processes are straightforward: some processes form rocks, others break them down. The rock cycle operates over geologic, as opposed to human, time. This Activity enables students to investigate the rock cycle with a physical model that simulates geological processes.

Preconceptions

Ask students to draw what they understand the rock cycle to be.

• All rock formed in the same way.
• It is impossible for one type of rock to change into another type of rock.

- Heat or pressure cannot alter the characteristics or properties of rock.
- Earth's soil has always been present, and it does not change.
- Granite, an igneous rock with a large grain size, forms at Earth's surface.
- Rocks form or change into another rock type in just a few years; otherwise, we could not know how they form or change.

What Students Need to Understand

- The rock cycle occurs slowly over geologic time. Most changes occur so slowly that people cannot observe them.
- Rocks on Earth's surface decompose, or are broken down, by chemical and mechanical weathering.
- Most sedimentary rocks form when layers of sediments are squeezed together (compacted and cemented) beneath Earth's surface.
- High pressure, such as is found at converging plate boundaries, causes changes in rock that result in metamorphic rock.
- Igneous rock is formed when magma cools and solidifies.

Time Management

This Activity will take approximately 150 minutes. On Day 1, introduce the Activity and complete Part 1. On Day 2, complete Part 2, Part 3, and steps 1–4 of Part 4. On Day 3, complete step 5 of Part 4 and the conclusion. Allow time for discussion and cleanup.

Preparation and Procedure

Pull out the materials and try this beforehand so you know what the pitfalls might be, especially those related to the safety of students using hot plates.

At the beginning of this Activity, ask students to draw and label a diagram of a rock cycle. This will allow you to understand what their preconceptions are.

Extended Learning

- Have students investigate possible consequences of weathering rocks of different composition, specifically limestone and granite. Could sand be derived from one of these rocks? Why do caves form in limestone?
- If students live in an area where there are cemeteries at least 100 years old, have them visit and observe the condition of the grave markers made of stone. Do they show signs of weathering (e.g., crumbling stone, difficult or impossible-to-read inscriptions)? Do all markers that are about the same age show the same amount of weathering? Why not? Have students speculate why rock that weathers easily is often used for markers. (It is easy to carve.)

SAFETY ALERT

1. Be careful when working with the hot plate and melted crayons—skin can be burned.

2. Use tongs to move the "sandwich" of melted wax—never pick it up with bare hands—it is hot and can burn skin.

3. Personal protective equipment must be worn during the entire lab Activity.

4. Handle the hot plate and melted crayon rock fragments with extreme care.

5. Be extremely careful not to spill the molten crayon on anyone or anything.

6. Wash hands with soap and water upon completing the lab.

- Have students plan a trip to a location where they are likely to be able to observe igneous rock in the process of forming. Where could they go to observe this? Specifically, what might they be able to see? Would there be any danger in doing this?
- The fundamental difference between chemical and mechanical weathering is that the former produces new (different) minerals, while the latter results in smaller particles of the original minerals. Have students think about the effects of chemical and mechanical weathering on wood, animal carcasses, and rocks. Emphasize that while chemical and mechanical weathering affect different substances at different rates, they are nevertheless the primary agents by which all Earth's organic and inorganic matter is broken down.

Interdisciplinary Study

- The word "metamorphose" or "metamorphosis" is used in many ways. Have students investigate some of these ways, and either report their findings to the class or write a short essay about this topic.
- In addition to rock cycle, the word *cycle* is used for many things: life cycle, business cycle, ring cycle, carbon cycle. Ask students to give you a written explanation of "cycle," and a list of cycles that they experience in their lives. (Items should be included even if the word *cycle* usually is not included, for example, "night and day.")
- Some rock, such as coal, is a valuable resource that often is obtained by strip mining. Have students investigate strip mining. What is it? Why is it done? What problems can strip mining cause? Can these problems be eliminated or minimized?
- The Earth Materials List (**Table 8.1**) matches common objects with the raw materials from which they are produced. Bring some of these objects to class and play "20 Questions" to see if students can identify the Earth materials from which objects were produced. This should help students understand that many materials that we use every day are derived from common or relatively common rocks and minerals, and from petroleum.

Table 8.1: Common Objects Made From Earth Materials: Rocks, Minerals, Petroleum

Common Objects	Earth Materials
Aluminum can	Aluminum ore (e.g., mineral bauxite)
Automobile	Iron ore (e.g., magnetite), aluminum ore, quartz, etc.
Battery	Minerals galena (lead), sphalerite (zinc), etc.
Compact disc or LP record album	Petroleum (oil)
Gold jewelry	Gold ore
Silver jewelry	Silver ore
Tin can	Iron ore, tin ore
Glass	Mineral quartz
Roads	Rock, sand, petroleum (oil)
Clothes (some)	Petroleum (oil)
Pottery and many dishes	Clay, feldspar minerals
Plastics (most)	Petroleum (oil)
Gasoline	Petroleum (oil)
Pennies	Minerals sphalerite (zinc), cuprite (copper)
Table salt	Mineral halite
Building materials: Concrete—sand and rocks (e.g., limestone and shale) Bricks—clay and sand Steel—iron ore, titanium ore, manganese ore	The materials for concrete and bricks are very common Earth materials.

Differentiated Learning

- Ensure that all students can discern the different colors of crayon.
- For students who need concrete examples, refer to Activity 7 for pairs of rock that reflect changes within the rock cycle. For example, use shale and slate, limestone and marble, and granite and sandstone.

Answers to Student Questions

1. Weathering: Chemical weathering can occur when a chemical change takes place in which bonds between substances in the rock are weakened or broken. Mechanical weathering occurs when a physical force acts upon a rock, causing it to break. Weathering was simulated in this Activity by shaving the crayons, as described in Part 1.

Connections

Climate influences both the weathering and deposition of sedimentary rocks. Limestones, for instance, weather in humid climates (e.g., Kentucky) but stand as prominent palisades in arid climates (e.g., much of Montana). Salts precipitate and form sedimentary rock deposits called evaporites in arid climates where evaporation rates are high. Have students investigate global areas to learn where evaporites are forming now.

2. High pressure and perhaps heat must significantly alter the rock. This could happen where sedimentary rock on one plate collides with another plate.

3. In Part 1, the crayons shaved into small pieces represent weathering. The placement of the shavings in layers in Part 2 represents the deposition of rock fragments in sedimentary layers. The pressure placed on the crayon shavings models the compaction of sediment caused by the weight of sedimentary layers above, which creates the sedimentary rock. The increased pressure in Part 3 is analogous to how metamorphic rocks form. The heating of the crayons in Part 4 represents the changes that occur as a result of rock material melting, and then forming igneous rock. Student answers regarding the model's strengths and weaknesses will vary. Encourage students to list a variety of strengths and weaknesses, including similarities and differences between rocks and crayons, and how long it takes for rocks to be altered through the rock cycle compared to how long it takes for crayons to melt and become solid again.

4. It is not likely that changes described by the rock cycle and simulated in this Activity will be observed by students within their lifetimes because of the extreme lengths of time required for most of the processes to occur. The only rock people might have the opportunity to see being created is igneous rock formed as a result of volcanic activity, such as those that form regularly in Hawaii.

Assessment

- At the end of this Activity, ask students to redraw or revise the rock cycle that they drew at the beginning.
- Ask students to reflect in writing what they know about the processes of change from one part of the rock cycle to another.

Activity 9 Planner

Activity 9 Summary

Students explore the physical properties of Silly Putty and a slurry of cornstarch and water. These substances are a physical model of rocks in the asthenosphere, solid rocks that flow slowly—or deform plastically.

Activity	Subject and Content	Objective	Materials
Solid or Liquid?	Properties of rock in the asthenosphere	Investigate and observe how a substance can, under certain conditions, behave like a solid and, under other conditions, behave like a liquid.	**Part 1**—Data tables for all: **BLM 9.1** **Part 2**—Each group will need: Silly Putty, hammer, data tables for all: **BLM 9.2**, board, safety glasses for all, lab aprons **Part 3**—Each person will need: Mystery Substance X, towels for cleanup

Time	Vocabulary	Key Concepts	Margin Features
50 minutes or less	Glaciers	II: Movement of plates	Safety Alert!, Fast Fact, What Can I Do?, Connections

Scientific Inquiry	Unifying Concepts and Processes
Experimenting	Change and rate of applied stress

Solid or Liquid?
Rock Behavior Within Earth

Background

What is a solid, and how does it behave? Let's consider a common solid—ice made from water. Anyone who has ever dropped an ice cube on a floor likely discovered that ice is a rigid and brittle solid, meaning that it is stiff (not flexible) and that it breaks easily. But, ice changes its behavior or properties under different conditions. Valley **glaciers** are "rivers of ice" that flow downhill slowly because of gravity. If you were to walk onto a glacier and examine the ice, you would observe that it is rigid and brittle, like ice in a refrigerator. However, if you could go at least 50 m below the surface of the ice, you would find that it is no longer rigid and brittle. Because of the pressure of the ice above, ice below approximately 50 m is flexible and nonbrittle—this behavior is sometimes called plastic. This plastic ice even flows very slowly, typically a few tens of meters each year. For emphasis, let's repeat this: Ice is a solid, but under pressure it can flow.

The ability of a solid to flow under certain conditions is not limited to ice. Solid rock that makes up lithospheric plates that cover Earth is rigid and brittle. But, under the lithosphere, solid rock of the asthenosphere is hot and at high pressure. Because of these conditions, this rock is not rigid and not brittle. Like ice that is under pressure, the asthenosphere rock is flexible and plastic—and it flows.

The word *fluid* sometimes confuses people. In common usage, *fluid* often is a synonym for *liquid*. However, fluid simply means

> ### Vocabulary
> **Glacier:** A slowly flowing river of ice or a huge sheet of ice (e.g., continental glacier).

Objective
Investigate and observe how a substance can, under certain conditions, behave like a solid and, under other conditions, behave like a liquid.

Topic: phases of matter
Go to: *www.scilinks.org*
Code: PSCG099

something that is able to flow. Liquids certainly flow, but so do gases, as well as solids under certain conditions. Thus, we could describe the asthenosphere as being fluid because it flows and, strictly speaking, this word usage is correct. Because people sometimes think a fluid must be a liquid, it is a good idea to try to make it clear that the asthenosphere is solid rock (except for a very small amount of molten rock that is present at some locations) (**Figure 9.1**).

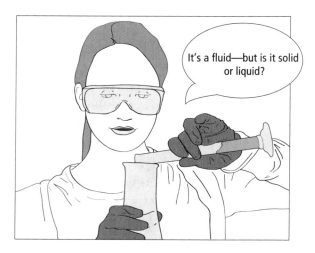

It's a fluid—but is it solid or liquid?

Figure 9.1
Trying to determine if a fluid is solid or liquid

Misuse of the word *fluid* illustrates the importance of using words correctly. If you use a word incorrectly or inconsistently, you can be confusing to others.

In this Activity, you will learn about two unusual substances—Silly Putty and Mystery Substance X—to help you understand the behavior of rocks at Earth's surface and below the surface.

Procedure

Part 1

1. Think about the following solids: rocks, books, and shoes. What characteristics do they share? From your group's discussion, complete the Typical Solid section of the table in **BLM 9.1**.
2. Now, think about the following typical liquids: water, pancake syrup, and motor oil. What characteristics do they share? From your group's discussion, complete the Typical Liquid section of the table in **BLM 9.1**.

Part 2

3. Send a member from the group to pick up the materials for this Activity.
4. Roll the Silly Putty into a ball and bounce it off the table. Pull it, stretch it, mash it. Record your observations on **BLM 9.2**. Does the Silly Putty display qualities more like a solid or a liquid?
5. Roll the Silly Putty into a ball and place it on top of your board. Place the board on the floor, in an open area away from your desks and chairs. You are about to test some of Silly Putty's other qualities.

Materials

Part 1
• data tables for all: **BLM 9.1**

Part 2
Each group will need

• Silly Putty
• hammer
• data tables for all: **BLM 9.2**
• board
• safety glasses for all
• lab aprons

Part 3
Each person will need

• Mystery Substance X
• towels for cleanup

Time

50 minutes or less

6. Before continuing, have everyone in your group (and nearby) put on safety glasses and lab aprons. Select one person to use the hammer. The tester should kneel by the Silly Putty ball and wait for the group's signal.

7. When everyone in the group is safely out of range of the hammer and ready to observe, the group should signal the tester to strike the Silly Putty with one hard swing of the hammer. What happened to the Silly Putty? Record your observations on **BLM 9.2**.

8. The tester should peel the Silly Putty off the board, roll it back into a ball, and repeat the experiment several times using different amounts of force each time. Before each trial, be sure everyone is at a safe distance from the tester and hammer. Record your observations on **BLM 9.2** after each trial.

9. After several trials, the tester should peel the Silly Putty off the board, roll it back into a ball, and place it on a piece of paper. Set the paper and Silly Putty in a place where it can rest undisturbed for at least 30 min. Someone in the group should carefully make a circle on the paper to document the ball's circumference. Record the time. (Note: Any source of gentle heat will speed up the change that you should observe; a lighted lamp with its bulb close enough to the Silly Putty to provide some warmth usually works well.)

10. Leave the Silly Putty undisturbed for 30 min. While waiting, return the other materials to your teacher and go on to Part 3.

Part 3

11. Obtain a small amount of Mystery Substance X. Examine this material—work it in your hands. What are its qualities? When does it have qualities typical of solids? When does it have qualities typical of liquids? Describe the qualities of Mystery Substance X on **BLM 9.2**.

12. Roll Mystery Substance X into a ball, and then break the ball apart. Let each piece of the ball rest in one hand. Describe the qualities of Mystery Substance X on **BLM 9.2**.

13. When you are sure you have fully investigated Mystery Substance X's qualities, dispose of it according to your teacher's instructions. Be sure to wash your hands and clean your lab area.

14. Check the time elapsed in the Silly Putty experiment in Part 2. After 30 min., observe the Silly Putty. Has its shape changed? To help answer this question, make a second circle around the Silly Putty. Handle the Silly Putty to learn if other qualities you observed earlier have changed. Record your observations on **BLM 9.2**. Discuss the changes you observe (if there are any) with members of your group. Is Silly Putty a solid or a liquid?

SAFETY ALERT

1. Safety glasses and lab aprons should be worn throughout the Activity.

2. The person using the hammer must be careful that no one is too close when the hammer is raised in order to swing and strike the test material.

3. Wash hands with soap and water upon completing the lab.

Fast Fact

Astronauts supposedly used Silly Putty on the *Apollo 8* mission, the first manned mission to orbit Earth's Moon. The story is that its adhesive properties helped them keep tools from floating around the capsule. There are many non-NASA links that make this claim, including one by the company that makes Silly Putty.

Activity 9

What Can I Do?

Glaciers exist in Alaska and the contiguous United States. You could research where you can still see them and plan a trip—real or hypothetical—to see a glacier. Where would you go? Have the glaciers there changed in size in recent years? How have they changed? How would you get there? Who would you take with you on this adventure?

Questions and Conclusions

1. When you bounced, mashed, and struck the Silly Putty with a hammer, did it react like a typical solid or like a typical liquid? Explain your answer.

2. When left undisturbed for 30 min., what happened to the ball of Silly Putty? Is this reaction typical of a solid or a liquid? Explain your answer.

3. How is Silly Putty different than typical solids, such as rocks, books, and shoes?

4. When you worked Mystery Substance X with your hands, what did you observe? Explain why this might have occurred.

5. How is Mystery Substance X different from a liquid such as water, pancake syrup, or motor oil?

6. Apply your understanding of Silly Putty and Mystery Substance X to Earth's asthenosphere. How can knowing that solids are not always rigid and brittle help you understand plate tectonics?

7. If Silly Putty or Mystery Substance X were used to model Earth's asthenosphere, what would be the strengths and weaknesses of each?

Typical Solid	Characteristics
Rocks	
Books	
Shoes	

Typical Liquid	Characteristics
Water	
Syrup	
Motor Oil	

Silly Putty—Student Observations:

Mystery Substance X—Student Observations:

Solid or Liquid?
Rock Behavior Within Earth

What Is Happening?

The behavior of seismic or earthquake waves demonstrates that both lithosphere and asthenosphere are almost entirely solid rock, as is the mantle below the asthenosphere. Only at the depth of the mantle-core boundary, about 2,900 km below Earth's surface, is there a layer of molten material.

Just below the lithospheric plates, in an area called the low velocity zone (LVZ), there is a very small amount of dispersed molten material, perhaps as little as 1% of the volume of the rock. The LVZ is characterized by unusually low seismic wave velocity. Even though the asthenosphere is mostly solid rock, its high temperature makes the rock weak and soft, or flexible (nonrigid) and plastic-like (nonbrittle); therefore, it flows very slowly. (It is the weakness of the rock that slows the seismic waves.) This fluid behavior of the asthenosphere is markedly different from that observed for the rigid and brittle rock that makes up lithospheric plates at and near Earth's surface. The plastic astheno-sphere below the lithospheric plates may be what allows the plates to move.

Any rock will melt if its temperature is raised to a high enough temperature. However, the melting point of a rock is also a function of the pressure on the rock. The temperature of the rock that makes up the asthenosphere is just below the melting temperature for this rock. This causes the rock to have its unusual plastic-like quality, allowing it to flow. In general, as pressure increases on a material, its melting temperature increases.

How Do We Know This?

How do we know whether Earth's interior is solid, liquid, or both?
Earthquake or seismic waves, and waves created by explosions, are used to tell if places deep within Earth are solid or liquid. There are different kinds of seismic waves, including P-waves and S-waves. P-waves can travel through any kind of material; S-waves travel only through solids. If an earthquake occurs on one side of Earth, the P-waves reach the opposite side of Earth, but the S-waves do not. This means that part of Earth's interior must be liquid. Detailed studies of these waves have shown that Earth is almost entirely solid from the surface to the outer core, and that the outer core is liquid, but the inner core is solid.

Objective

Investigate and observe how a substance can, under certain conditions, behave like a solid and, under other conditions, behave like a liquid.

Key Concept

II: Movement of plates

Materials

Part 1
• data tables for all: **BLM 9.1**

Part 2
Each group will need

• Silly Putty
• hammer
• data tables for all: **BLM 9.2**
• board
• safety glasses for all
• lab aprons

Part 3
Each person will need

• Mystery Substance X
• towels for cleanup

Time

50 minutes or less

Preconceptions

Ask students, "What does 'fluid' mean to you?"

- Except for the rocky crust, Earth is molten.
- Earth is completely solid.
- Molten rock or magma comes from a molten layer just below Earth's crust.
- Molten rock that forms volcanoes comes from Earth's core.
- Magma forms when rock is subjected to great pressure deep within Earth.
- Continents move on top of molten rock.
- Liquids can flow, but solids cannot.
- All fluids are liquid.

What Students Need to Understand

- Earth's plates are rigid, brittle, and solid rock that moves on the top of the asthenosphere.
- The asthenosphere is not liquid molten rock. It is almost entirely hot solid rock.
- The solid rock of the asthenosphere is flexible and plastic-like, causing it to flow very slowly.
- Some solids have qualities or behaviors similar to those usually shown by liquids; some liquids have qualities or behaviors similar to those usually shown by solids.
- Using careful and precise language can be very important in science, as well as in many other disciplines and activities.

Time Management

Students can do this Activity, including setup and cleanup, in 50 minutes or less. However, they will need a 30-min. interval for Part 2 of the procedure.

Preparation and Procedure

You will need to assemble materials and mix Mystery Substance X before class. Mystery Substance X is a slurry of water and cornstarch in a ratio of two or three parts cornstarch to one part water. You are trying to create a very thick sludge.

Try the Activity before having students do it to ensure that you know what to expect. The experience will help you address safety concerns and prevent mishaps.

Extended Learning

- Students usually enjoy opportunities to experiment with variations of this Activity. Many recipes are available for "slimes"—substances exhibiting qualities typical of both solids and liquids.

- Place a mound of Mystery Substance X on a table or lab bench, and put two blocks of wood side by side on top of it. As the cornstarch begins to flow, the two blocks of wood will move apart, carried along by the moving cornstarch underneath. Using this demonstration, students can explore how the rigid plates that make up Earth's surface can be carried about by material flowing underneath.

- Encourage students to seek information about other substances that mix qualities typical of both solids and liquids. Suggest that they investigate *thixotropic* substances (fluid materials that are liquid when stirred or shaken but become semisolid or solid when allowed to stand).

- Earth gets hotter going from surface to core. Have students look for information about why Earth's interior is so hot. And, if it is so hot, why isn't everything in Earth's interior molten?

Interdisciplinary Study

- Have students research and read the poem "Earthquake" by Kokan Shiren. Ask them to describe how Shiren's earthquake resulted in things similar to or different than what they have observed about solids and liquids. Also, ask them to describe the mood of the poem. Have them investigate liquefaction, a phenomenon that sometimes occurs during earthquakes and always occurs when you tap your foot on wet sand at the edge of the ocean.

- Have students think and write about how they feel when substances and objects exhibit unexpected qualities and characteristics, and when events take unexpected turns.

- Glass is another material with some unusual properties. Ask students to investigate what glass is and how it is made. Have them make a list of different ways in which glass is used.

- Ask students to think about a time when they or someone with them incorrectly used a word when speaking with someone, and that misused word caused some type of problem. Did the misuse cause a disaster? Was it funny? Was it sad? Or, was it just an inconvenience? Explain what happened.

Differentiated Learning

- Scientifically inclined students can investigate non-Newtonian fluids, of which Silly Putty is an example.
- Other students might benefit from a review of the properties of solids, liquids, and gases.

Answers to Student Questions

1. When bounced, pulled, and stretched, Silly Putty behaves largely as a typical solid. If left alone, it changes its shape without breaking, which is a quality typical of liquids. When hammered, Silly Putty fractures or breaks, as would a typical solid.

2. When left undisturbed for 30 min., Silly Putty slowly flows and spreads out. The bottom of the ball flattens. This fluidity is a quality typical of liquids.

3. Typical solids do not exhibit the fluid qualities of Silly Putty; they cannot easily be stretched.

4. When worked vigorously by hand, Mystery Substance X reacts more like a typical solid than a typical liquid. It crumbles, rolls into a ball, and can be broken in half. In this instance, Mystery Substance X reacts like a typical solid.

5. Mystery Substance X exhibits qualities of a typical solid under certain conditions. When worked vigorously it exhibits qualities of a typical solid, but when left alone it exhibits qualities of a typical liquid.

6. Earth's asthenosphere is an atypical solid: it flows. Most geologists believe a flowing asthenosphere allows or causes overlying lithosphere plates to move.

7. Answers will vary. Of course, the asthenosphere or mantle is not made of either Silly Putty or Mystery Substance X. Students should recognize that the environment within Earth's asthenosphere is quite different than that of the classroom, or Earth's surface in general. Also, flow within the asthenosphere is extremely slow—much slower than the flow observed for either of these substances.

Assessment

- For a summative assessment, you can grade answers to questions.
- You can also ask students to create a concept map based on what they have learned about solids, liquids, gases, and fluids.

Activity 10 Planner

Activity 10 Summary

Students study properties of Earth's tectonic plates and the ways they interact atop the asthenosphere using a physical model—a Milky Way candy bar.

Activity	Subject and Content	Objective	Materials
Edible Plate Tectonics	Plate tectonics: interaction	Investigate how plates move on Earth's surface, and observe how some geologic features form as a result of this movement.	Each student will need: one Milky Way bar or similar type of product, towels for cleanup

Time	Key Concepts	Margin Features
15 minutes	I: Geological patterns and lithospheric plates II: Movement of plates	Safety Alert!, Fast Fact, Connections

Scientific Inquiry	Unifying Concepts and Processes	Historical Context
Modeling, visualizing	Influence of physical properties on change	Evolving theories

Edible Plate Tectonics

Plates Move and Interact

Background

Plate tectonics is geology's central theory and one of the most important in science. It provides explanations for many of Earth's major geological processes and physical features. It explains, for example, the distribution of earthquakes and volcanic activity throughout the world. It also explains how many of Earth's surface features form and how they change. For example, mountain ranges form where plates move together, causing continents on plates to collide. Also, where one plate slides or sinks beneath another plate, ocean trenches and chains of volcanoes form. In addition, where plates move apart, volcanic mountains form, creating mid-ocean ridges; rift valleys also may form where plates move apart. This Activity uses an unusual physical model to introduce some of the interactions and features that occur at plate boundaries.

To consider how plate tectonics "works," remember that the outer part of Earth consists of plates made of solid, rigid, and brittle rock. Some of these plates are larger than continents, while others are smaller. Although plates touch, they really are not connected to each other, and they move independently on top of the asthenosphere. Plates interact in different ways at different types of plate boundaries, resulting in many events and features. Investigating plate interactions and the consequences of these interactions is what many geologists do.

We will look specifically at possible causes of plate motion in Activity 11. At this point, it is sufficient to say that several hypotheses exist that explain plate motion. Earth scientists do agree that properties of the asthenosphere

Topic: plate tectonics
Go to: *www.scilinks.org*
Code: PSCG111

Objective

Investigate how plates move on Earth's surface, and observe how some geologic features form as a result of this movement.

Activity 10

Materials

Each student will need

- one Milky Way bar or similar type of product
- towels for cleanup

Time

15 minutes

SAFETY ALERT

1. Students who are allergic to ingredients such as nuts in candy bars should let their teacher know before the Activity is started.

2. Never eat food used in the lab Activity or bring any other food or drink in to the lab.

3. Wash hands with soap and water once the Activity is completed.

play a major role in the movement of the overlying plates. Asthenosphere is almost entirely solid rock, but extreme heat and pressure make it soft and plastic-like, and able to flow very slowly.

Procedure

1. Obtain a small Milky Way candy bar and a paper towel from your teacher.
2. Carefully unwrap the candy bar. Use your fingernail to make a few cracks across the middle of its top. The cracked chocolate represents or models the cracks or boundaries between plates of Earth's lithosphere.
3. Hold the candy bar with its top facing up, with your left thumb and forefinger holding the sides of one end, and your right thumb and forefinger holding the sides of the other end.
4. Slowly stretch the candy bar, pulling it apart a few centimeters at most. The chocolate should separate, exposing the caramel. The exposed caramel represents new material that can rise to Earth's surface and form new igneous rock.
5. Slowly push the stretched candy bar back together again. The brittle chocolate may crumble. "Mountain ranges" may form when pieces of chocolate or "plates" collide. Alternatively, one chocolate "plate" may slide beneath another.
6. Again, slowly pull the candy bar apart and push it back together. Do this until you have a good sense of how plates can be moved about by the motion of the caramel underneath. When the plates are pulled apart, material from beneath could move to the surface (although this may not happen with the candy bar). When plates are pushed together, they can collide, or one can slide beneath another.
7. Once you have finished, pull the candy bar completely apart. Look at its exposed interior and think of the candy bar as a model of Earth's layers. The top layer of chocolate represents Earth's brittle lithosphere, broken into plates. The caramel and nougat represent the asthenosphere, where the material is solid yet still able to flow (**Figure 10.1**).
8. After answering the questions below, dispose of your model as instructed by your teacher. Be sure to clean up and wash your hands.

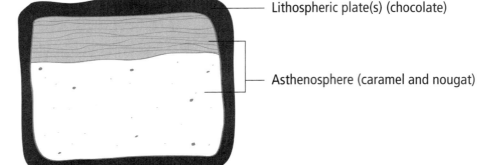

Lithospheric plate(s) (chocolate)

Asthenosphere (caramel and nougat)

Figure 10.1
Candy bar tectonics— demonstrating plate movement and interactions

112

Questions and Conclusions

1. Describe the consistency of the candy bar layers. How do they compare and contrast with one another?

2. Describe what you observed when the candy bar was pulled apart. What might you expect to see at a place on Earth where two plates are moving apart?

3. Describe what you observed when the stretched candy bar was pushed together. What might you expect to see at a place on Earth where two plates collide?

4. Using the candy bar as a model for a portion of Earth, what do each of the candy bar layers represent?

5. From your study of this model and plate tectonics, explain why earthquakes occur frequently along the boundaries between plates.

6. One limitation of this model is that fingers pulling and pushing, and not natural geologic processes, cause the "plate" motion. What natural processes might cause the motion of Earth's plates?

Fast Fact

If you made a model train layout at the same scale as this Milky Way candy bar model of Earth's outer layers, the whole train layout would fit on the head of a pin, with room to spare. For reference, while an HO train set is at the scale of 1:87, the Milky Way model is at about the scale of 1:50,000,000.

Teachers' Guide to Activity 10

Edible Plate Tectonics
Plates Move and Interact

What Is Happening?

Middle-school students sometimes have difficulty understanding plate tectonics. The idea of entire continents moving over Earth's surface can be a hard one to accept—it was even for many scientists in the past. This simple demonstration provides another visual and physical introduction to plate motion and some of its effects.

As is discussed even more thoroughly in other Activities, the outer part of Earth is a relatively brittle layer called plates or lithosphere. Beneath the plates is a layer—the asthenosphere—in which solid rock actually flows, although this flow is slow, usually several centimeters each year.

In this Activity, a Milky Way candy bar models the relationship between plates and asthenosphere. The outer top layer of the candy bar—the brittle chocolate—represents plates. The next layer, caramel, represents the flowing material in the upper asthenosphere. The layer below the caramel, the nougat, represents the lower asthenosphere where flow also occurs, but perhaps not as readily as in the upper asthenosphere.

A drawback of this model is that continents, which are embedded in lithospheric plates, are not represented by anything on or in the candy bar. (Note that a continent is the top part of a plate where the rock has lower density than the plate beneath continents and the plate below oceans.) The model does convey interactions between asthenosphere and lithosphere, and it is this relationship that is important for students to grasp.

Objective
Investigate how plates move on Earth's surface, and observe how some geologic features form as a result of this movement.

Key Concepts
I: Geological patterns and lithospheric plates
II: Movement of plates

Materials
Each student will need
• one Milky Way bar or similar type of product
• towels for cleanup

Time
15 minutes

How Do We Know This?

How do we know that plates move and interact?

Nowadays, Global Positioning System (GPS) is used to determine the amount and direction of movement of plates in real time. Interaction is indicated by the fact that the present-day occurrence of most earthquakes and volcanic eruptions occurs at or very close to boundaries between plates. Before GPS became available, we could see abundant evidence of earlier plate interactions, for example, Appalachian Mountains, Himalayas, and distribution of ancient volcanoes.

Students might want to know why testing hypotheses is so difficult, and why geologists do not all agree. These are good questions, but there are no easy answers. However, these questions could provide an opportunity to discuss the way geologists, among other scientists, actually perform science, and to refresh students' memories about the scientific method. This Activity might also provide an opportunity to discuss how new technologies enable today's geologists to test hypotheses in ways that earlier geologists could not.

Preconceptions

Ask students to describe what they think they know about tectonic plates and the way plates move. Students could do this as a class discussion, as a journal entry, as a Think-Pair-Share, or as a concept map.

- Plates move but one plate has no effect on another plate.
- Earthquakes that occur at plate boundaries cause mountain ranges.
- Continents or plates can never join together to form a larger continent or plate.
- Plates move, but continents do not.
- Mountains never form when plates diverge or move away from each other.
- Plate motion has no effect on the appearance of Earth's surface.
- When two plates move toward each other, nothing happens because movement is so slow.
- Continents can move but everything else stays in the same place.

What Students Need to Understand

- Earth's interior is layered, and each layer has different properties.
- Earth's lithosphere is brittle and is broken into a number of plates, some large and some small.
- The asthenosphere is not liquid, molten rock. It is solid rock at relatively high pressure and temperature. High pressure and temperature change the properties of the rock and cause it to be a solid that can flow.
- Certain kinds of plate motion produce characteristic geological features, such as mountain ranges, deep ocean trenches, volcanoes, and rift valleys.
- Certain kinds of plate motion produce geological events, such as volcanic activity and earthquakes.

Time Management

Students can complete this Activity in about 15 minutes.

Preparation and Procedure

Chill the candy bars enough for the chocolate to be brittle. No other special preparations are required. To ensure that the candy bars will perform as expected, go through the Activity prior to the start of class. A note of caution: Candy must be used in classrooms only under close supervision.

Alternative Preparation

An alternative approach for this Activity that can work well is to do the Activity as a demonstration while students watch.

Extended Learning

- Have students design and test other models that will illustrate concepts important to plate tectonics. In designing new models, students must first identify those aspects of plate tectonics critical to understanding the geologic processes involved. Students also should identify strengths and weaknesses of their models.
- Ask students to investigate where continent-continent plate collisions in the past produced mountains. Where are these mountains today?
- Ask students if they know where plates are sliding beneath other plates today. They could investigate what else is happening at these locations.
- At some plate boundaries, plates just slide past each other. Ask students to cite some examples where this happens, and describe what geologic events may occur there.

Interdisciplinary Study

- In the early 1900s, Alfred Wegener and F. B. Taylor proposed the theory of continental drift (see Reading 1: Plate Tectonics for more on the origin of continental drift theory). At the time, their ideas met with derision and were rejected by a majority of the scientific community. It was not until the 1950s and 1960s that mounting evidence—largely provided by technological advances in undersea exploration—led to widespread acceptance of a theory of plate tectonics, a theory that is a direct descendant of Wegener and Taylor's original hypothesis. Have students study the development of the theory of plate tectonics, paying particular attention to how accumulated evidence from many disciplines affects a theory's acceptance or rejection. Have students explore both the good and bad effects of scientists' reluctance to accept theories that seem to challenge generally accepted knowledge.
- Have students discuss how scientists use the words *hypothesis* and *theory*. Do they mean the same thing? Do nonscientists use the words in the same way? If not, how are these words used?

> ## SAFETY ALERT
>
> **1.** Some students may be allergic to components in the candy bar. Always check with the school nurse first. If relevant allergies exist, this might be better done as a demonstration by the teacher.
>
> **2.** Never eat food used in the lab Activity or bring any other food or drink in to the lab.
>
> **3.** Wash hands with soap and water once the Activity is completed.

- This Activity demonstrates a use of candy to explain aspects of geological sciences. Ask students to think of other ways that candy has been used to convey ideas or feelings. Ask them to make a list of other ways that candy is used.
- Ask students to try to find out if candy is available in all cultures. If not, why? And, if not available, are there substitutes that are used in a similar way to how we use candy?
- Sugar, at least in the United States, often comes from sugar cane or sugar beets, and can be produced from maple trees. Have students investigate these sugars. Where are they produced? Is one better than another? Is one more fattening than another? Is there a region or soil type that is best for growing these different sources of sugar?
- Have students investigate the nutrition—or lack of nutrition—in the candy bar that they used as a model.

Connections

Although plate tectonics explains the occurrence and location of volcanoes on Earth, no other planetary bodies in our solar system have convincing evidence for equivalent processes. However, we do know they have volcanoes and other mountains. Have students investigate Earth-type volcanoes on other planetary bodies (e.g., Venus and Mars), or other types of volcanoes (e.g., ice volcanoes on the moon Titan).

Differentiated Learning

- For concrete thinkers, this Activity uses a physical model to make abstract knowledge more concrete. Help these students compare and contrast the model with reality.
- For highly verbal students, you can discuss the equivalence of a model with an analogy, simile, or metaphor in literature.

Answers to Student Questions

1. The outer layer of chocolate on the candy bar is brittle and can be broken easily into pieces. The caramel and nougat are much less brittle. Caramel and nougat can change shape by stretching or compressing, while the chocolate breaks instead of undergoing a change in shape.
2. The chocolate fractured into a number of pieces. Where the pieces were not touching, caramel could be seen beneath the chocolate. Where two plates are pulled apart, such as at the crest of a mid-ocean ridge, a rift valley may form. The rift valley along the crest of the mid-Atlantic Ridge is an example.
3. When the Milky Way candy bar was pushed together, chocolate pieces were forced upward and formed ridges, or pieces of chocolate were forced to slide beneath other pieces. Where two plates collide, mountain ranges may form. The Himalayas were formed when the plates carrying Asia and India collided. At other locations where continents are not present, one plate slides beneath another, resulting in an oceanic trench (extremely deep water). Such areas are called subduction zones. The Marianas Trench in the western Pacific Ocean is an example. Volcanoes commonly form above subduction zones.

4. The chocolate represents Earth's outer layer, the plates or lithosphere. The caramel and nougat represent the asthenosphere, beneath the lithospheric plates.

5. Plate motion causes plates to move together, to move apart, or to slide alongside one another. Rock along plate boundaries either periodically breaks or moves suddenly, resulting in earthquakes.

6. Current explanations for plate motion will be explored in Activity 11. At this point, encourage students to develop as many plausible explanations and models as possible. Ask how each might be tested.

Assessment

• You can grade answers to questions, but this Activity is engaging enough that an informal class discussion about what students saw and what the model represented will probably suffice.

• You could ask students how their understanding of plate tectonics changed as a result of this Activity.

Activity 11 Planner

Activity 11 Summary

Students conduct experimental trials involving a drop of food coloring moved by convection in a pan of water to observe convection cells. Students record their observations on this model and relate what is observed in the pan to what might be happening in Earth's asthenosphere.

Activity	Subject and Content	Objective	Materials
Convection	Heat transfer within Earth's mantle	Investigate and observe how material moves within a convection cell, and consider how your observations might pertain to Earth's interior.	Each group will need: indirectly vented chemical splash goggles, aprons, and gloves for each student; room-temperature water; hot water (about 70°C); towels for water spills; food coloring in small containers; basin or sink for used water; plastic pan; pipette or medicine dropper; four foam cups; one cup lid; two sheets of white paper; data sheets for each student

Time	Vocabulary	Key Concepts	Margin Features
50 minutes	Convection, Experiment, Density	I: Geological patterns and lithospheric plates II: Movement of plates	Safety Alert!, What Can I Do?, Fast Fact, Connections, Resources

Scientific Inquiry	Unifying Concepts and Processes	Technology	Historical Context
Experimenting	Density differences and heat transfer	Convection in technology	Evolving theories

Convection
Transfer of Heat From Earth's Interior

Background

Earth's surface is covered by seven or eight large plates of solid rock and about an equal number of smaller plates (specific numbers depend on the definition of "large"). A single plate can be 8,000 km across and average 100 km in thickness. These brittle and rigid plates move independently. They can move because the layer beneath them—the asthenosphere—is hot and soft, and flows even though it is solid rock.

But, what is the source of the heat that causes this solid rock to flow? In this Activity, you will build models of **convection** cells in water, **experiment** with them, and consider convection cells as a way of bringing heat to rock that is close to Earth's surface. This heat from Earth's interior, directly or indirectly, is the driving force for plate tectonics. Reading 1: Plate Tectonics expands on the topic of plate tectonics.

Much of the heat that affects Earth comes from the Sun, but the interior of Earth also provides heat that makes plates move, mountains and volcanoes form, and so on. In the last few decades of the 20th century, most Earth scientists thought that convection currents within Earth were directly responsible for plate motion. The idea was that rock heated up deep within Earth, causing the rock to have lower **density**; thus, the rock would rise toward the surface. Because the outer part of Earth is cooler, the rock would cool and become denser again. This increased density would cause it to sink. Once deep within Earth, the rock would become hot and less dense, and this

Vocabulary

Convection: Movement of material because of differences in density.

Experiment: A trial to see what happens when you change a variable or to test a hypothesis.

Density: Mass divided by volume.

Objective

Investigate and observe how material moves within a convection cell, and consider how your observations might pertain to Earth's interior.

Topic: heat convection
Go to: *www.scilinks.org*
Code: PSCG121

Activity 11

Materials

Each group will need

- indirectly vented chemical splash goggles, aprons, and gloves for each student
- room temperature water
- hot water (about 70°C)
- towels for water spills
- food coloring in small containers
- basin or sink for used water
- plastic pan
- pipette or medicine dropper
- four foam cups
- one cup lid
- two sheets of white paper
- data sheets for each student

Time

50 minutes

convection cycle or cell would be repeated. (A crude analogy would be currents created in a pan of water on a hot stove.)

In this convection cell model, hot rock is brought to the surface at spreading centers (divergent boundaries) where it melts, then cools to form new rock; lateral motion of the cells causes plates to move horizontally, and downward motion of the cells drags the plates into Earth's interior. However, as Earth scientists developed 3-D images of Earth's interior from earthquake records, they realized that this simple convection cell model cannot explain everything that actually happens. There must be something else going on, and what that might be is still under discussion.

Procedure

Setup

1. Select a group member to pick up your tray of supplies. Put on the goggles, aprons, and gloves.
2. Clear off the tray and line it with white paper. This will make observing your convection cell easier.
3. Place three of the four foam cups upside down on the paper, forming a triangle. The fourth cup eventually will be placed right side up amid the other three, as in the apparatus shown in **Figure 11.1**.

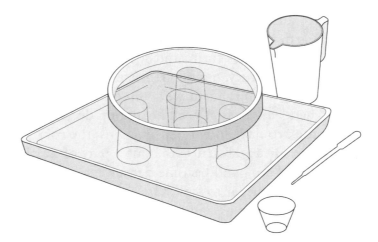

Figure 11.1
Experimental setup for convection cells Activity

4. Add room-temperature or cooler water to the clear plastic pan so that it is 1/2 to 2/3 full.
5. Place the pan on top of the three upside-down cups.
6. Leave the apparatus undisturbed until there are no ripples in the water.

Trial 1

In Trial 1, you will observe the movement of food coloring with no heat source. You will compare the results of future experiments to this experiment.

7. After the water is still, place a small drop of food coloring at the bottom of the pan, in the center. To do this, put food coloring in your pipette. Carefully wipe off any excess coloring on the outside of the pipette. Place the pipette tip at the bottom of the water at the pan's center (**Figure 11.2**). Take care not to create any movement in the water as you insert and remove the pipette; when moving the pipette into and out of the water, use slow up-and-down motions only. Slowly release one very small drop of coloring.

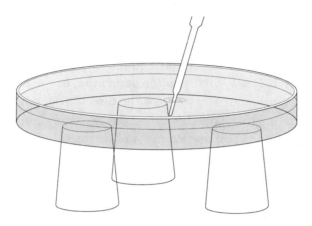

Figure 11.2
Adding food coloring to center and bottom of pan

8. Observe the water for about 2 min., viewing it both from above and from the sides. To improve your observations, hold a piece of white paper behind the pan. Record your observations on **BLM 11.1**. In the space provided, draw what you see happening to the distribution of the food coloring. Use arrows to show the direction of movement.

9. After recording the results of this control experiment, gently swirl the water to disperse the food coloring. You only need to replace the water in your pan if it is too dark for further observations.

Trial 2

In Trial 2, you will observe the movement of food coloring when you place a heat source directly below the pan's center, as in **Figure 11.3**.

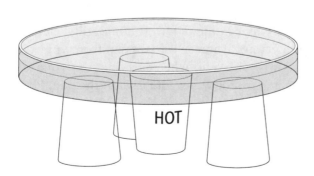

HOT

SAFETY ALERT

1. Indirectly vented chemical splash goggles, aprons, and gloves are required.

2. Immediately wipe up any spilled water—slip and fall hazard.

3. Wash hands with soap and water upon completing the lab.

Figure 11.3
Placement of hot water for convection cell Activity

10. After the food coloring from Trial 1 has dispersed, allow the water to become still again.

11. Select one person from the group to get hot water in a foam cup from your teacher. Cover the hot water tightly with a lid when carrying it to your table.

12. Be careful not to disturb the still water in the pan; gently slide the cup of hot water underneath your pan. Place the cup directly underneath the center of the pan (**Figure 11.3**).

13. As in Trial 1, place a small drop of food coloring in the bottom center of the water (**Figure 11.1**). Remember to release the drop slowly.

14. Observe the water for about 2 min. Record your observations on **BLM 11.1**. Draw what you see happening to the distribution of the food coloring, using arrows to show the direction of movement.

15. After completing Trial 2, remove the cup containing the hot water from underneath the pan and empty it as directed by your teacher. Replace the pan water with clean, room-temperature water.

Trial 3

In Trial 3, you will observe the movement of food coloring with a heat source placed under the center of the pan, as in Trial 2. But, in this experiment, the food coloring will be placed on the bottom roughly halfway between the pan's center and its perimeter, as in **Figure 11.4**.

Figure 11.4
Adding food coloring to bottom of pan midway between center and edge

16. Allow the water in the pan to become still. Select one person from the group to get hot water in a foam cup from your teacher. Cover the hot water tightly with a lid when carrying it to your table. As in Trial 2, gently slide the cup of hot water underneath the pan. Place it directly underneath the pan's center.

17. Place a small drop of food coloring on the pan's bottom roughly halfway between the center and the perimeter. Remember to release the food coloring slowly to avoid disturbing the water.

18. Observe the water for about 2 minutes. Record your observations on **BLM 11.1**.

19. When your observations and recording are complete, gently swirl the water to disperse the food coloring. You only need to replace your pan's water if it is too dark for further observations. Remove the cup containing the hot water from underneath the pan and carefully empty it as directed by your teacher.

Trial 4

In Trial 4, you again will observe the movement of food coloring with the heat source placed under the center of the pan. As in Trial 3, the food coloring will be placed roughly halfway between the pan's center and perimeter. However, instead of being inserted on the pan's bottom, the food coloring now will be placed on the water's surface, as in **Figure 11.5**.

Figure 11.5
Adding food coloring to pan midway between center and edge, at surface of water

20. Allow the water to become still as you did in Trials 2 and 3. Select one person from the group to get hot water in a foam cup from your teacher. Cover the hot water tightly with a lid when carrying it to your table. Gently slide the cup of hot water underneath the pan's center.

21. For this trial, place a small drop of food coloring roughly halfway between the pan's center and edge. But, this time place the drop directly on the water's surface.

22. Observe the water for about 2 minutes. Record your observations on **BLM 11.1**.

23. After completing your observations and recording, discard the water as directed by your teacher. Place all experimental materials on the tray and return them to the spot chosen by your teacher. Clean up.

Questions and Conclusions

1. Review the results of the four trials within your group. Compare Trial 1 (the control experiment) to the other trials. What effect does the heat source have on Trials 2, 3, and 4?

2. For each trial, describe the location in the pan where the current flowed toward the heat source. Where did it flow away from the heat source?

3. For each trial, where in the pan was the food coloring flowing upward? Where was it flowing downward?

What Can I Do?

Convection cells work because of different densities—hot rock in the mantle, but water in this Activity. Galileo exploited the principle of density in his design of a thermometer, in 1593. With the help of an adult, try to make one for yourself. Search online for "homemade Galilean thermometer jar" for instructions that use baby food jars and a large vase. You could substitute other containers (e.g., film canisters for baby food jars). To improve accuracy, use a laboratory balance for your mass measurements.

Activity 11

Fast Fact

Although water freezes—turns to a solid—at 0°C, it is densest at 4°C. Some examples of water temperatures and densities are

0°C, 0.99984 g/cm³
4°C, 0.99997 g/cm³
40°C, 0.99222 g/cm³
70°C, 0.97777 g/cm³
100°C, 0.95837 g/cm³

4. This Activity models one of the mechanisms geologists think might drive plate tectonics. In this model, what does the water represent? What does the hot water in the cup represent?

5. In this model, nothing represents plates. To include them, what could you add and where should they be placed?

6. Assuming that this model accurately represents Earth, explain how plates are moved about on Earth's surface. Why do land masses or continents move when their underlying plates move?

7. The currents in the water normally cause the food coloring to move at a rate of 2–3 cm or more per minute. How does this compare to the rate estimated for tectonic plate motion?

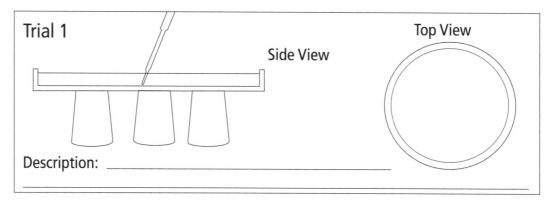

Trial 1

Side View

Top View

Description: _____
_____

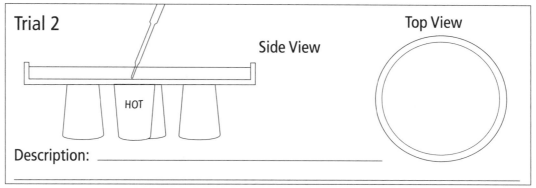

Trial 2

Side View

Top View

HOT

Description: _____
_____

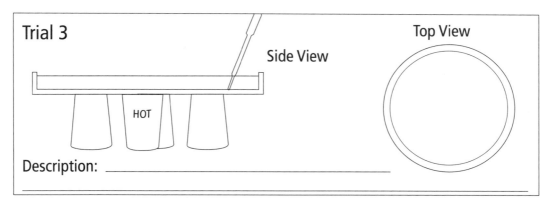

Trial 3

Side View

Top View

HOT

Description: _____
_____

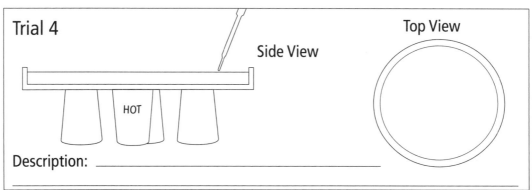

Trial 4

Side View

Top View

HOT

Description: _____
_____

Convection
Transfer of Heat From Earth's Interior

What Is Happening?

Convection is a way to transfer heat from one place to another. Heating a pan of water produces simple convection cells. When heated from underneath, water nearest the heat source expands, becoming less dense than the cooler water around it. The less dense water rises upward away from the heat source and begins to cool as it rises. By cooling, it increases in density and sinks. The cycle of heating and rising, cooling and sinking, establishes convection currents in the water. The combined system of currents is called a convection cell. However, take care to distinguish between the solid asthenosphere and the liquid model used here. Make sure students understand that the asthenosphere is solid, not molten.

Until recently, most geologists believed convection to be the driving force behind plate tectonics: High temperatures within Earth caused convection in the mantle, and these currents brought new rock to the surface, moved plates-plus-continents, and caused old parts of plates to return to Earth's interior. However, three-dimensional imaging of Earth's interior (seismic tomography) shows that simple convection cells are unlikely to exist and thus they probably cannot explain plate motion. Instead, a force called slab pull may be the primary cause of plate motion: As the new rock of a plate moves away from a spreading center or mid-ocean ridge, it becomes older and colder. As it becomes colder, it becomes denser, and this increase in density may be sufficient to pull the plate or slab into the mantle—hence the term *slab pull*.

Even if simple convection cells are not the direct cause of plate motion, convection undoubtedly is vital to plate tectonics because it brings significant heat to the upper mantle. This heat causes the solid rock of the asthenosphere to be soft and plastic, and to flow very slowly (similar to the behavior shown by substances observed in Activity 10). These properties permit rigid and brittle plates to move on top of the asthenosphere.

How Do We Know This?

How do we know that the deep interior of Earth is extremely hot?
   The outer core must be molten because S-seismic waves that travel only through solids do not enter the outer core. Despite very high temperatures, the inner core is solid due to very high pressures.

Objective

Investigate and observe how material moves within a convection cell, and consider how your observations might pertain to Earth's interior.

Key Concepts

I: Geological patterns and lithospheric plates
II: Movement of plates

Materials

Each group will need

- indirectly vented chemical splash goggles, aprons, and gloves for each student
- room temperature water
- hot water (about 70°C)
- towels for water spills
- food coloring in small containers
- basin or sink for used water
- plastic pan
- pipette or medicine dropper
- four foam cups
- one cup lid
- two sheets of white paper
- data sheets for each student

Time

50 minutes

Preconceptions

Ask students, "What do you think of when you hear the word *convection*?" (If students talk about ovens, ask them if they know how convection ovens work.) Or, "What do you understand about convection and how it relates to density?"

- Heat has no effect on the volume or density of material.
- Heat can melt rock, but it does not cause materials to move.
- Continents always move on top of molten rock.
- Earthquakes cause plates to move.
- Magma forms when rock is subjected to great pressure deep within Earth.
- Plates are all moving in the same direction.

What Students Need to Understand

- Convection is a way for heat to be moved from one place to another.
- Geologists believe convection makes plate tectonics possible, but convection probably does not propel plates.
- Flow of the solid asthenosphere is very slow, much slower than the flow of water in this Activity.
- The asthenosphere is not liquid molten rock. It is solid rock but it can slowly flow.

Time Management

This Activity can be completed in 50 minutes.

Preparation and Procedure

Before class, gather the materials and do this Activity yourself. This will ensure that you know what to expect. You can then troubleshoot better, and predict and prevent safety issues. Use any standard size foam cups; all four cups must be the same size. Clear plastic pans also can vary in size. One convenient source is a garden supply store; drainage trays for plant pots make good pans. Place a few drops of food coloring in small containers. Warning: Food coloring can stain. Therefore, caution students to use care to avoid spilling it on clothing, furniture, or the floor.

Because working with hot water can be dangerous, you should be in charge of the heat source. When students are ready for the hot water, one student from each group should bring a foam cup and lid to you. Pour the water, make sure the lid is tight, and caution students to walk carefully to their group. Using tightly fitting lids reduces the risk of spills and burns.

SAFETY ALERT

1. Indirectly vented chemical splash goggles, aprons, and gloves are required.

2. Immediately wipe up any spilled water—slip and fall hazard.

3. Wash hands with soap and water upon completing the lab.

To engage students at the beginning of this Activity, you could display a lava lamp on your desk. This would certainly catch their attention. Otherwise, or in addition, ask students questions in the Preconceptions section.

Extended Learning

- Students could place drops of food coloring elsewhere in the pan and observe the results. Water could be at various temperatures, or placed elsewhere beneath the pan. If possible, substitute rheoscopic fluid for the water and the food coloring. This can be an effective way to observe convection currents; the material that makes the currents visible will not dissipate.
- Ask students to investigate other types of density currents that can exist in nature (e.g., salt and fresh water, mud and water, magmas of different densities). Where do you find these in nature? Could these be modeled in the classroom?

Interdisciplinary Study

- Have students find out about convection ovens. How do they differ from conventional ovens? What are the advantages? What are the disadvantages?
- Ask students to investigate tomography, ways of obtaining images of interiors of objects. Magnetic resonance imaging (MRI) and computer-aided tomography (CAT) scans of humans are well known, but similar imaging also can be used on the entire Earth, tombs, and many other objects. Have students investigate some nonmedical and nonscience fields in which this type of imaging has been or could be used.
- Students could also investigate the role convection plays in heating and air conditioning for homes, and so on.

Differentiated Learning

Convection cells depend on differences in density, and density is a concept some students struggle with. To make density intuitive for these students, have handy at least two samples of the same volume but with different mass. You might find these materials with physical science supplies.

Answers to Student Questions

1. Students should see the flow of water in response to their placing a heat source under the pan of water.
2. The current was flowing toward the heat source along the bottom of the pan. The current was flowing away from the heat source directly above it, and then along the surface of the water.

Connections

Convection drives a variety of phenomena in meteorology and oceanography. Have students investigate other examples of convection and convection cells. In addition to exploring other examples, students could investigate the relative rates of movement within different convection cells. For an animation of convection cells in the atmosphere, search for "Teachers' Domain: Convective Cloud Systems" at *www.teachersdomain.org/ resource/ess05.sci.ess. watcyc.convective/*.

Resources

www.teachersdomain.org/
resource/ess05.sci.ess.watcyc.
convective/

3. The food coloring flowed upward in the center of the pan, away from the heat source. It flowed downward along the outer perimeter of the pan.

4. The water represents the asthenosphere, which is actually solid rock. Due to extremes of heat and pressure within Earth, the asthenosphere can flow slowly. The hot water in the cup represents the heat sources deeper within Earth's interior.

5. The plates might be represented by a piece of Styrofoam or cardboard floating on the water's surface.

6. In the convection model, heat from Earth's interior causes convection currents within the asthenosphere. Lithospheric plates move along with the underlying asthenosphere, and thus are carried in the same direction as the asthenosphere flows. Where the asthenosphere flows to the west, for example, the overlying plate moves to the west. If the flow is downward, the plate slides down into the asthenosphere and becomes part of it. If the flow is upward, material from the asthenosphere is added to the lithospheric plates.

7. Scientists have determined that many plates move at a rate of 2–3 cm/yr, whereas the water in this experiment may move at a rate of 2–3 cm/min. Over the course of one year, the plates will move 2–3 cm while the water would move about 10–15 km. Thus, the water has a velocity more than 500,000 times that of the plates.

Assessment

- For informal assessment as a class discussion, you can ask students to explain why a hot air balloon rises or how a lava lamp works.
- For formal or summative assessment, you can grade students' answers to questions, or you can ask students to draw and label a convection cell like that from one of their trials.

Activity 12 Planner

Activity 12 Summary

Students analyze the consequences of plate tectonics on continents by modeling the breakup of Pangaea via a flip book.

Activity	Subject and Content	Objective	Materials
A Voyage Through Time	Breakup of Pangaea	Model the breakup of the supercontinent Pangaea and the subsequent movement of continents.	Each student will need: a copy of the three map sheets, colored pencils or crayons (red, orange, yellow, green, blue, purple, tan), scissors, current world map showing terrain such as mountains and seafloor (this could be on display only)

Time	Vocabulary	Key Concepts	Margin Features
50 minutes	Supercontinent	I: Geological patterns and lithospheric plates II: Movement of plates III: Geological phenomena and plate tectonics	Fast Fact, What Can I Do?, Connections, Resources

Scientific Inquiry	Unifying Concepts and Processes	Technology	Historical Context
Modeling, predicting	Evolution of landmasses	Animation	History of Earth

A Voyage Through Time

Pangaea Breakup and Continent/Plate Movement

Background

A continent is part of a lithospheric plate; therefore, it moves in the same direction and at the same speed as the plate. In a sense, a continent is a passenger on a plate. Two plates, and thus two continents, can move toward each other (convergent boundary), move away from each other (divergent boundary), or move alongside each other (transform boundary or fault). Lithospheric plates—and continents—probably have been moving for billions of years. Because of this motion and interaction between plates, the shape and position of landmasses today—of continents and islands—is much different than in the past. Earth is an ever-changing planet!

About 280 million years ago, plates and continents came together and formed a **supercontinent** called Pangaea (pan-GEE-uh). Geologists have reconstructed the approximate shape and size of Pangaea by comparing rocks from all over the world and by using many different kinds of data. Pangaea existed for about 80 million years, then it split or rifted into smaller continents, and then these continents (and their plates) gradually moved apart.

Here is what we think happened to form Pangaea—and what could happen again. Continents can join together to form a larger continent at convergent plate boundaries.

Vocabulary
Supercontinent: Unusually large land area formed from most or all of the continents that existed prior to formation of this large landmass.

Fast Fact
The mountains in the Great Smoky Mountains National Park were formed when North America collided with Africa during the formation of Pangaea. The Blue Ridge region was shoved westward, up and over underlying rocks, to form a mountain chain probably as majestic as today's Himalayas. After hundreds of millions of years of erosion, what is left are the mountains in the Great Smoky Mountains National Park. Each year, 8 to 10 million people visit, making this the most visited national park in the United States.

Objective
Model the breakup of the supercontinent Pangaea and the subsequent movement of continents.

Activity 12

Topic: pangaea
Go to: *www.scilinks.org*
Code: PSCG136

Figure 12.1 shows two continents, A and B, separated by an ocean basin. This ocean basin will gradually become smaller because plate motion and subduction is causing the plate on the left to go down into Earth's interior. As the ocean basin becomes smaller, continents A and B move closer together, and eventually the ocean basin disappears and they collide (**Figure 12.2**). The lower part of the plate may go into Earth's interior, but continental rocks have low density and thus they mostly stay at the surface where the collision between plates may force them up to high elevations (e.g., the Himalayan Mountains, created by a collision between India and Asia).

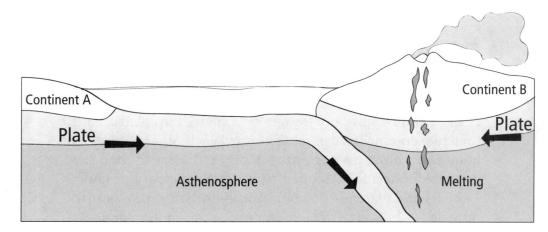

Figure 12.1
Convergent plate boundary with shrinking ocean basin and two continents (A and B), which are moving closer together. Arrows show directions of plate movement.

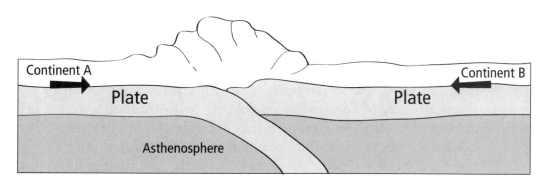

Figure 12.2
Convergent plate boundary with collision between two continents (A and B). Collision produced fold mountains and one continent from A and B. Arrows show directions of plate movement.

After a supercontinent has formed, the forces that brought plates and continents together may shift directions; continents—and plates—may be pulled apart forming divergent boundaries or rift zones (**Figure 12.3**). This is what happened to Pangaea. Geologists have been able to chart the changing positions and shapes of continents since Pangaea broke apart. Rifting or splitting of continents and plates is not something that happened only long ago. Today, rift zones are developing in several places around the world, including the Great Rift Valley in East Africa. **Figure 12.3** shows an example of rifting at early stages (e.g., parts of East Africa). As time passes, the rift valley will become wider, and an ocean basin with new ocean floor may form at this location. The continents will then move apart (like North America and Europe are doing today).

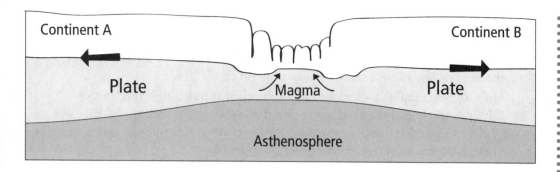

Figure 12.3
Continent and plate split
or rifted at divergent plate
boundary. What was one
continent and one plate
has split into two plates
and two continents. Arrows
show directions of plate
movement.

Although continents may appear to be fixed in position, actually they are still moving. This has been shown conclusively by use of GPS and other modern surveying techniques. North America is moving several centimeters farther away from Europe and closer to Asia each year. If the plates continue on their present course, North America will bump into Asia in a few hundred million years! Australia is heading northeast toward the equator at about the same rate. Africa and Europe continue to move toward each other. Plate movement is occurring today and will continue to occur into the future.

In this Activity, you will follow the movement of continents over the past 200 million years, beginning with the breakup of Pangaea. A flip-book model shows how the ancient continents moved and how today's continents arrived at their current positions.

Procedure

1. Your teacher will provide three map sheets (**BLM 12.1**), with a total of 20 frames. These frames are reconstructed maps of the continents that existed on Earth at a specific time. The interval between successive frames is approximately 10 million years. Frame 20 depicts continents as they are today.

2. Beginning with frame 20 and working backward, identify the continents listed in **Table 12.1**. Color the continents as indicated in **Table 12.1**. Continue back in time until you can no longer identify the individual continents.

Table 12.1: Color Guide for Continents

Landmasses	Color
North and South America	Yellow
Australia	Tan
India	Orange
Africa	Green
Europe and Asia	Red
Antarctica	Blue
Greenland	Purple

Materials

Each student will need

- a copy of the three map sheets
- colored pencils or crayons (red, orange, yellow, green, blue, purple, tan)
- scissors
- current world map showing terrain such as mountains and seafloor (this could be on display only)

Time

50 minutes

3. Beginning with frame 1 and working forward as far as you can, identify the supercontinent Pangaea. Color this land mass green.

4. Cut out each of the frames along the dotted lines. When all are cut out, stack them in order, 1–20. Frame 1 should be on top.

5. Hold the rectangles along their left side, then flip through the frames. Observe the continents changing position. You are modeling the breakup of Pangaea and the movement of continents over 200 million years, arriving at the formation of our present-day continents.

Questions and Conclusions

1. What event began to occur about 200 million years ago?

2. During your coloring of the frames, in which frame did you locate the first appearance of the following continents:

   North America? _____

   Australia? _____

   India? _____

   Europe? _____

   Antarctica? _____

3. In which frame did you locate the final breakup of Pangaea? Why did you choose that frame and not another?

4. What causes continents to move across Earth's surface?

5. When two plates collide and have continents at their colliding edges, the rocks are pushed together, forming a mountain range. Using a world map, identify two locations where mountain ranges exist and where you hypothesize plate collisions occurred.

6. Explain why continents do not go into Earth's interior when plates collide and one plate sinks or slides under the other.

7. If mountain ranges can form where plates are colliding, what would you hypothesize might occur where plates are separating? Apply your hypothesis to identify locations on a world map where plates might be separating.

What Can I Do?

To explore the breakup of Pangaea further, visit a museum about science and nature such as the Smithsonian Institute's National Museum of Natural History in Washington, D.C., or this website: *www.scotese.com/*.

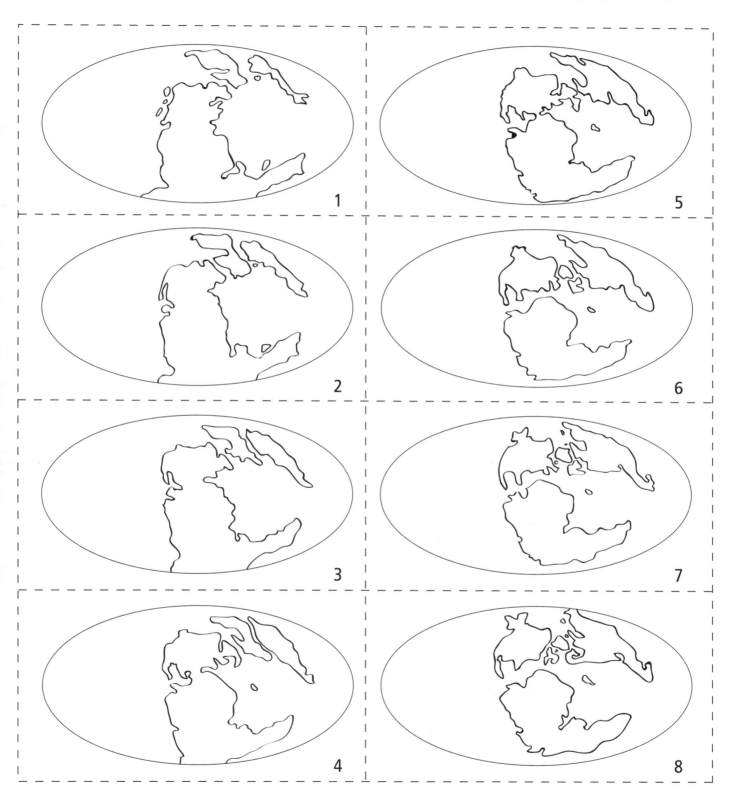

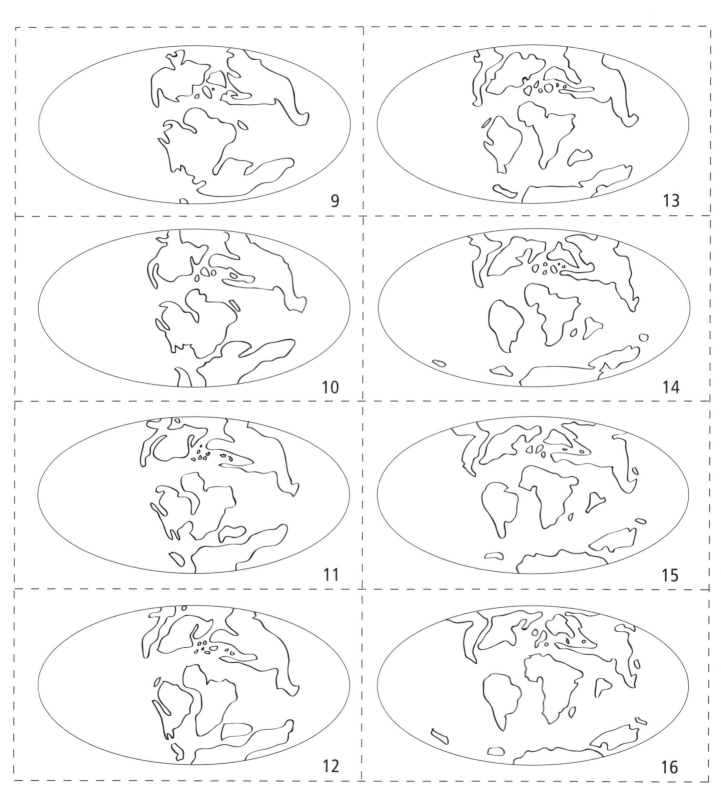

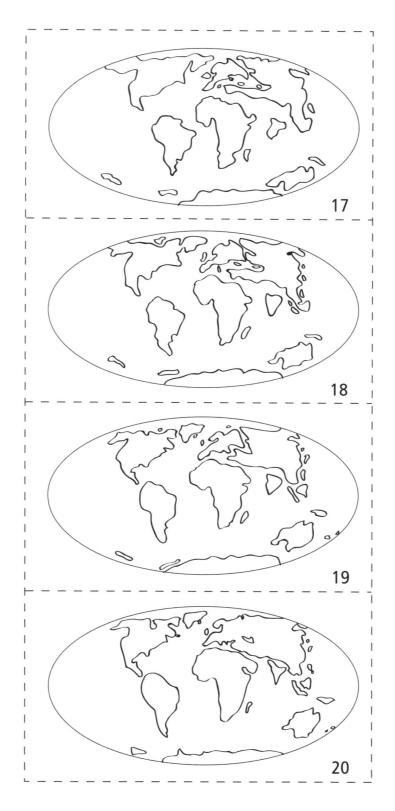

A Voyage Through Time
Pangaea Breakup and Continent/Plate Movement

What Is Happening?

Earth's lithospheric plates may have been in motion since early in Earth's history. Continents are integral parts of most plates, and they move as plates move. Several large continents came together to form one supercontinent, Pangaea (pan-GEE-uh), approximately 280 million years ago. Pangaea started to break up roughly 200 million years ago when the lithospheric plate(s) beneath it began to break up and move apart. Since that breakup, these plates have continued to move, carrying pieces of former Pangaea with them. The positions we observe today for Earth's continents are the result of this motion. Earth's plates continue to move.

When two plates move together, often a subduction zone is formed, with one plate sinking beneath the other. For example, a subduction zone currently exists along the western coast of South America, and it has produced a deep trench in the ocean floor. Because material making up continents is less dense than the material making up the rest of the plates, continents themselves generally are not subducted. Instead, they may be pushed together at subduction zones. This is one form of mountain building, and it can be observed in the formation of the Himalayan Mountains.

Objective

Model the breakup of the supercontinent Pangaea and the subsequent movement of continents.

Key Concepts

I: Geological patterns and lithospheric plates
II: Movement of plates
III: Geological phenomena and plate tectonics

Materials

Each student will need

- a copy of the three map sheets
- colored pencils or crayons (red, orange, yellow, green, blue, purple, tan)
- scissors
- current world map showing terrain such as mountains and seafloor (this could be on display only)

Time

50 minutes

How Do We Know This?

How do we know that a supercontinent called Pangaea even existed, let alone that it broke up about 200 million years ago?

The present-day shape of most of the continents suggests that they might have once been joined. But, the really convincing evidence comes from magnetic data preserved in rocks from each continent. This information indicates that the continents were all in about the same place on Earth's surface about 200 million years ago. In addition, ages and other characteristics of the rocks on each continent support the idea that the continents were joined. See Reading 1: Plate Tectonics to learn about more evidence for the existence of Pangaea.

Preconceptions

Ask students what they know about how plate motions have affected the positions of continents over geologic time.

- A continent can never split into smaller continents.
- A plate can never split into smaller plates.
- Continents float on top of the oceans.
- Plate boundaries are always at edges of continents.
- Plates and continents are totally separate features of Earth.
- Plates used to move, but now they are staying in the same places.
- The shape of a continent or a plate can never change.
- Earth has not existed long enough for continents to have moved.

What Students Need to Understand

- Continents, and the plates they are a part of, have been moving on Earth's surface for at least hundreds of millions of years. They continue to move today at rates of a few centimeters each year.
- Because plates move and interact, and because forces that move plates sometimes change, both plates and continents have changed size, shape, and position on Earth.
- Landmasses that became the present continents once were part of the supercontinent Pangaea.
- Low-density continental rock (tops of some plates) is too buoyant to sink into the asthenosphere along subduction zones.

Time Management

This Activity can be completed in 50 minutes.

Preparation and Procedure

No special preparation is required for this Activity. To improve the flip book's performance, use heavyweight paper or card stock when reproducing the map frames. You could do this Activity without adding color to as many maps (**BLM 12.1**) as the Procedure stipulates. While the flip books certainly look better if color is added, coloring can take considerable time.

Extended Learning

- Ask students if they can determine the directions of plate movement based on different motions observed in the frames. From this, students may be able to anticipate future changes in the positions of continents. Using these predictions, create additional frames for the flip book for the next 100 million years. Might a new Pangaea form at some point in the future?

- Los Angeles is on the Pacific plate and San Francisco is on the North American plate. The Pacific plate is moving north 2 cm/yr relative to the North American plate. Since Los Angeles is about 600 km south of San Francisco now, when should they be next to each other? In coming up with an answer, what assumptions are being made? The North American and Pacific plates actually are moving in about the same direction. If this is the case, how can the Pacific plate be "moving north 2 cm/yr relative to the North American plate"? (Hint: Think about relative movement.)

- The Appalachian Mountains are believed to have formed by continent-continent collisions at plate boundaries, but today these mountains are thousands of kilometers from a plate boundary. If the Appalachians did form at a plate boundary, what must have happened since that time?

- Other supercontinents are believed to have existed prior to Pangaea. Suggest that students search for information about these very ancient landmasses. Where were they? What are they called? How is their existence known or suspected?

Interdisciplinary Study

- Flip books are a basic type of animation. How are students' flip books similar to early forms of "motion pictures"? How are "modern" types of animations made?

- Have students investigate the use of animation in fields other than science (e.g., sports, history, education). What are advantages of animation? What are disadvantages of animation?

- The motion of continents and smaller landmasses had profound effects on the history of life. For example, after South America and Africa separated (approximately 130 million years ago), primates evolved into two separate lineages: the so-called "old" and "new" world groups. Have students investigate differences among animal groups separated by continental movement.

- Ask students to investigate what life on Pangaea might have been like 200 million years ago before this ancient continent started to break apart. How would it have changed after the breakup?

Differentiated Learning

Make sure that students can discern differences among the colors used in the flip book, and change colors if needed. An alternative would be to use stippling or cross-hatching for some of the colors.

Connections

The climate of a region depends on many factors including latitude, global wind patterns, and proximity to oceans. Ask students to describe how plate tectonics can explain the evidence for ice sheets in what is now India and for tropical plants in what is now Antarctica.

Answers to Student Questions

1. The breakup of the supercontinent Pangaea began to occur.

2. Answers will vary because identifying a continent's first appearance is somewhat arbitrary. During discussions of their decisions, you should encourage students to state their choices and explain the reasoning behind them.

3. Answers will vary. Encourage students to think in terms of geologic time in their estimations.

4. The movement of the lithospheric plates on which the continents "ride" causes continental drift.

5. Possible locations of plate collisions and related mountain building include the Himalayan mountain range (Nepal), the Zagros range (Iran), and the Appalachian Mountains (North America). Rather than searching for actual locations of plate collision and mountain building, students should use their flip books to identify collision locations and thus suggest plausible locations for mountain building.

6. Continents are not subducted because the material that composes them is less dense than the material composing their underlying plates. Less dense material rises above and generally stays above more dense material.

7. Answers will vary. Heat and volcanic activity often form volcanic mountains at divergent boundaries; the Mid-Atlantic Ridge and Mid-Pacific Rise are good examples. Another geologic feature commonly found where plates are moving apart is a rift or rift valley. Examples are the Atlantic–Indian Ocean Rift off the southern tip of Africa, the Mid-Atlantic Ocean Rift down the central Atlantic Ocean, and the Red Sea and Great Rift Valley of Eastern Africa.

Assessment

- For formal summative assessment, you can grade students' answers to the questions.

- For less formal assessment, you can ask students to describe what they learned from this Activity, either as a class discussion, as a small group conversation, or as a written exercise. You can ask them specifically what they now know about the positions of continents over time.

Resources
www.scotese.com/

Activity 13 Planner

Activity 13 Summary

Students model a volcanic eruption by melting crayons inside a plaster of paris model. They use a hot water bath to melt the wax, which rises through a tube they made with string in the plaster of paris.

Activity	Subject and Content	Objective	Materials
Magma and Volcanoes	Volcanic eruption	Create a model of a volcano with magma that rises to Earth's surface.	For each volcano model, students will require: two wax crayons, 25 cm of string, beaker (50–100 mL), scissors, paper cup (300 mL), plaster of paris (100–150 mL), hot plate, wire gauze, spoon, pan to boil water, water, tongs, indirectly vented chemical splash goggles, aprons, and gloves

Time	Vocabulary	Key Concepts	Margin Features
100 minutes	Tephra, Magma, Viscous	I: Geological patterns and lithospheric plates III: Geological phenomena and plate tectonics	Fast Fact, Safety Alert!, What Can I Do?, Connections

Scientific Inquiry	Unifying Concepts and Processes	Personal/Social Perspectives
Modeling	Modeling to illustrate a process	Cultural interpretation of volcanic events

Magma and Volcanoes

Model of a Volcano

Background

In 1980, Mount St. Helens in the Cascade Range in Washington State erupted violently, spewing **tephra** (ash and other materials) more than 20 km into Earth's atmosphere. Ash from Mount St. Helens traveled around the world. The explosion knocked down trees more than 25 km away and rattled windows in houses and office buildings 160 km away. Still, compared with many historic eruptions, such as Vesuvius in Italy and Krakatoa in Indonesia, Mount St. Helens' eruption was minor.

Volcanoes that erupt violently are located most often near converging plate boundaries. Where plates converge and one plate slides beneath the other, a chain of volcanoes forms above the sinking or down-going plate. **Magma** and lava associated with this kind of volcano are **viscous**, which means they are very thick and do not flow easily. Gases in the magma build up pressure inside the volcano, and eventually the volcano may explode. Mount St. Helens is this type of volcano; it is associated with the convergent plate boundary separating the Juan de Fuca and North American plates.

Where plates diverge, volcanic activity is usually in the form of relatively gentle eruptions, mostly lava flows. This is because magma and lava formed at divergent boundaries are relatively low-viscosity fluids—that is, they flow easily. Volcanoes associated with divergent boundaries are located

Vocabulary

Tephra: Solid material blown out of a volcano. It can include ash, pumice, dust, cinders, and other materials.

Magma: Molten rock that is below Earth's surface.

Viscous: When a liquid is thick and flows slowly.

Fast Fact

Hot ash from Mount Vesuvius buried the Roman town of Pompeii in 79 AD. It was undiscovered for 1,500 years and then was rediscovered several times before the first archeological excavations in the 19th century. From historical documents and archeological relics such as coins, household goods, and the remains and molds of fruits, pets, and humans, we can now reconstruct the way people lived—and died—in Pompeii.

Objective

Create a model of a volcano with magma that rises to Earth's surface.

Activity 13

Materials

For each volcano model, students will require

- two wax crayons
- 25 cm of string
- beaker, 50–100 mL
- scissors
- paper cup, 300 mL
- plaster of paris, 100–150 mL
- hot plate
- wire gauze
- spoon
- pan to boil water
- water
- tongs
- indirectly vented chemical splash goggles, aprons, and gloves

Time

100 minutes

SAFETY ALERT !

1. Indirectly vented chemical splash goggles, aprons, and gloves are required.

2. Pertinent safety procedures and required precautions for hazardous materials' MSDSs will be reviewed with students prior to doing this Activity.

3. Be careful to quickly wipe up any spilled water on the floor—slip and fall hazard.

primarily under oceans, where they form mid-ocean ridges. Iceland formed from this type of volcano as a result of repeated lava eruptions. Volcanoes at that location grew larger and larger until they were above sea level.

But, what makes magma rise to Earth's surface in the first place? Rocks and minerals melt when they become sufficiently hot. Magma forms below Earth's surface, and it is less dense than the unmelted rock around it. Magma's lower density causes the magma to rise toward and sometimes to Earth's surface. In this Activity, you will construct a model of an active volcano, with magma rising to the surface.

Procedure

Part 1 should be completed a day in advance to allow the plaster of paris to harden overnight.

Part 1

1. Remove paper from the crayons. Break a crayon into pieces and put the pieces in a glass beaker. Put on the indirectly vented chemical splash goggles, aprons, and gloves. Carefully warm the beaker on wire gauze on the hot plate until the crayon melts. Beakers must not go directly on the hot plate.

2. Hold the string at one end and use the spoon to push it into the melted wax until the string is completely coated. Then remove the string and let it cool.

3. Break the other crayon into three or four pieces and bundle the pieces together using the wax-covered string. Leave at least 5 cm of string sticking out of the bundle.

4. Mix the plaster of paris and water in the paper cup. The mixture should be about the consistency of soft ice cream and should fill 1/3–1/2 of the cup.

5. Use the spoon to push the crayon bundle into the plaster of paris mixture. The bundle should be completely covered and should not touch the bottom or sides of the cup. Loop the string around a pencil to support the bundle and keep it from sinking to the bottom of the cup (**Figure 13.1**).

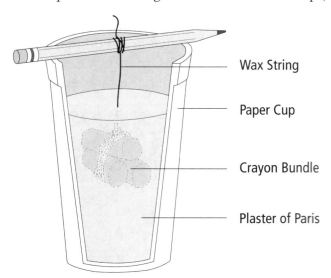

Wax String

Paper Cup

Crayon Bundle

Plaster of Paris

Figure 13.1
Experimental setup for model of volcano—Part 1

150

6. Holding the pencil, tap the cup on the table to make any air bubbles rise to the top of the plaster of paris. Try to be sure that the bundle of crayons is not touching the bottom or sides of the cup.

7. Clean your work area and let the plaster of paris harden overnight. To remove wax from the beaker, melt it with hot water, pour out the water, and wipe out the beaker before the wax hardens again.

Part 2

8. After the plaster has hardened and you are ready to make the volcano erupt, tear away the paper cup from around the hardened plaster.

9. Cut off the string close to the surface of the plaster.

10. Put on your indirectly vented chemical splash goggles, apron, and gloves and wear them throughout the rest of the Activity. Use tongs to place the plaster in a pan of boiling water with the string end up. Be careful not to splash the hot water on yourself—it will burn your skin! For the best results, the surface of the plaster should be about 1.5 cm above the surface of the water (**Figure 13.2**).

11. Observe and think about what happens as the wax "magma" inside the plaster "volcano" becomes hot and then melts.

12. When the "eruption" is completed, turn off the hot plate. Let the water stop boiling and cool. Once the water has cooled, use the tongs to remove the volcano carefully from the pan. Discard the volcano, empty the water from the pan, and clean any remaining wax from pan, tongs, and hot plate. Make sure the hot plate has had enough time to cool before attempting to clean it.

Topic: volcanic eruptions
Go to: www.scilinks.org
Code: PSCG151

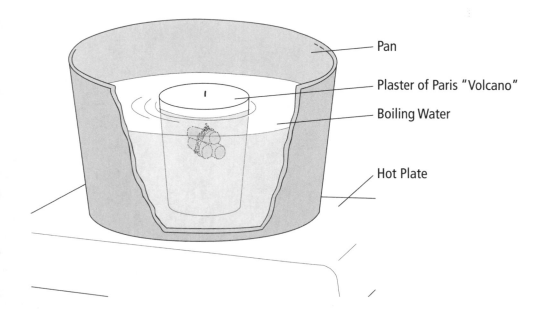

Pan

Plaster of Paris "Volcano"

Boiling Water

Hot Plate

Figure 13.2
Experimental setup for model of volcano—Part 2

Activity 13

What Can I Do?

You can monitor active volcanoes. In any given year, at least one volcano threatens or destroys communities. To monitor them, keep an eye on the news and search online for "global volcanism program." Then consider how you could help the victims of the volcano—are you willing to help relief programs in any way?

Questions and Conclusions

1. Why did the wax from the crayons inside the model volcano rise to the surface when the volcano was placed in the pan of boiling water?

2. What causes magma to rise to Earth's surface in a real volcano? How effective are the wax crayons in the plaster of paris model in portraying the action of real magma?

3. When the volcano model was prepared, you worked to remove air bubbles from the plaster. What do you think would have happened if there still had been a lot of air spaces in the plaster surrounding the bundle of wax crayons?

4. What might have happened if there had been no waxed string (no opening to the surface) in the plaster to relieve the pressure from the expanding crayon? Is this situation (the absence of a vent for magma and steam pressure) possible in a real volcano? What would be the result?

Magma and Volcanoes
Model of a Volcano

What Is Happening?

Molten rock is less dense than the same rock that is solid, and thus molten rock tends to rise toward Earth's surface, where it may form volcanoes. Although almost all rock beneath Earth's surface is solid, when it is subjected to different conditions of heat and pressure, the rock may melt. This molten rock normally contains a significant amount of gas (mostly water vapor).

Much of Earth's magma originates at depths of 100–200 km below the surface. At these depths, high pressures keep gases dissolved in the magma (analogous to gases dissolved in an unopened bottled soft drink). But, as magma rises toward the surface where pressures are lower, gases form bubbles (as happens when a soft drink bottle is opened). In magma, as pressure decreases, the increasing gas bubble volume makes the magma even less dense than the surrounding rock. This may allow the magma to continue moving upward.

Volcanic gases undergo a huge increase in volume when magma rises to Earth's surface, and it is expansion of these gases that is the primary cause of explosive eruptions. Experimental studies show that if 1 m³ of magma containing 5% dissolved water were suddenly brought from depth to the surface, the result would be a mixture of water vapor and magma with a volume nearly 700 times greater than the initial volume—from 1 m³ to 670 m³! The expanding gas bubbles can cause explosive eruptions that produce pieces of volcanic rock known as tephra (ash and larger pieces). The most abundant gas released from volcanoes is water vapor (H_2O), followed by carbon dioxide (CO_2), and sulfur dioxide (SO_2).

How Do We Know This?

How do we know when a volcano with an explosive eruption history will next have a potentially dangerous eruption?

The short answer is that we do not know for certain. Thus far, we are unable to predict the time and severity of volcanic eruptions. But, the volcano may provide clues suggesting a new eruption in the not-too-distant future. These clues may include a new release of gases (or increased gas emission), sudden release of minor amounts of ash or lava, an increase of minor earthquake activity due to stress buildup, and inflation as measured by high-resolution GPS units. Unfortunately, these things do not tell us when an eruption will occur, and they are not even proof that there soon will be an eruption.

Objective

Create a model of a volcano with magma that rises to Earth's surface.

Key Concepts

I: Geological patterns and lithospheric plates
III: Geological phenomena and plate tectonics

Materials

For each volcano model, students will require

- two wax crayons
- 25 cm of string
- beaker, 50–100 mL
- scissors
- paper cup, 300 mL
- plaster of paris, 100–150 mL
- hot plate
- wire gauze
- spoon
- pan to boil water
- water
- tongs
- indirectly vented chemical splash goggles, aprons, and gloves

Time

100 minutes

This Activity uses wax crayons in a plaster of paris volcano to simulate rock as it is heated, melts, expands, and flows to the surface.

Preconceptions

Ask students what their image of a volcano is—how does it look and what do they think comes out of it? You also can ask them whether any eruptions have been in the news lately. What do they know about those eruptions?

- The addition of heat to rocks causes them to become denser.
- Molten or solid rock within the Earth cannot rise toward or to Earth's surface.
- Volcanoes are hills or mountains on Earth's surface, but we do not know how they form.
- Earthquakes are the cause of all volcanic eruptions and volcanoes.
- Molten rock that forms volcanoes comes from Earth's core.
- The Mid-Atlantic Ridge formed as a result of a collision between two plates.

What Students Need to Understand

- Solid rocks and minerals deep within Earth may melt, forming magma, when subjected to new conditions of heat and pressure.
- Magma is usually less dense than the rock from which it forms.
- Since magma is usually less dense than the rock surrounding it, it tends to rise toward Earth's surface.
- If magma reaches Earth's surface, it may erupt as gentle lava flows or explosively as tephra; in both cases, volcanoes may form.
- Gases, especially water vapor, are important products of volcanic activity.

Time Management

This Activity can be completed in 100 minutes. The plaster of paris must have time to harden between classes. To save time, you might choose to do this Activity as a demonstration or to prepare all the volcanoes beforehand.

Preparation and Procedure

Before asking students to do this Activity, do it yourself to check for and troubleshoot potential safety and logistical issues.

Once all the materials are distributed, have students begin constructing their model volcanoes. Have students wear goggles, aprons, and gloves throughout this Activity. Remind students that beakers must not go directly on the hot plate. Make sure that a string is used as a vent in all volcanoes. If no string

SAFETY ALERT

1. Indirectly vented chemical splash goggles, aprons, and gloves are required.

2. Review MSDS for plaster of paris prior to use and share precautions with students.

3. Be careful to quickly wipe up any spilled water on the floor—slip and fall hazard.

4. Be careful when working with the hot plate and melted crayons—skin can be burned.

5. Wash hands with soap and water upon completing the lab.

is used, there will be no pathway for the melted crayon to flow to the surface, and if pressure becomes high enough, the model could explode (although simple cracking may be more likely). Using goggles, aprons, gloves, and string for a volcanic vent should minimize risk. Stress to students the importance of ensuring that the plaster contains no air bubbles when left to harden overnight. Air bubbles will interfere with the volcano's eruption by creating spaces in the plaster for the crayon to flow into as it expands.

Before any volcanoes are actually erupted, ask students what they think will happen to the crayons when the volcano is heated. Someone will probably say that they will melt. This will illustrate that a change in physical state, such as melting, may occur when conditions of temperature or pressure change. As the crayons melt, the wax will expand and rise to the surface along the string.

Explain to students that a similar process occurs deep within Earth when rocks and minerals are heated. They melt, forming magma, which is less dense than the surrounding rock. If the magma is sufficiently less dense and fluid, it can rise to the surface and erupt. When the time comes to "erupt" the volcanoes, make sure students are wearing indirectly vented chemical splash goggles, aprons, and gloves, and that they use extreme caution around the hot plates and boiling water.

Extended Learning

- Some of the volcanoes and eruptions listed in Reading 2: Volcanoes would be good subjects for student investigations. If they wish to learn about a relatively recent eruption in the United States, the 1980 Mount St. Helens eruption would be appropriate.

- Students could learn more about products of volcanic activity, such as kinds of rock and gas, and other materials. Do these materials have any economic value?

- Some rock associated with volcanoes contains older mineral and rock fragments. This means the fragments rose to the surface with the magma, or rose through the magma, and then were frozen in place when the magma cooled and solidified. But, these fragments normally are denser than magma. How could they rise to the surface? (Magma contains dissolved gases, and these gases may help carry the mineral and rock fragments to Earth's surface. An easy-to-perform classroom demonstration will help students understand how this could happen. Place several raisins in a beaker filled halfway with clear, carbonated soft drink or carbonated water. Bubbles should form on and adhere to the outside of the raisins and carry them to the surface. There the bubbles will be released into the atmosphere and the raisins will sink, where the process will begin again.) How might this explain the fragments in volcanic rocks?

- Let students investigate why the plaster of paris became hard. How is this type of plaster made?

Interdisciplinary Study

- Some societies have rejected or ignored scientific explanations of volcanic activity, preferring traditional views based on their cultural heritage. Have students investigate different kinds of cultural interpretations of volcanic activity.
- Investigate how volcanoes or volcanic products have been used in or as works of visual art. Also, in what ways have volcanoes been featured in literature?
- Usable heat can be obtained from Earth in a number of ways (e.g., hot springs, geysers, heat pumps). What are some of the different ways in which this heat is used? In what parts of the world is this done?
- Gases come from Earth's interior to the surface when volcanoes erupt. What normally happens to these gases after they reach the surface? Did this happen in the past? How might this relate to the fields of oceanography and atmospheric science?

Answers to Student Questions

1. The crayon expanded as it was heated and melted. The string provided a path to the surface.
2. Solid rock expands when it melts, resulting in material with a lower density than the original rock. This difference in density usually causes the molten rock to rise toward Earth's surface. Rising gases may also help carry it upward. The wax crayons fairly effectively model this process. However, volcanoes do not have "wicks" for the molten material to follow to the surface.
3. The expanding crayon would have filled the spaces rather than flowed to the surface.
4. The volcano might have exploded as the crayons melted and expanded. Yes, this situation is possible in the case of real volcanoes (e.g., explosive volcanoes). Or, the rock may simply crack, and the cracks then could provide passageways for magma to reach Earth's surface.

Assessment

- After students erupt their model volcano, ask them what their image of a volcano is now. How does the model compare to videos they have seen— or even volcanoes or volcanic eruptions they have seen?
- You could have students make a concept map of a volcano or volcanic eruptions—as a group or as an individual project.
- You can also grade answers to student questions for a formal assessment.

Activity 14 Planner

Activity 14 Summary

Students experiment with stacks of sugar cubes to explore the stability of structures during earthquakes.

Activity	Subject and Content	Objective	Materials
Shake It Up	Earthquakes' effects on structures	Compare how well various construction designs withstand the effects of an earthquake.	Each group will need: two books (same size), one shoe box lid or tray, 20 sugar cubes, pencil or crayon, ruler, Student Worksheet

Time	Key Concepts	Margin Features
50 minutes	I: Geological patterns and lithospheric plates III: Geological phenomena and plate tectonics	Safety Alert!, What Can I Do?, Fast Fact, Connections, Resources

Scientific Inquiry	Unifying Concepts and Processes	Technology	Personal/Social Perspectives	Historical Context
Experimenting	Rapid energy transfer	Design of structures	Natural hazards	Analyzing historical earthquakes

Shake It Up
Activity

Earthquakes and Damage to Buildings

Background

Nearly all locations on Earth experience occasional earthquakes, although most of them are not large enough to cause significant damage. But, people living near plate boundaries often experience earthquakes, and sometimes those earthquakes do cause significant loss of life and huge amounts of damage.

Damage and loss of life due to earthquakes could be significantly reduced if people avoided living in areas where a lot of earthquakes occur. This is not likely to happen. However, by using certain construction designs and materials, we can build more earthquake-resistant buildings. Such designs and materials can be expensive, and people must weigh the costs of using them against the possibility that a potentially damaging earthquake will actually occur in their area. In 2010, Haiti was devastated by an earthquake in part because of poor building practices. In contrast, Baja California, Mexico, experienced a stronger earthquake, also in 2010, yet structures in nearby southern California, with strict building codes, suffered minor damage.

In this Activity, you will use sugar cubes to investigate and compare the effects of an earthquake on different construction designs. You also will learn some of the things that people need to consider when constructing buildings in areas where there are frequent earthquakes.

Table 14.1 lists devastating earthquakes that occurred from 2000 to 2010. Each earthquake resulted in at least 1,000 deaths. Many of these deaths were caused by buildings collapsing on people.

Topic: earthquake damage
Go to: *www.scilinks.org*
Code: PSCG159

Objective

Compare how well various construction designs withstand the effects of an earthquake.

Activity 14

Table 14.1: Devastating Earthquakes, 2000–2010, That Caused 1,000 or More Deaths

Year Month/Date	Location	Deaths	Magnitude	Some Details
2001 01/26	Gujarat, India	20,085	7.6	166,836 injured; 339,000 buildings destroyed; 783,000 damaged. Due to Indian plate pushing north into Eurasian plate.
2002 03/25	Hindu Kush, Afghanistan	1,000	6.1	At least 1,700 houses destroyed or damaged. Landslides blocked many roads.
2003 05/21	Northern Algeria	2,266	6.8	10,261 injured; 180,000 homeless; over 43,500 buildings affected. A tsunami caused damage in the Balearic Islands, Spain.
2003 12/26	Southeastern Iran, Bam area	31,000	6.6	30,000 injured; 75,600 homeless; 85% of buildings damaged or destroyed. Largest earthquake in this area in over 2,000 years.
2004 12/26	Sumatra, Indonesia	227,898	9.1	3rd-largest earthquake since 1900. 1.7 million people displaced by earthquake and subsequent tsunami in 14 countries in S. Asia, E. Africa. Tsunami 51 m high.
2005 03/28	N. Sumatra, Indonesia	1,313	8.6	Over 300 buildings destroyed. Tsunami at least 3 m high caused by earthquake.
2005 10/08	Pakistan (and adjacent India)	86,000	7.6	Over 69,000 injured; 4 million people homeless. Landslides damaged roads and highways, cutting off access to the region.
2006 05/26	Indonesia	5,749	6.3	38,568 injured; 600,000 people displaced; 127,000 houses destroyed; 451,000 damaged; loss estimated at US$3.1 billion.
2008 05/12	Eastern Sichuan, China	87,587	7.9	374,177 injured. 45.5 million people affected, including 5 million homeless. 5.4 million buildings destroyed, 21 million damaged. Total economic loss US$86 billion. Landslides created 34 lakes threatening 700,000 people downstream.
2009 09/30	Southern Sumatra, Indonesia	1,117	7.5	1,214 injured; 181,665 buildings affected; 451,000 people displaced. Landslides disrupted power and communications.
2010 01/12	Haiti	222,570	7.0	300,000 injured; 1.3 million displaced; 97,294 houses destroyed and 188,383 damaged. Felt in Bahamas, Cuba, Virgin Islands, Florida, Colombia, and Venezuela.
2010 4/13	Southern Quinghai, China	2,698	6.9	12,135 injured; 15,000 buildings damaged.

Source: Data from U.S. Geological Survey Earthquakes Hazards Program: *http://earthquake.usgs.gov/earthquakes/world/world_deaths.php*

Procedure

1. Use the ruler to locate the center of the shoe box lid or tray. Mark this center point with the pencil or crayon (**Figure 14.1**). This center point will be the epicenter for the earthquakes you will create.

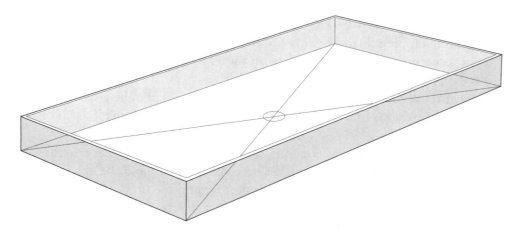

2. Stand the two books upright (as they would go on a shelf), and rest the shoe box lid or tray on top. Space the books so the ends of the lid or tray are each resting on one book (**Figure 14.2**).

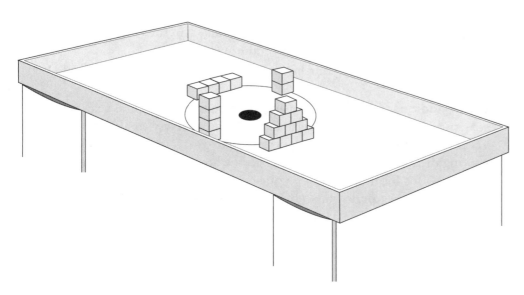

3. Place the sugar cubes at various spots near the center of the lid or tray, but not at the ends of the tray over either book. Use the following configurations:
   • four cubes side-by-side and touching
   • two cubes, one on top of the other
   • four cubes in a stack, like a tower
   • 10 cubes stacked like a pyramid

Project Earth Science: Geology, Revised 2nd Edition

Materials

Each group will need

• two books (same size)
• one shoe box lid or tray
• 20 sugar cubes
• pencil or crayon
• ruler
• Student Worksheet

Time

50 minutes

Figure 14.1

Shoe box lid or tray for earthquake experiment

SAFETY ALERT

Students should never eat food used or brought into the lab.

Figure 14.2

Setup for earthquake experiment: shoe box lid or tray, wide books for support, and sugar cubes for buildings

Activity 14

The center of each sugar cube structure should be approximately 5 cm from the earthquake epicenter. Do not worry about measuring 5 cm exactly. Just place the structures the same distance from the epicenter.

4. Lightly tap the underside of the lid or tray directly beneath the epicenter. Continue tapping lightly until one of the sugar cube structures topples. Make a note of which structure topples first under the heading Trial A on the Worksheet (**BLM.14.1**).

5. Continue tapping the lid or tray progressively harder until all the sugar cube structures have toppled. Note on the Worksheet the order in which they topple.

6. Repeat the trial using the same designs. Place the sugar cube structures in the same positions on the lid or tray. Record the results under Trial B on the Worksheet.

7. In Trial C, choose one of your four designs, and make multiple structures of that design. Vary the distance between the structure and the epicenter. Place one structure directly over the epicenter and the other(s) at varying distances from it. Record the distance from each structure to the epicenter on the Worksheet. Also note which design you used.

8. Lightly tap the underside of the lid or tray directly beneath the epicenter. Continue tapping gently until one of the structures topples. Make a note of which one topples first under Trial C on the Worksheet.

9. This time, rather than continuing the earthquake until all the structures topple, take note of the damage done to the other structures immediately after the first structure toppled. Did they slide? Are the cubes now misaligned? Record your findings on the Worksheet.

10. Repeat Trial C to verify your findings. Record the results under Trial D on the Worksheet.

11. Create additional earthquakes using your own experimental sugar cube structure designs. As you experiment, remember to try to alter only one variable at a time. For example, design your own structure and place it at varying distances from the epicenter to see how it withstands an earthquake at the various locations. Design your own data collection sheet to record data from your experiment so that others may easily understand it. Repeat the experiment as often as time allows. Record subsequent trials on your own data collection sheet.

12. When you are done, clean your area and return the materials to their proper places.

13. Your teacher may ask each group to present the findings from their experimental trials.

Questions and Conclusions

1. Which structure toppled first during Trial A?
2. Why do you think it was first to topple?
3. Which structure toppled last during Trial A?
4. Why do you think it was last to topple?
5. Were the results for Trial B the same as the results for Trial A? If so, why? If not, how and why did they differ? Were all of the test conditions exactly the same? What changes in the conditions could have changed the results?
6. Using the data you collected from Trials A, B, C, and D, as well as the data collected from your own experimental trials, what general predictions can you make about how the structure of a building affects its stability during an earthquake? Do you think your prediction would apply to a real building? What differences between the sugar cube structures and real buildings might affect the accuracy of your predictions?
7. Buildings with designs and materials that minimize the potential for earthquake damage tend to be somewhat more expensive than buildings constructed in conventional ways. Using these more expensive construction procedures can increase costs in communities where earthquakes occur. What factors should people in high-risk earthquake areas consider when deciding how much protection against earthquake damage to include in their building construction designs and materials? What benefits could offset a higher cost of construction?
8. Earthquakes cannot be prevented or controlled, but occasionally there are possible warning signs, such as bulging or tilting of the ground, increases in the number of small tremors, changes in well-water levels, and sudden changes in the speed of vibrations in the bedrock of Earth's crust. Because earthquake prediction is still unreliable, people's safety may depend upon their ability to react quickly and take necessary precautions at the earliest sign of an earthquake. Can you think of circumstances that might hinder a person's efforts to react quickly to signs of an earthquake?
9. Sugar cubes are not buildings. What are some of the weaknesses of using sugar cubes to model the effects earthquakes have on buildings? What are some of the strengths?

What Can I Do?

Devise a plan by which your family can get in touch with each other if you are separated in an earthquake. Have a backup plan that does not rely on cell phones.

Fast Fact

In 1886, a major earthquake flattened Charleston, SC, and even toppled chimneys and rang doorbells 250 miles away in Raleigh, NC.

Trial A: Standard Designs	
Structure Type	Order in Which It Toppled
Trial B: Standard Designs	
Structure Type	Order in Which It Toppled
Trial C: Distance From Epicenter	**Design Chosen:**
Order in Which It Toppled	Result/Damage
Distance	
Trial D: Distance From Epicenter	**Design Chosen:**
Order in Which It Toppled	Result/Damage
Distance	

Shake It Up
Earthquakes and Damage to Buildings

What Is Happening?

Virtually all locations on Earth experience earthquakes at some time or other. People living near plate boundaries live in active seismic areas and they may experience earthquakes frequently. Earthquakes in such areas also tend to be more intense. Almost always, the damage at or near the epicenter of an earthquake will be more severe than in areas farther from the epicenter. Of course, the number, size, and types of structures in an area, and the degree to which the population is prepared to react to an earthquake, are all important factors.

Table 14.2 lists major earthquakes that have occurred in the United States through 2010. The listings for Alaska and California should not be surprising because these locations are close to plate boundaries. But, major earthquakes also have occurred in Washington, Oregon, and Missouri. As well, major earthquakes with magnitudes slightly less than 7.5 (and thus not included in the table) have occurred in Massachusetts and in South Carolina. These past events indicate that it is a good idea for all of us to understand the possibility of being harmed by earthquakes and to have some knowledge of how damage can be minimized.

Objective
Compare how well various construction designs withstand the effects of an earthquake.

Key Concepts
I: Geological patterns and lithospheric plates
III: Geological phenomena and plate tectonics

Materials
Each group will need

- two books (same size)
- one shoe box lid or tray
- 20 sugar cubes
- pencil or crayon
- ruler
- Student Worksheet

Time
50 minutes

How Do We Know This?

How do we know that earthquakes will continue to occur in places where they have been common in the past?

Most of these locations are at or close to plate boundaries. Interactions between plates cause stresses within rocks to increase, and these can be expected to result in additional earthquakes. A typical pattern is that stresses increase, an earthquake occurs, and this reduces the stresses; then stresses increase again, and eventually there is another earthquake.

Table 14.2: Largest Earthquakes in the United States Through 2010 (ranked by magnitude)

	Location	Year	Month/Day	Magnitude
1.	Prince William Sound, Alaska	1964	03/28	9.2
2.	Cascadia subduction zone, WA, OR, CA	1700	01/26	~9
3.	Rat Islands, Alaska	1965	02/04	8.7
4.	Andreanof Islands, Alaska	1957	03/09	8.6
5.	East of Shumagin Islands, Alaska	1938	11/10	8.2
6.	Unimak Islands, Alaska	1946	04/01	8.1
7.	Yakutat Bay, Alaska	1899	09/10	8.0
8.	Denali Fault, Alaska	2002	11/03	7.9
9.	Gulf of Alaska, Alaska	1987	11/30	7.9
10.	Andreanof Islands, Alaska	1986	05/07	7.9
11.	Near Cape Yakataga, Alaska	1899	09/04	7.9
12.	Ka'u District, Island of Hawaii	1868	04/03	7.9
13.	Fort Tejon, California	1857	01/09	7.9
14.	Rat Islands, Alaska	2003	11/17	7.8
15.	Andreanof Islands, Alaska	1996	06/10	7.8
16.	San Francisco, California	1906	04/18	7.8
17.	Imperial Valley, California	1892	02/24	7.8
18.	New Madrid, Missouri	1811	12/16	7.7
19.	New Madrid, Missouri	1812	02/07	7.7
20.	New Madrid, Missouri	1812	01/23	7.5

Source: Data from U.S. Geological Survey Earthquakes Hazards Program:
http://earthquake.usgs.gov/earthquakes/states/10_largest_us.php

While earthquakes cannot be prevented or controlled, sometimes there are warning signs, such as bulging or tilting of the ground, increases in the number of small tremors, changes in well-water levels, and sudden changes in the speed of seismic waves (vibrations that emanate from the source of an earthquake). The time of day or night that an earthquake occurs can be a crucial factor affecting human preparedness. A warning network may be largely ineffective in the middle of the night, for example. A building in which many people work during the day poses danger to those people during an earthquake that occurs during daytime. Highway bridge collapse and other damage pose particular threats during times of heavy traffic.

Damage caused by earthquakes can be reduced by not locating buildings in high-risk areas. However, economic and population factors may make building in such areas unavoidable. Certain construction designs and materials can be used to minimize structural damage. These techniques, however, tend to be expensive; and for public buildings and highways, usually they must be paid for through increased taxation. In deciding how to build, the protective value of earthquake-resistant construction must be weighed against the extra costs of this type of construction.

In this Activity, students use sugar cube structures to investigate and compare the effects of an "earthquake" on different building designs. This Activity is designed to encourage and facilitate discussion on earthquake preparedness, including weighing the costs of special construction techniques against the likelihood of an earthquake's occurrence.

Encourage students to be aware of the various components of the scientific method they are employing in this Activity. These include experimentation and observation, repetition, hypothesis formulation, variability, and data collection and reporting.

Preconceptions

Ask students if they know specific cases of earthquake damage to structures that harmed people. In what way were the structures damaged? How were people hurt? If students offer many examples, organize their stories in a table or with a concept map. Categories of information could include kinds of structure, construction materials, and specific damage (e.g., building ornamentation shaken loose, facades crumbling, fire or water damage, etc.).

- Earthquakes only cause damage in places where earlier earthquakes occurred.
- Earthquakes are caused by changes in weather or climate, or phases of the Moon.
- Earthquakes occur only close to oceans and at edges of continents.
- The rotation of Earth on its axis causes all earthquakes.
- Earthquakes occur randomly, not in discernible patterns.
- Earthquakes cause plates to move.

What Students Need to Understand

- Earthquakes occur all over the world, but they occur most frequently and with greater intensity in active seismic regions, especially along and near plate boundaries.
- Earthquakes cannot be prevented or controlled, but some construction designs and materials will lessen the risk of property damage and loss of life.
- In general, it is not good to be inside a building during a major earthquake because the building may collapse.
- For specific locations, the cost of building structures that can better withstand earthquakes usually must be weighed against the likelihood of a damaging earthquake's occurrence.
- Earthquake preparedness is important, especially in areas where seismic activity frequently occurs.

Time Management

Students can complete this Activity in 50 minutes.

Preparation and Procedure

Collect the materials and divide them among the groups. Before distributing the materials to each group, stress the fact that earthquakes occur almost everywhere around the world, but that people living at or near plate boundaries are in active seismic regions. In such areas, earthquakes occur more frequently than in other areas, and they may be especially intense. The damage that results from a given earthquake depends on many variables, including the response readiness of the population, the number and types of structures, and the materials of which those structures are built.

Inform students that some buildings, because of their construction, sustain less damage during an earthquake than others. However, such structures can be more expensive to build. Explain to students that they are about to perform an experiment that will allow them to compare the types and amounts of damage that different structural designs may sustain during an earthquake. At the conclusion of the experiments, have students report their findings to the class.

Extended Learning

- Ask students to find information about what they could experience if an earthquake of magnitude 7 were to occur where they live. Have them make a list of things that would or could happen. They also could describe what they would try to do during and after the earthquake.
- Have students learn whether there have been earthquakes where you live, and, if so, when, what the magnitude was, where the epicenter was, and how much damage occurred. If there have been local earthquakes, students could build a local version of **Table 14.1**.
- Have students investigate damage caused by one or more major earthquakes (such as those listed in **Table 14.1** and **Table 14.2**). They might compare the damage done to different types of structures, or to similar structures at different distances from the earthquake's epicenter.
- Discuss what the components should be of a successful prediction of an earthquake (date and approximate time, specific location, and approximate magnitude).
- Have students obtain information about the types of data that geophysicists have used to try to predict earthquakes. How successful is earthquake prediction?

- Have students investigate emergency preparedness and response plans in your community. By contacting local and regional emergency-response officials, as well as organizations dedicated to disaster response and victim relief such as the American Red Cross and the Federal Emergency Management Agency (FEMA), students could gain valuable insight into the relationship between civic responsibility, humanitarian aid, and emergency preparedness. The class might want to perform a mock earthquake-response drill.

Interdisciplinary Study

- We now know that earthquakes are caused when rock beneath Earth's surface suddenly breaks or shifts position; exploding volcanoes also can cause earthquakes. However, a number of cultures have had quite different and interesting views about causes and consequences of earthquakes. What are some of these views?
- Some geometric shapes are inherently more stable than others. Architects and engineers have incorporated these shapes in designing structures that can better withstand shock waves created by earthquakes. Have students investigate which geometric shapes exhibit stability, and how architects and engineers use them. They should be able to find pictures of some of these structures.
- Select a major earthquake, such as the one in San Francisco in 1906, or the one in Lisbon, Portugal, in 1755. How did life in this city change after the earthquake? What changes were made in the city? How quickly did the city recover from the devastation caused by the earthquake?

Differentiated Learning

For students who enjoy thinking about design, engineering, or construction, you can direct them to software for Google SketchUp—at no cost—for designing or depicting three-dimensional structures.

Answers to Student Questions

1. Usually, the four-cube, stacked structure will be the first to topple.
2. It is the least stable geometric design—it is tall and spindly.
3. In most cases, the pyramid will be the last to topple.
4. It has the most stable geometric design—it has a wide base and a low center of mass.
5. Answers may vary. If results from Trials A and B were the same, all test conditions were the same. If results were not the same, something in the test conditions differed between the two trials. Answers will vary as to what test conditions were changed. These are possible changes that could affect the

Connections

Seismologists and ocean-ographers together try to prevent human catastrophes from happening as a result of earthquakes. As we have seen repeatedly, earthquakes cause collateral damage far from an epicenter via tsunamis rolling across oceans. Fortunately, tsunamis take time to travel across oceans. You can ask students to learn about tsunami warning systems—their historical effectiveness and their current configuration. Search for "Tsunami Warning" at *www.weather. gov/ptwc/*.

results: structures were placed in different locations; tapping was done at a different location; tapping was done with a different intensity; structures were "built" in different ways.

6. Generally, the taller or narrower a building, the less stable it will be during an earthquake. Answers will vary as to predictions for real buildings. Differences that may affect the accuracy of predictions might be the degree of "connectedness" of building sections as opposed to the degree of "separatedness" of sugar cubes; the sinking of building foundations below ground level as opposed to the setting of sugar cubes directly on top of the shoe box lid or tray; earthquake-resistant construction methods that may be used in real buildings. Flexible materials are able to move during an earthquake without breaking as readily; rigid or brittle construction materials usually break or crumble. Thus, wooden buildings and buildings that are properly reinforced with steel may survive an earthquake, while masonry structures (brick, concrete blocks) often are destroyed.

7. Answers will vary. Possible factors are cost, whether or not funds are available to construct a more resistant structure; the purpose of the structure—a hospital or school may need to be especially earthquake-resistant; how many people will occupy the structure at one time; the history of earthquake activity and damage to structures in the area.

8. Answers will vary. There are many actual and potential circumstances that could hinder a person's reaction to an earthquake. Some of the most significant circumstances include the following:

   • The time of day or night when an earthquake occurs. A warning network might not be effective in the middle of the night, when most people are asleep. A building such as a school or office, where many people work during the day, may pose danger to more people during an earthquake that occurs during the day than one that occurs during the night. Highway bridges pose a special threat during a time of day with heavy traffic loads.

   • Crowded conditions, such as in a stadium or sports complex. Such conditions may prohibit people from reaching exits. Crowds under any circumstances pose dangers if panic occurs.

   • Lack of warning signs, such as early tremors, preceding a major earthquake.

   • Confinement in an enclosed area, such as a subway, bus, automobile, or room, when an earthquake occurs.

   • People with hearing deficiencies who are unable to hear warnings that might be broadcast by radio, or who are physically unable to leave a building quickly.

9. Answers will vary, but encourage students to try to come up with a list of strengths and weaknesses for the model.

Assessment

- As students do their experiments, circulate to ask questions and offer suggestions about changing one variable at a time.
- For summative assessment, you could ask students or groups of students to develop a concept map designing structures to be safe in earthquakes.
- Alternatively, you could ask students to write: "If I were building a home, how would I build it to be safe in an earthquake?"
- Or, you could grade students' answers to questions.

Resources

http://earthquake.usgs.gov/earthquakes/world/world_deaths.php

http://earthquake.usgs.gov/earthquakes/states/10_largest_us.php

www.weather.gov/ptwc/

Activity 15 Planner

Activity 15 Summary

Students make a triple-decker, soy butter with raisins and jelly sandwich to model sedimentary rock formations. They take core samples with a straw, fold the sandwich into synclines and anticlines, and cut it to simulate faulting. From this Activity, students learn about the practice of sampling and the logic of deciphering a geological history.

Activity	Subject and Content	Objective	Materials
Study Your Sandwich	Deforming rocks	Investigate core sampling techniques geologists use to collect information about rock formations and their relative ages, and geologic structures.	Each group will need: one slice white bread, one slice whole wheat bread, one slice dark rye bread, two tablespoons jelly, two tablespoons soy—not peanut or almond—butter mixed with raisins, two paper plates, plastic knife, measuring spoon, clear plastic straws

Time	Vocabulary	Key Concepts	Margin Features
50 minutes	Sedimentary rock, Rock formation, Core sampling	I: Geological patterns and lithospheric plates III: Geological phenomena and plate tectonics IV: Rocks and minerals	Safety Alert!, Fast Fact, What Can I Do?, Connections

Scientific Inquiry	Unifying Concepts and Processes	Historical Context
Visualizing in 3-D	Analyzing models of rock structures	Chronology of rock formation and deformation

Study Your Sandwich

Sedimentary Rock Layers, Structures, and Relative Ages

Background

About three-fourths of Earth's land areas are covered by **sedimentary rock**, rock that typically forms in horizontal layers primarily from the debris of other rocks. Geologists obtain information about the history of a particular area by studying the area's rock layers or formations. A **rock formation** is what geologists call a distinctive unit of rock that formed in a particular area at a specific time. Geologists study rock formations so they can learn what an area was like when the rock layer formed, and how an area has changed over geologic time.

Rock formations are easy to study when they are exposed, such as along road cuts or cliffs. But, many rock formations are not exposed, and can be deep within Earth. Geologists have had to develop special techniques to study them. One technique involves drilling into the rock layers at a given location and pulling out specimens of all the rocks that formed there. This is called **core sampling**. By obtaining specimens from many of the rocks in an area, geologists can construct a chronology (timeline) of geologic events for that area.

Vocabulary

Sedimentary rock: Rock that forms from fragments of other rocks or fossils, or that crystallized from salts dissolved in water.

Rock formation: A distinctive rock unit that formed in a particular geographic area.

Core sampling: A technique used by geologists to get information about rock formations, involving drilling into Earth and pulling out specimens of rock from a formation's many layers.

Objective

Investigate core sampling techniques geologists use to collect information about rock formations and their relative ages, and geologic structures.

Topic: rock formation/deformation
Go to: *www.scilinks.org*
Code: PSCG173

Activity 15

Materials

Each group will need

- one slice white bread
- one slice whole wheat bread
- one slice dark rye bread
- two tablespoons jelly
- two tablespoons soy— not peanut or almond— butter mixed with raisins
- two paper plates
- plastic knife
- measuring spoon
- clear plastic straws

Time

50 minutes

In this Activity, you will use a sandwich as a model for a rock unit made of sedimentary layers. You will learn about the special technique of core sampling, and how geologists use the information they get from core sampling to construct geologic timelines for specific areas.

Procedure

1. Pick up a tray of materials from your teacher.
2. The ingredients used to create your sandwich represent layers of rock. Name each ingredient to represent a layer of rock. For example, white bread could represent sandstone, and soy butter with raisins could represent a conglomerate. Record the name on **BLM 15.1**, and create a graphic symbol for each layer. You will use these symbols later in the Activity on some of the diagrams that you make.
3. Place the dark rye bread on a paper plate. Next, spread soy butter with raisins onto the dark rye bread. Add the whole wheat bread, the jelly, and the white bread. Your sandwich represents a rock formation with five layers of rock (**Figure 15.1**). How do the layers in your sandwich differ? How do you think rock layers differ?

Figure 15.1

Sandwich: dark rye bread (bottom), then soy butter with raisins, whole wheat bread, jelly, white bread (top)

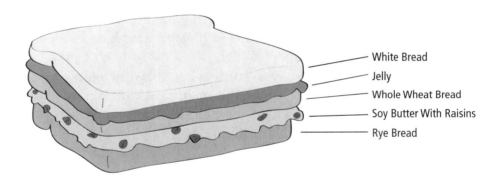

- White Bread
- Jelly
- Whole Wheat Bread
- Soy Butter With Raisins
- Rye Bread

SAFETY ALERT

1. Never eat food used in the lab Activity or bring any other food or drink in to the lab.

2. Wash hands with soap and water upon completing the Activity.

4. The relative ages of the various rock layers are important for geologists to determine. In the rock formation represented by your sandwich, which layer represents the oldest rock layer? Where is it located? Explain your answer.
5. It is important to note that while geologists sometimes find rock layers flat and horizontal like your sandwich, often the layers are bent or broken. To illustrate this, take your sandwich, holding the white bread at the top, and bend it so that it forms an arch (**Figure 15.2**). Label **Figure 15.2(b)** with the symbols for each of the rock layers that you created on **BLM 15.1**. Rock formations that form an upward-pointing arch are called anticlines.

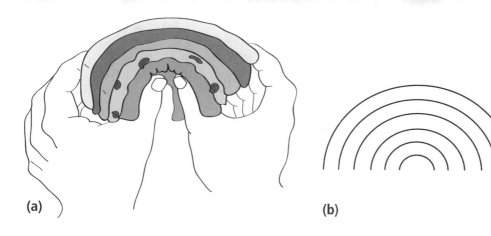

Figure 15.2
(a) Bent sandwich with arch pointing up, and (b) bent layers representing an anticline (label these layers with symbols)

6. Now bend your sandwich to form a trough, again holding the white bread at the top (**Figure 15.3**). As you did above, label this diagram with your rock layer symbols from **BLM 15.1**. Rock formations that form a downward-pointing trough are called synclines.

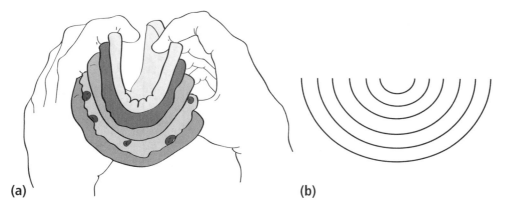

Figure 15.3
(a) Bent sandwich with trough pointing down, and (b) bent layers representing a syncline

7. Geologists want to know the relative ages of the various rock layers within the overall rock formation, and the sequence of events that affected the rocks. Which is the oldest layer in your rock formation? Which is the youngest? Was the formation deformed—bent upward or downward—before or after the original layers formed?

8. Keeping the white bread at the top, one person in your group should carefully bend the sandwich again to form an arch (anticline) as shown in **Figure 15.4**. Other members of the group should then use clear plastic straws to take three core samples at the three points indicated on the figure. Push the straw into the sandwich from top to bottom, making sure to keep the straw in a vertical position, regardless of whether the rock layers in your sandwich are horizontal or not. Make sure that you keep the core oriented correctly so that you remember which end is the top of the core sample (you could mark the top of the straw to help keep the orientation correct).

9. After you have finished taking the three core samples, sketch the results of your sampling in the empty cylinders in **Figure 15.4**, labeling the diagrams using the symbols you created on **BLM 15.1**.

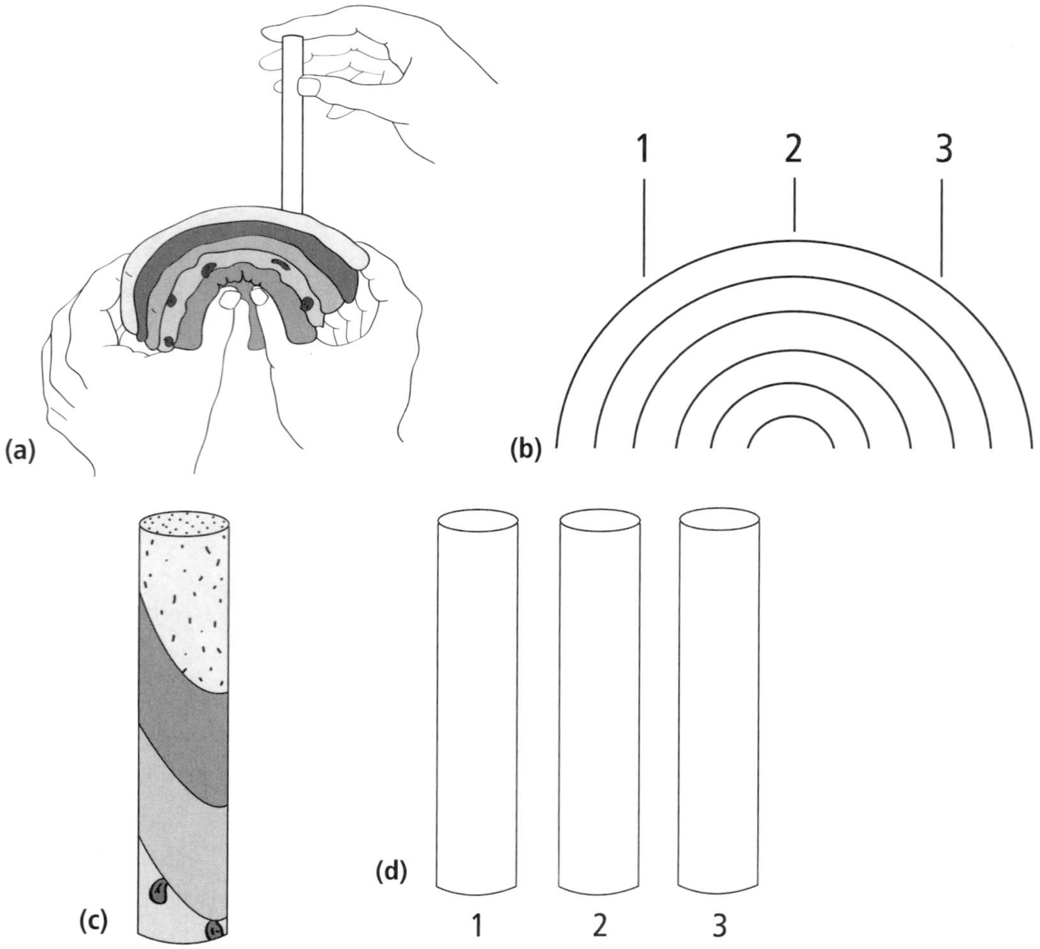

Figure 15.4

(a) Bent sandwich with arch pointing up, and bent layers representing an anticline

(b) Bent layers representing an anticline, with three places for core samples (1, 2, 3)

(c) Example of core sample

(d) Cylinders (plastic straws) for displaying core samples from sandwich

10. Repeat step 8, but this time bend the sandwich downward to form a trough (syncline) (**Figure 15.5**). Sketch the results of your core samples, using the appropriate symbols from **BLM 15.1**, in the empty cylinders in **Figure 15.5**.

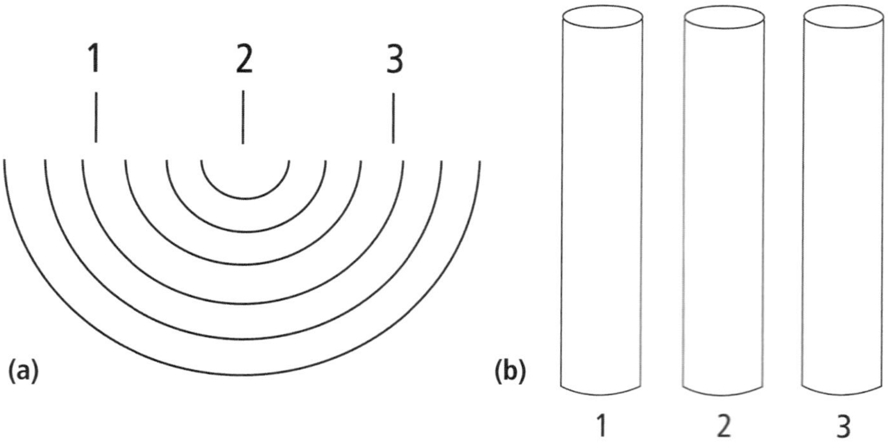

Figure 15.5

(a) Bent layers representing a syncline, with three places for core samples (1, 2, 3).
(b) Cylinders (plastic straws) for displaying core samples from sandwich

11. Sometimes rock formations can be completely broken, rather than just bent. To simulate this, cut your sandwich in half. Holding one of the halves in each of your hands, keep the halves close together, but slowly move one half up or down a few centimeters relative to the other. Do the layers match up anymore? In space A of **BLM 15.2**, draw a side view of what you observe.

12. What you have just created with your sandwich halves is a simulation of a vertical fault. Movement of rock layers along a vertical fault can cause earthquakes. Another type of fault is called a lateral fault. Simulate a lateral fault with your sandwich model by setting the sandwich on a flat surface with the halves touching, and then sliding the two halves past one another. Movement of rock layers along lateral faults also can cause earthquakes. In space B of **BLM 15.2**, draw a side view and a top view of your lateral fault.

13. Again, observe your sandwich. Which is the oldest rock layer? Did the faulting occur before or after the original layers were formed?

Questions and Conclusions

1. Describe the order of events that produced the samples seen in the cores you took in step 8 (from the anticline). Which layer was formed first, second, and so on, and when did significant deformational events occur?

2. Describe the order of events that produced the results observed in step 11 (vertical faulting).

3. How are the chronologies described in questions 1 and 2 similar? How are they different?

4. For the set of core samples shown in **BLM 15.3**, create a cross-sectional diagram in the box provided of what the rock structure from which they were pulled might look like. Describe a possible chronology of events leading to this particular rock structure.

5. How accurate a picture could you make if you had only one of the core samples shown in **BLM 15.3**? What does your answer tell you about the importance of having a lot of data or making a lot of observations before reaching a conclusion?

6. Why might it be important for geologists to locate faults?

7. For what reasons might it be important to know what is under Earth's surface?

Fast Fact

Geologists even drill cores through frozen lakes that fill impact craters above the Arctic Circle in Siberia. Dr. Julie Brigham-Grette, for example, was part of an international team that first had to pump water on Lake El'gygytgyn to make the ice thick enough to support the drill rig. Then they cored through the ice into sediment to learn about global climate change. They drilled into the rock below because its structure formed from the impact of an asteroid. You can learn more about Dr. Brigham-Grette's work as lead U.S. scientist on this project by searching online for "Brigham-Grette EARTH" at *www.earthmagazine.org/earth/article/36b-7da-7-14*.

What Can I Do?

When you are riding around in a car, look out the window for places where the road cuts through a hill. There you often can see sedimentary rock formations in what we call road cuts. Look to see if the rocks in the road cuts lie flat, tipped, or even are folded. How do you think they become that way?

Ingredient	Rock Name	Symbol

BLM 15.2: Drawings of Sandwich Broken by Faults

Date_____

A	B

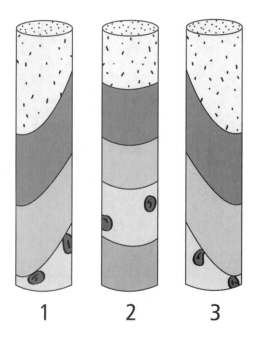

1   **2**   **3**

Core samples shown in the order and orientation in which they were taken from Earth

Study Your Sandwich
Sedimentary Rock Layers, Structures, and Relative Ages

What Is Happening?

This Activity is designed to give students an opportunity to investigate core sampling, one of the techniques geologists use to study rock formations. Students will also learn how geologists use the data they get from core sampling to construct a chronology of geologic events in a particular area.

Geologists cannot always see rock formations at Earth's surface. In such situations, with sufficient funding, they can drill cores (core sampling) to gather information about what lies beneath Earth's surface. As with all sampling

How Do We Know This?

How do we know when a sequence of sedimentary rocks forms that the lowest layer is the oldest layer and the uppermost layer is the youngest?

To understand why the bottom layer is the oldest, it may be best to try to visualize the formation of a sequence of layers of sediment that later become layers of sedimentary rock: Imagine a large body of water (ocean or lake) to which a stream brings a large amount of sand. The sand is deposited on the ocean bottom because the stream slows when it enters the ocean and can no longer carry the sand. Minor currents in the ocean spread the sand out, and eventually it has a smooth or essentially flat upper surface; we will call this first deposit of sand Layer A. Then more sand or some other type of sediment, such as clay, is added to the ocean, and the spreading and smoothing process is repeated. This could happen again, and again. Which layer was there first? Layer A, and thus it has to be the oldest. After the sediments are deposited, the grains are cemented and squeezed together to form sedimentary rock layers (e.g., sandstones, shales).

But, there could be a complication: Collisions between plates can significantly deform rocks, sometimes even resulting in a sequence of sedimentary rocks being overturned (youngest at the bottom). Fortunately, most sedimentary rocks have features on their surfaces and within the layers that make it possible to tell if this overturning has taken place. Examples would be a snail shell with the bottom filled with mud, or raindrop impressions preserved on the upper surface of a layer of what was once mud.

Objective

Investigate the core sampling techniques geologists use to collect information about rock formations and their relative ages, and geologic structures.

Key Concepts

I: Geological patterns and lithospheric plates
III: Geological phenomena and plate tectonics
IV: Rocks and minerals

Materials

Each group will need

- one slice white bread
- one slice whole wheat bread
- one slice dark rye bread
- two tablespoons jelly
- two tablespoons soy— not peanut or almond— butter mixed with raisins
- two paper plates
- plastic knife
- measuring spoon
- clear plastic straws

Time

50 minutes

techniques, the number of samples and the locations where they are taken are important variables in determining how accurate a picture can be obtained using the samples.

To understand the geological history of an area, we must understand the relative ages of the layers of rock present. The oldest layers are found at the bottom and the youngest layers at the top, unless the sequence has been overturned. Also, layers of rock that are bent or broken indicate that a deformational event occurred after horizontal layers formed. A sense of chronology of geologic events is an important concept for students to learn and appreciate.

This Activity is a highly simplified illustration of the many processes involved in creating geologic structures from rock formations. Emphasize to students that this is just an introduction. There can be many complexities involved in the formation of sequences of rock layers; for example, rock layers can be overturned, and weathering and erosion might remove some rock layers at that location.

Preconceptions

Ask students what they understand about how sedimentary rocks form. The issue is whether students understand that sedimentary rocks typically form underwater in flat layers that build up over time.

- In a sequence of layered rocks, all of the layers are the same age.
- During the formation of sedimentary rocks, sediments always are deposited on continental rocks.
- Bending of layers of sedimentary rock is extremely unusual.
- The oldest rock layer is always the one at the top.
- Changes to the appearance of Earth's surface are always very slow.
- It is impossible for one type of rock to change into another type of rock.

What Students Need to Understand

- Sedimentary rocks generally form in horizontal layers, with the oldest layer on the bottom. If in a different order, the layers have been deformed or even overturned by later events.
- Mountain-building events may bend or break sedimentary layers after they are formed. The forces that cause such events also may cause earthquakes.
- The kinds of rocks that are present, and the characteristics of those rocks, provide information about the geological history of a location, including ancient environmental conditions.

Time Management

This Activity can be completed in 50 minutes.

Preparation and Procedure

No special preparations are required for this Activity. The bread you select should be firm, day-old bread, or something similar. Fresh, soft breads do not hold up well enough to produce clear core samples. You might want to practice with the bread you are planning to use, and even have students practice taking core samples several times before proceeding with the graphic representations.

Answers to Procedure Questions

Procedure #3. Student answers might include that layers in their sandwiches differ in composition, color, texture, and thickness, among other differences. Rock layers differ for many of the same reasons, but age is a major difference.

Procedure #4. The oldest layer is on the bottom and the youngest layer is on top.

Procedure #7. The oldest layer is on the bottom and the youngest layer is on the top. The disruption of layers occurred after the layers were formed.

Procedure #13. Again, the oldest layer is on the bottom and the youngest layer is on the top. The faulting occurred after the layers were formed.

Extended Learning

- Most sedimentary rocks form on the ocean floor. It can be very difficult for students to visualize and accept that many times in the past, North America's interior was covered by inland seas. Have students investigate the sedimentary rocks that cover much of the middle portions of the United States. What rocks are there? What characteristics indicate that they formed on the seafloor?

- A common preconception is that anticlines cause hills and mountains, while synclines cause valleys. However, this is not true. Anticlines often form valleys, and synclines often form mountains. What is important to the formation of a mountain or valley is how resistant the rock at the surface is to weathering and erosion—if resistant, mountains result; if easily weathered and eroded, valleys result. Have students investigate to see if there is a correlation between resistant rocks such as sandstone and the formation of mountains. Students also could determine what rocks are easily weathered and eroded, and thus occur under valleys (e.g., Shenandoah Valley).

- Anticlinal and synclinal structures in rocks can range from microscopic in size to many hundreds of kilometers across. Large structures include the Cincinnati Arch and Nashville Dome, and the Michigan Basin and Williston Basin. Ask students to find information about the rocks in one of these areas, and try to determine if the rock structure there is anticlinal or synclinal. (Hint: Arch and dome are anticlinal structures, and basin is synclinal.)

- Ask students to imagine an area where the dominant rock is the igneous rock granite (if possible, have a sample on display). This rock typically contains the minerals feldspar, quartz, and mica (usually biotite). Given the right circumstances and enough time, weathering and erosion could convert this granite into the sedimentary rock sandstone. Most of this sandstone would be quartz from the granite. Have students make up a sequence of events that would have to happen for the granite to be converted into sandstone. (They probably will need to look up information on the minerals in the granite, and their behavior during weathering.)

- Actual core sampling requires considerable effort and expense to drill through Earth's layers. Have students investigate how far down geologists have been able to drill for the purpose of extracting samples. Use this investigation to reinforce students' understanding of geological distances and the actual depth from Earth's surface to Earth's interior layers (e.g., asthenosphere, mantle, core).

Interdisciplinary Study

- Determining a sequence of events is important not only in geology but also in virtually every human activity. Learning to analyze evidence and data to produce a plausible sequence of events is a skill that takes practice to perform well. **Figure 15.6** shows two sets of animal tracks. Have students look at the tracks, and see if they can determine what happened to the two animals. Have them write a short explanation of what happened; they also should construct a timeline based on the chronology of their narrative. Also have students give alternate explanations if they think these are possible.

- Core sampling is a way of obtaining data, but expense and time necessarily limit information that can be obtained. Ask students to investigate sampling in general: What does "representative" mean? List different types of sampling. Why is sampling done? How do people determine what samples to take? What are typical limiting factors in obtaining data? How can you be confident that the samples obtained actually are representative of what has been sampled?

Differentiated Learning

You can challenge students with spatial skills by asking them to sketch a map as if the rocks in **BLM 15.3** had partially eroded. Draw a horizontal line halfway down the cores and ask students to draw the pattern of rock formations they would see if they were soaring overhead. This is called a

Connections

While geologists core downward to gather data, meteorologists float balloons upward. Twice a day, meteorologists release weather balloons with probes and transmitters (radiosondes) to collect temperature, humidity, and barometric pressure through the air column. They do it worldwide at about 800 places. Have students learn about the weather balloons in the context of sampling data where scientists cannot go.

plan view or map view. You also can give these students real geological maps and cross sections to explore. Geologic maps from the Appalachian Mountains or Grand Canyon are both fascinating and beautiful.

Figure 15.6
Two sets of animal tracks

Answers to Student Questions

1. Answers will vary depending upon the names of the various rock layers. The bottom layer is the oldest and the top layer is the youngest. The folding to produce the anticline occurred after all horizontal rock layers were formed.

2. Answers will vary depending upon the names of the various rock layers. The bottom layer is the oldest and the top layer is the youngest. The break in the formation to produce the vertical fault occurred after all horizontal rock layers were formed.

3. The chronologies are similar in that both begin with sediments being deposited in horizontal layers, horizontal rock layers being formed from the sediments, followed by an event that deformed the rock formations. The chronologies are different in the type of disruptive event that occurred.

4. Answers will vary depending upon the names and symbols of the various rock layers. The bottom layer is the oldest and the top layer is the youngest. The folding of the rock formation layers to produce the anticline occurred after all horizontal layers were formed.

5. With only one core sample, it would be impossible to know the position of

the rocks in adjacent locations. You would not be able to distinguish among synclines, anticlines, or faults. Scientists always must consider the amount and accuracy of available data when drawing conclusions based on that data. Limited data and inaccurate data can lead to inaccurate conclusions.

6. Where faults are found, there may be earthquakes created by movement of rock along the faults. Also, valuable mineral deposits are sometimes found along faults.

7. Answers will vary. Possibilities include locating valuable mineral resources or fuels, finding reliable supplies of water, and determining where earthquakes or volcanic eruptions might occur.

Assessment

- For informal formative assessment, monitor students as they do this Activity to make sure that they do not get too frustrated with the spatial aspects of interpreting their cores.
- For summative assessment, you can grade students' answers to questions, but you can also ask them to interpret the geological sequence of events from a simple cross section.

Readings

Introduction

The following Readings on Plate Tectonics, Volcanoes, Earthquakes, and Rocks and Minerals elaborate on the concepts presented in the Activities. The Reading on Careers in Geology and Geosciences provides a resource for you to help students know what geologists do and how to become one. The Readings were written especially for this volume with the teacher in mind.

Plate Tectonics

What We Mean by Plate Tectonics

Early investigators suggested that continents had not always been in their current positions, and this idea was called continental drift. As evidence accumulated, it was recognized that much more of Earth moves than just continents. *Plate tectonics* became the name of this new realization and theory.

The modern theory of plate tectonics states that the outer part of Earth consists of relatively thin, rigid pieces called plates (some of which include the continents), and that these plates continually move, although slowly. It might be helpful to think of Earth as a very large hard-boiled egg whose shell has been cracked into a few pieces that somehow move over the egg white's surface. Depending on how one defines "large" and "small," there are about seven large plates and about twice that many smaller ones that move and interact at their boundaries (**Figure R1.1**). Each plate is about 100 km thick and has a surface area of thousands of square kilometers. Different plates move with different velocities, ranging from about 1–20 cm/yr.

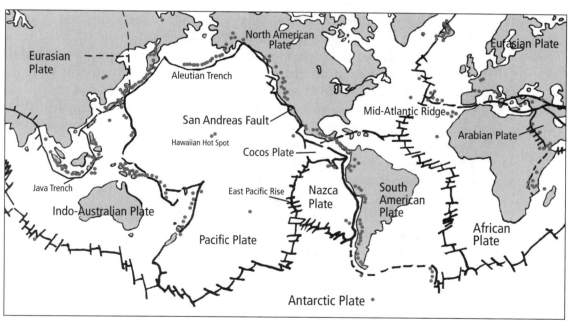

Figure R1.1   Map of world with major lithospheric plate boundaries and locations of active volcanoes

Development of a Unifying Theory

The theory of plate tectonics helps explain many geological phenomena, especially the existence and distribution of earthquakes, volcanoes, and mountain ranges. Plate tectonics provides a unifying theory that explains large-scale geologic change over long stretches of time. It helps us understand why Earth's geological formations currently appear the way they do, and it also helps scientists predict changes in Earth's form that may occur in the future.

Modern world maps hold the same clues to continental movement that early theorists noticed from maps that charted European naval exploration after the 15th century. Francis Bacon wrote in the early 1600s about the "good fit" between the shapes of coastlines of the "old" and "new" worlds. Over 200 years later, Antonio Snider noted similarities among certain plant fossils collected in Europe and America. He also recognized the apparent fit between continental coastlines and suggested that the continents had once been a single, huge landmass. Then, in 1885, Eduard Suess found the same rock formations on several southern-hemisphere continents. The formations were identical in sequence and type, so they almost certainly formed at the same time and place. Since that could not have happened on different continents separated by oceans, Suess concluded that they must have once been a single landmass.

Continental drift was first proposed as a distinct scientific theory by F. B. Taylor and Alfred Wegener in the early 1900s. Their hypotheses, developed independently of one another, were based on evidence similar to that discussed above and included the suggestion of a single landmass in the past. While the theory of continental drift attracted much attention, the insufficiency of hard evidence and the absence of an explanation as to how the continents moved hindered its acceptance among the international scientific community. Although the theory of continental drift was not universally accepted in the early 1900s, continuing curiosity and improving technology gradually provided sufficient evidence to support it. (Note: In the early part of the 1900s, the theory of continental drift was much more accepted in Europe than it was in North America.) Below is some specific information about two additional examples of evidence that supports continental drift: (1) distribution of fossils of plants and animals that were unlikely to have crossed oceans, and (2) ancient magnetic patterns preserved in rocks.

Fossil Records

Seeds of an extinct fern *(Glossopteris)* were found in South Africa, Australia, and India. Because the seeds were large, biologists thought it unlikely that they could have been dispersed by wind or water. Fossil remains of an extinct fresh-water reptile, *Mesosaurus*, were found distributed in areas of eastern South America and western South Africa. Fossils of the land reptile *Lystrosaurus* were found in Antarctica, India, and Africa. *Cynognathus* fossils, also land-dwelling reptiles, were found in South America and Africa. The distribution of all these

organisms could best be explained by one large continent, as shown in
Figure R1.2. The ages of rocks on the continents, geologic structures such as
mountain ranges, and distribution of unusual glacial deposits also match up
if these continents were joined together as shown. The specific examples cited
are not the only lines of evidence, but these have proven to be compelling.

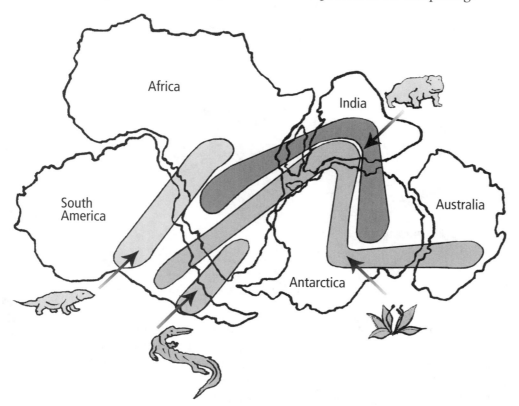

Figure R1.2
Distribution of fossils of
a land plant and three
nonmarine reptiles that
lived over 200 million years
ago. Today, these fossils are
found on widely separated
continents. This figure is
based on information from
the U.S. Geological Survey.

Paleomagnetism (ancient magnetism)

Some types of rocks are weakly magnetic. When they were formed, iron-
bearing minerals within them became aligned parallel to Earth's magnetic field
of the time. When these rocks crystallized, iron-bearing minerals that were
aligned like a compass needle with magnetic poles were "frozen" in place.
Figure R1.3 shows three hypothetical continents: A, B, and C. The arrow on
each continent shows the direction of magnetic north for rocks of a specific
age on that continent. However, this direction is significantly different for each
of the continents! In other words, the arrows do not point toward a single
position for the magnetic north pole. Based on **Figure R1.3**, it appears that
magnetic north was in three different places at the same time, or that there
were three entirely different magnetic north poles. Neither of these situations
is possible.

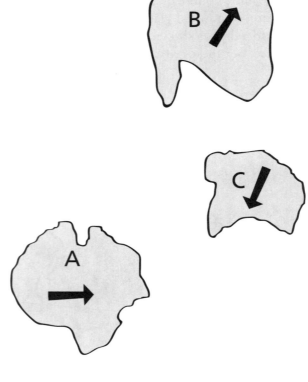

Figure R1.3
Three continents, A, B, C, include rocks of the same age, but the position of magnetic north recorded in these rocks is in different locations (see arrows). How could magnetic north have been in different places at the same time?

If each continent moved with respect to the other continents after the rocks were formed, that would account for the apparent existence of three ancient magnetic north poles. In **Figure R1.4**, the continents in **Figure R1.3** have been moved so the arrows point toward one place—a single magnetic north pole. This is analogous to maps of Earth that show the southern continents reassembled into Gondwana. Thus, using paleomagnetism, geologists have demonstrated that continents moved over time a significant distance. Furthermore, from high-resolution GPS data, we know they continue to move.

Figure R1.4
These are the same hypothetical continents as in **Figure R1.3**, but they have been moved so that the magnetic north arrows for rocks of the same age on each continent now point to the same spot.

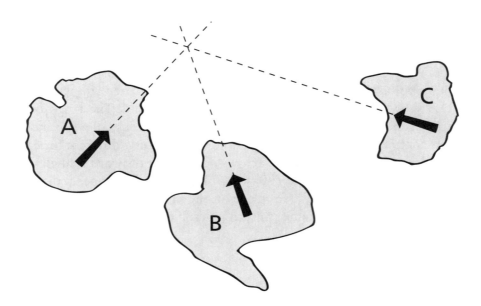

Ages of Seafloor Rocks

So far, we have looked at several types of evidence that support the idea that continents have moved. Overwhelming evidence for continental movement—now called plate tectonics—began to accumulate in the 1950s. With more sophisticated technology, scientists systematically explored the world's seafloors. They discovered long ridges of undersea mountains formed of basalt, an igneous rock (**Figure R1.5**). Ridges occur on all the world's seafloors, and rise as much as three kilometers above the adjacent seafloor. Running along the crest of each of these mountain ranges is a feature called a rift valley. A rift valley is a crack or series of cracks in Earth's crust that occurs in places where the plates are being pulled apart; in the Atlantic and Indian Oceans, rift valleys lie roughly midway between the continents. For this reason, many of these ranges are called mid-ocean ridges. The Mid-Atlantic Ridge is perhaps the best known mid-ocean ridge. In a few places, these ridge-and-rift systems cut across continents: the Red Sea lies in a huge rift valley.

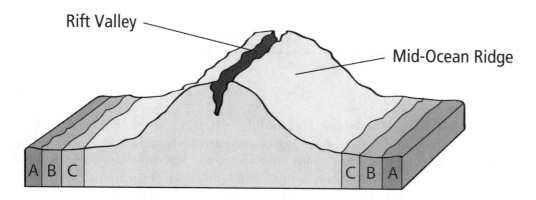

Rift Valley — **Mid-Ocean Ridge**

A B C   C B A

Figure R1.5
This is a cross-section of a mid-ocean ridge, showing a rift valley at the top of the ridge. A, B, and C on both sides of the ridge are locations of rocks of different age: oldest, A; intermediate age, B, youngest, C; the rocks directly below the rift valley are younger than those at C.

Seafloor Spreading

In the early 1960s, further exploration of seafloor geological features revealed even more evidence supporting plate tectonics. The age of rocks from the seafloor was found to increase moving away from the ridges and toward the continents. In several places along mid-ocean ridges (see **Figure R1.5**), samples of rock obtained by drilling, at Location C, for example, were found to be younger than samples taken from Location B, and those were younger than samples from Location A. Where there is weakness in Earth's crust, like at the rift valleys, magma can rise, even to Earth's surface. This may be more easily understood if we think of three discrete episodes of movement of magma through Earth's crust and examine the results (**Figure R1.6**).

Reading 1

Figure R1.6

In **Figure (a)**, magma forms new igneous rocks (A) at a mid-ocean ridge or spreading center. **Figure (b)** shows that at a later time than the formation of rocks at A, magma forms new igneous rocks at B; the rocks formed initially (A) have moved away from the ridge. **Figure (c)** shows that at a later time than the formation of rocks at A and B, magma forms new igneous rocks at C; the earlier rocks (A and B) have moved away from the ridge. This movement is called seafloor spreading.

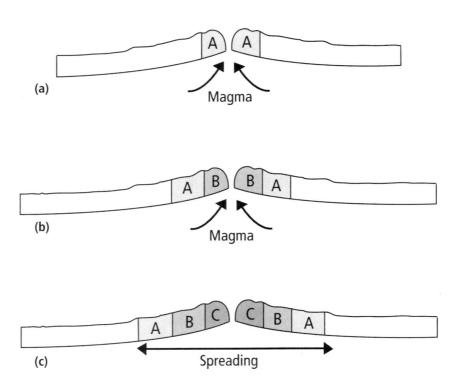

(a) Magma

(b) Magma

(c) Spreading

Topic: lithosphere
Go to: *www.scilinks.org*
Code: PCSG194

From this series of diagrams (**Figures R1.6a, b, c**), we see that igneous rock forms first at Location A and then moves away from the crest of the ridge; rock then forms at B, and then at C. This phenomenon is called seafloor spreading. Specific evidence for this process is provided by the ages of the rocks that form the seafloor, as well as by the magnetic patterns preserved in those rocks. As new rock is added to the oceanic crust at the ridge, it records the characteristics of Earth's magnetic field at that time. As oceanic crust moves in both directions away from the ridge, the magnetic minerals contain and preserve the record of periodic changes in Earth's magnetism; this clearly demonstrates the movement of the seafloor. Since the seafloor is part of the lithospheric plates, and the continents are also part of the plates, if the seafloor is moving, then the plates and continents also must be moving.

The relationship of seafloor, continents, and the upper part of Earth's interior is shown in a more detailed sketch of two diverging lithosphere plates (**Figure R1.7**). The continental and oceanic portions of Earth's crust form part of the lithosphere, the relatively rigid or brittle outer portion of Earth. When new oceanic crust forms at mid-ocean ridges, both the older oceanic crust and the continents riding atop the plates move.

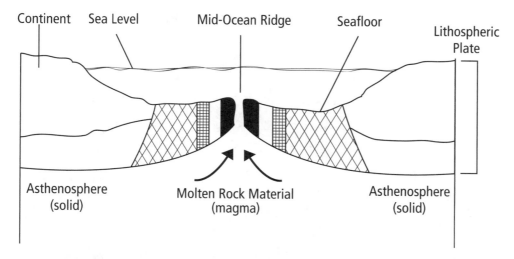

Figure R1.7
Cross-section of a mid-ocean ridge (e.g., Mid-Atlantic Ridge), showing lithospheric plates and oceanic and continental crust, seafloor, and two continents. The plates would be moving away from the mid-ocean ridge.

Convection Cells—Cause of Plate Motion?

Scientists do not completely agree about what causes plate motion. For many years, most investigators accepted the idea that convection currents or cells within Earth's interior provide the driving mechanism for plate movement. Convection currents or cells are common phenomena in water and air. They are initiated when a liquid or gas is heated, becomes less dense, and thus rises. As it rises, the liquid or gas loses heat and becomes cooler and denser; this increased density eventually causes the liquid or gas to sink. This process forms a convection cell, and material within the cell continually moves. (An example of a convection cell would be the currents established in a pan of water on a hot stove.)

Convection currents also can occur in hot solids like those in Earth's mantle, although their motion is very slow. Earth's interior is hot enough for the outer core to be molten. Heat rising from the interior creates convection within the mantle. The size and distribution of these cells are topics of debate among those who investigate the nature of Earth's interior. Although **Figure R1.8** shows convection cells that extend from the upper to the lower parts of the mantle (whole mantle convection), some investigators believe that there are two layers of convection cells within the mantle. In terms of plate motion, the idea is that convection cells bring hot rock up to spreading centers where it becomes magma, which then solidifies. Lateral motion of the cells carries the plates horizontally. Heat loss results in the downward motion of part of the cell, and this drags an edge of the plates into Earth's interior. The cycle repeats when the rock reheats at great depth.

Reading 1

Figure R1.8

Sketch of Earth showing possible deep convection cells. Upwelling of heat creates new igneous rock and mid-ocean ridges at Earth's surface. Convection may cause or at least contribute to the motion of lithospheric plates. Note that the lithosphere is not drawn to scale; its thickness is exaggerated for the sake of clarity. Modified from U.S. Geological Survey figures.

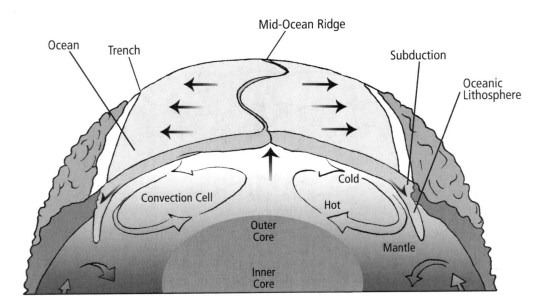

While exploring the seafloor in the 1950s, scientists also found deep, narrow trenches, such as the one along the western coast of South America. Trenches occur where one plate (the denser one) is subducted beneath another plate into Earth's interior; small amounts of the subducted material may melt, resulting in volcanoes above the subduction zone (for example, the Cascade or Andes Mountains), but most of the down-going plate remains solid and again becomes part of Earth's interior. Even though seafloors are continually spreading as new rock is added at mid-ocean ridges, rock is continually recycled at subduction zones at the same rate. Earth is not changing size because the amount of material added is the same as the amount removed. **Figure R1.8** shows the relationships among convection cells, plate motion, mid-ocean ridges, and subduction zones.

In the past few years, there has been increasing uncertainty that convection cells could result in the observed distribution and movement of lithospheric plates. As a result, other mechanisms to explain plate movement have been proposed.

Ridge Push and Slab Pull

Two alternative forces that have been proposed to explain plate movement are called ridge push and slab pull. Both forces are related to gravitational and thermal effects. Heat from deep within the mantle rises beneath mid-ocean ridges and causes the oceanic lithosphere to expand, thus creating an elevated ridge system; some melting of rock also occurs and this molten rock forms new igneous rocks at the ridges. Because of the elevation of the rocks at the ridge, the youngest edge of the lithospheric plate is at the top of an inclined surface. Gravity causes the plate to slide down this inclined surface over the plastic asthenosphere and push on the rest of the plate; hence the term *ridge push*. However, many investigators believe that this ridge push is insufficient to move a plate.

As seafloor moves away from a ridge, that rock moves away from the heat source at the ridge. Consequently, this rock cools and contracts, causing the part of the plate that is the farthest from the ridge to become the coldest and densest part of the plate. Eventually, the cold and dense edge of the plate may sink (be subducted) into Earth's interior under the influence of gravity. As it is subducted, small amounts of the plate may melt. Those magmas may rise above the subduction zone, forming igneous rocks, possibly in the form of volcanoes. As the plate sinks to greater depths, increasing pressures may convert some minerals into new and denser minerals. As the cold, dense, plate edge sinks into the mantle, it pulls on the remainder of the plate; hence the term *slab pull*. Slab pull is now considered by many geologists and geophysicists to be the main driving force for plate tectonics.

Plate Boundary Types

Different types of plate boundaries have different characteristics, and thus may cause rocks to behave and be affected in different ways. Interactions at plate boundaries result in earthquakes, volcanoes, deep-sea trenches, destruction of seafloor, uplift of continents, rifting of continents, formation of new seafloor, and deformation and metamorphism of rocks. Lithospheric plates have three types of boundaries:

Divergent boundary. This boundary occurs where two plates are moving away from each other, such as along mid-ocean ridges (**Figures R1.8** and **R1.9**), or on continental crust, such as in eastern Africa. There, what was once one plate is being split into two diverging plates along the East African Rift. The upwelling of heat from the Earth's interior and the generation of molten rock material create new crust at these boundaries. Earthquakes and volcanoes are frequent in such areas.

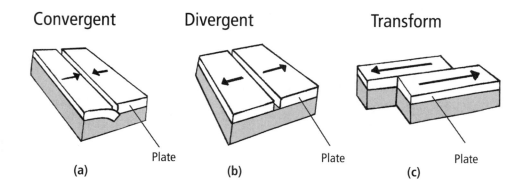

Convergent

Divergent

Transform

Plate
(a)

Plate
(b)

Plate
(c)

Figure R1.9
Sketches showing relative plate movements at convergent (**a**), divergent (**b**), and transform (**c**) fault boundaries. Arrows show direction of movement; plates move on the plastic asthenosphere.

Convergent boundary. This boundary is where plates move toward each other (**Figures R1.8** and **R1.9**). If a continent is on the edge of one of the colliding plates, the plate without the continent is denser and part of it will subduct beneath the continent-bearing plate; that rock is assimilated into Earth's interior. The diving plate creates a submarine trench at the subduction zone. Where two plates with continents collide, a mountain range can form. The Himalayas were formed in this way when the plate carrying India collided with the plate carrying China. The Appalachian Mountains formed many years ago as the result of several continent-continent plate collisions. Earthquakes commonly occur in areas of convergent plate boundaries. Igneous activity, including volcanoes, can occur, especially at a subduction zone.

Transform fault boundary. These boundaries occur where lateral movement along the fault dominates (**Figure R1.9**). The San Andreas Fault in California is a transform fault boundary. Movement along this fault caused major earthquakes in San Francisco in 1989 and in Los Angeles in 1994.

Conclusions

Lithospheric plates exist, move, and interact at plate boundaries. These interactions result in earthquakes and volcanic eruptions, volcanoes and mountain ranges, and igneous and metamorphic rocks. The exact mechanism of plate movement is still uncertain, but it may be due to a plate being pulled as the old, cold, dense part of the plate sinks into the mantle; many investigators now favor this slab-pull mechanism. Regardless of details as to how plates move, it is heat from Earth's interior that makes plate tectonics "work." The theory of plate tectonics provides a unifying explanation for many geological phenomena that in the past were not well understood. These include volcanic and earthquake activity, the formation of large mountain chains, and many features of the seafloor. Continuing investigations should result in an even better understanding of how and why Earth changes over time.

Volcanoes

Volcanic Eruptions and Volcanoes

Most volcanic activity is associated with a plate boundary where two plates converge or two plates move apart (diverge). While not all volcanic activity is related to plate boundaries (some volcanoes occur in the interior of plates, and some plate boundaries exhibit no volcanic activity at all), most of the frequently spectacular, sometimes destructive, volcanic eruptions are located at plate boundaries. The nature of a particular eruption, as well as the shape of the resulting volcano, if one forms, depends upon the proportion of gaseous, liquid, and solid material produced during the eruption, and the chemical composition of the magma. A summary of volcanic products follows.

Gases. Volcanic gases are primarily water vapor (steam) and lesser amounts of carbon dioxide. Other volcanic gases include hydrogen sulfide and compounds of chlorine, fluorine, and boron. The "smoke" frequently seen emerging from a volcano is not gas but actually a combination of condensing steam and volcanic dust.

Liquids. The liquid product of volcanic eruptions is lava, which can have a range of temperatures from about 700–1200°C. Lavas vary in chemical composition and physical properties; their chemical composition affects their viscosity, which in turn affects how fast and how far they flow before becoming solid. Lavas are classified according to silica (SiO_2) content: felsic (65–75% silica), intermediate (50–65% silica), and mafic (less than 50% silica). Felsic lavas tend to be quite viscous and explosive, and normally do not flow far, while mafic lavas are less viscous and less explosive and may flow long distances before becoming solid rock. Some lavas are so fluid that they spread out before solidifying and do not form volcanoes. Instead, they form thick layers of what is called flood basalt; examples cover significant parts of the northwestern United States, India, Siberia, and major parts of the seafloor. The chemical composition also determines the temperatures at which the lava crystallizes.

Solids. Solid volcanic products are called pyroclastics. These represent fragments of solidified magma within the volcano vent that are blown out when gas pressure increases. Pyroclastic fragments are usually classified by size, and range from volcanic ash (less than 2 mm) to volcanic blocks or bombs (greater than 64 mm).

While silica content determines the viscosity of lava, water content provides the potential for steam pressure that determines explosive force. Following is a consideration of silica and water content combinations to show how each affects eruption behavior and volcano shape.

Low water/low silica. This usually results in a relatively quiet, nonviolent eruption due to low viscosity. Essentially, horizontal layers of flood basalt may occur, or, if there is a volcano, it will be broad-based and have relatively gentle slopes; this is called a shield volcano. The Hawaiian Islands are good examples of shield volcanoes.

High water/high silica. This combination usually results in volcanoes with an explosive history. High viscosity from the high silica content inhibits the escape of steam bubbles until the rising magma is close to, or breaks through, Earth's surface. When this happens, steam bubbles expand due to decreased pressure, violently throwing out large amounts of gas and mostly solidified rock material. The steep-sided shape of a composite or stratovolcano (**Figure R2.1**) results from alternate eruptions of pyroclastics and viscous lava, and the accumulation of that material close to the vent (i.e., most of the pyroclastics quickly fall to Earth, and the viscous lava does not flow far before becoming rock).

Volcano Features

Volcanoes are formed when molten rock emerges through an opening, or vent, from Earth's interior. Such an opening may be above or below water. Lava is simply magma that has emerged from Earth's interior onto the surface. The accumulation of volcanic lava and rock debris around the vent forms a cone- or dome-shaped structure. **Figure R2.1** shows a composite or stratovolcano. Good examples are Mount St. Helens in Washington and Mount Vesuvius in Italy.

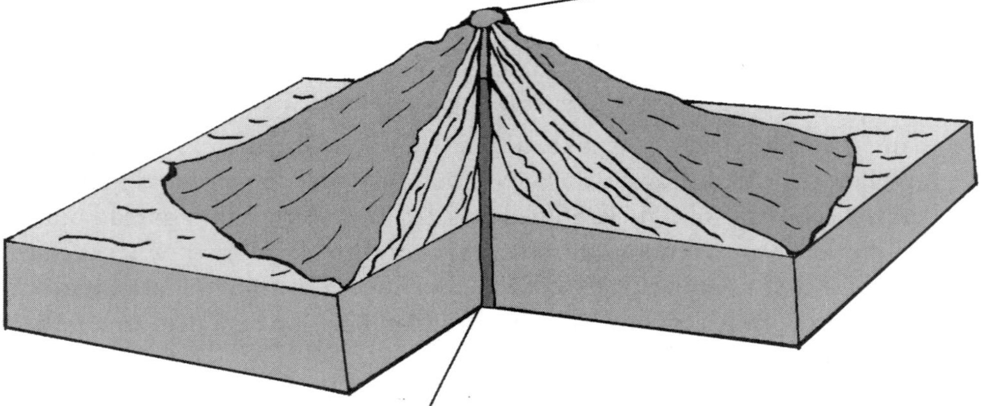

Figure R2.1
A volcano has built up from alternating eruptions of layers of lava and pyroclastics (ash and larger fragments); because of this "mix" of materials, this type of volcano is called a composite volcano.

A *crater* is a steep-sided, funnel-shaped depression at the top of a volcano. Sometimes the top of a volcano collapses or is removed by an eruption, resulting in a depression much larger than the previously existing crater. This geological feature is a *caldera* (**Figure R2.2**).

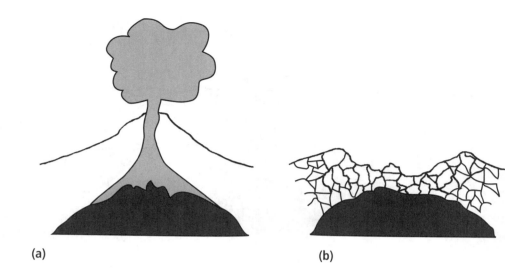

(a)
(b)

Figure R2.2
Figure (a) shows an erupting composite volcano or *stratovolcano*. The upper portion of one of these volcanoes may collapse, or may be removed by an explosion. The result is a large depression called a caldera at the top of the volcano, as shown in **Figure (b)**.

Zones of Volcanic Activity

Most volcanic activity occurs in areas where plate edges meet. If we plotted the locations of volcanic activity on a world map, we would find that most volcanic activity occurs in three distinct zones. The first zone runs almost continuously around the edge of the Pacific Ocean, incorporating New Zealand, the Philippines, Japan, and the Aleutians, and extends along the coasts of North, Central, and South America. Because of its roughly circular shape, this zone of volcanic activity has been called the "Ring of Fire," and it delineates the boundary of the Pacific Plate.

Another zone of volcanic activity extends east-west through the Mediterranean Sea into Asia. The third main zone extends from Iceland southward through the middle of the Atlantic Ocean, roughly paralleling the edges of the ocean-bordering continents. This zone occurs where two plates are diverging. Magma rising between the plates has resulted in the undersea volcanic mountain range known as the Mid-Atlantic Ridge.

Figure R2.3 depicts three different geological situations where plate movement may result in volcanic activity. When two plates converge beneath an ocean, as in A, one plate moves under the other into the asthenosphere, and some remelting of the downward-moving plate occurs. This remelting may trigger volcanic activity, resulting in the formation of volcanic islands like the Aleutians in the northern Pacific Ocean. The mid-ocean ridges, as in B, are chains of volcanic mountains formed by the intrusion of magma between two diverging plates. An example is The Azores in the Atlantic Ocean, volcanic mountains whose peaks protrude above the ocean's surface. When a plate moves beneath a thicker continent-bearing plate, as in C, and limited remelting occurs, volcanic activity may result at least as far as 150 km inland. The Cascade Mountains in the Pacific Northwest are an example of volcanic mountains formed in this manner.

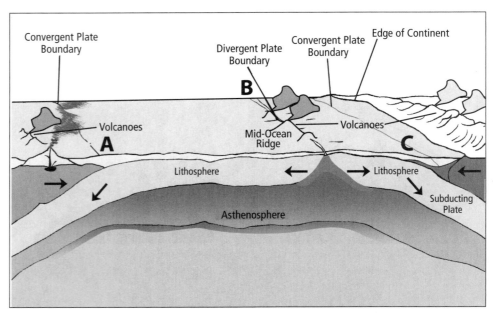

Figure R2.3
Volcanic activity at a mid-ocean ridge, and at subduction zones, one at a boundary where there is no continent, and one at a boundary where there is a continent.

Source: Adapted from the U.S. Geological Survey publication, "This Dynamic Planet," at *http://pubs.usgs.gov/gip/dynamic/dynamic.html.*

Hot Spots and Volcano Formation

Since the early 1900s, at least 90% of Earth's major volcanic eruptions have occurred near plate boundaries. A major exception has been continuing volcanic activity in Hawaii. The Hawaiian Islands are located far from any plate boundary. The Hawaiian Islands formed, and are still being formed, above a *hot spot*. Hot spots beneath a lithospheric plate melt rock that rises through the plate and forms a volcano. Hot spots are thought to be essentially stationary, and the plate above moves across them as shown in **Figure R2.4**.

Figure R2.4
Plate moving over a hot spot. An active volcano is above the hot spot. The volcanoes to the left of the hot spot are extinct. The volcano on the left side of the sketch is the older of the two.

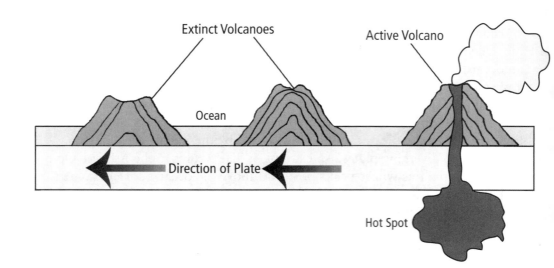

If a plate moves as shown in **Figure R2.4**, an active volcano eventually moves away from the hot spot and becomes inactive or extinct; then a new volcano forms above the hot spot. Continuing movement of the plate in a particular direction would result in a chain of volcanoes along the route of the plate's motion, with present-day volcanic activity occurring only where the plate is directly above the hot spot. The reasons for the existence and locations of hot spots are not well understood, but the heat that makes up the hot spot undoubtedly came from deep within Earth. There are at least 100 hot spots distributed around the world, including ones under Yellowstone National Park and Iceland.

From the ages of the rocks and locations of the islands and submarine volcanoes, we know that the Pacific Plate has been moving west-northwest for the last 43 million years. In Hawaii, the hot spot is currently under the active volcanoes of Mauna Loa and Kilauea, and there is a relatively new submarine volcano named Loihi forming about 35 km southeast of Mauna Loa. Continued volcanism is expected to eventually build a new island at Loihi. This volcano currently is about 1 km below sea level; based on recent amounts of volcanic activity, it is estimated that it will take 10,000 to 100,000 years for this volcano to reach the ocean's surface.

Impact on Humans

Volcanoes often have had a negative impact on people. One of the most devastating modern eruptions in terms of loss of life occurred on the island of Martinique in 1902. Mount Pelee, only 7 km from the town of St. Pierre, had been fairly quiet for about 200 years. In February, residents noticed a sulfurous odor in the air. In April, Pelee discharged a huge cloud of ash, and eruptions accompanied by loud rumblings grew more and more frequent. By then, some 2,000 of St. Pierre's 30,000 residents had sought safety off the island, but new people had moved into town from the countryside seeking refuge. During the first days of May, a series of eruptions resulted in accumulations of ash and dust about 0.5 m in thickness. A ship's captain anchored in the harbor who had seen Mount Vesuvius erupt in Italy in 1895 understood the danger and set sail immediately, but few others followed his example. On May 8, Mount Pelee erupted violently and a superheated cloud of ash and gases flowed down its slope at about 160 km/hr. St. Pierre was directly in the path of this fiery cloud, and all but two of the 30,000 inhabitants were killed by suffocation and burning. (Deaths from volcanic eruptions result primarily from burns inflicted by hot ash or suffocation by ash and gases.)

Contrary to popular belief, lava usually moves too slowly to pose a serious threat, although it does cause extensive property damage. An example of the destructive potential of lava did occur on the Icelandic island of Heimaey in 1973. Without any prior warning, a fracture or rift opened in the ground about 2 km from a small town called Vestmannaeyjar. Lava began to spew out in large quantities. Fortunately, the town's 5,000 residents were able to evacuate quickly. While there was no loss of life, nearly one-third of Vestmannaeyjar was

Topic: volcanic disasters
Go to: *www.scilinks.org*
Code: PSCG203

completely buried in lava. What began as a relatively small lava flow from a single rift ended four months later as a volcanic cone that was 225 m high and named Eldfell.

Mount Paricutin is another volcano that was observed at its birth. This volcano started in 1943 when a fracture developed in a farmer's cornfield in southwestern Mexico. One week later, it was a volcanic cone 168 m high. Within a year it had grown to 335 m. During nine years of activity, Paricutin ejected an estimated 3.6 billion metric tons of ash and lava. The 4,000 residents of a nearby village moved in time to escape personal injury, but all lost their homes to lava flows.

The Five Most Explosive Volcanic Eruptions in the Past 200 Years

Investigators at the Volcano Hazards Program of the U.S. Geological Survey have devised a Volcanic Explosivity Index (VEI) that describes the size and explosivity of a volcanic eruption (0 = nonexplosive, gentle eruption; 8 = colossally explosive; e.g., in Yellowstone 2 million years ago). For additional information about the VEI, see the following website from the Volcano Hazards Program of the U.S. Geological Survey: *http://volcanoes.usgs. gov/images/pglossary/vei.php*. Using this index, the five eruptions listed below are the most explosive of the past 200 years.

Tambora, 1815 (VEI = 7)
The Tambora eruption in what is now Indonesia was the largest explosive eruption in modern history. Tsunamis triggered by the explosion plus hot ash flows resulted in at least 60,000 deaths. Large amounts of volcanic ash were thrown into the atmosphere. The cool or cold summer of 1816, "the year without summer," has been attributed to that ash partially shielding Earth's surface from receiving a normal amount of solar radiation. The unusually cool temperatures resulted in crop failures and food scarcities in many parts of the world; average temperatures were 1 to 2.5°C below normal in New England and western Europe.

Krakatoa, 1883 (VEI = 6)
In 1883, a series of major eruptions destroyed the Indonesian island of Krakatoa. One of the explosions reportedly was heard about 5,000 km away, and a tsunami over 40 m high was created by the force of one of the eruptions. These eruptions also put large amounts of volcanic ash into Earth's atmosphere, causing red sunsets for several years afterward. Approximately 35,000 deaths resulted from these explosions, primarily as the result of tsunamis caused by the eruptions. Renewed volcanic activity in the depression created by the explosions has formed a new volcanic cone, named Anak Krakatoa, or Son of Krakatoa.

Novarupta, 1912 (VEI = 6)

The most explosive volcanic explosion of the 20th century occurred in a remote part of Alaska in 1912. In just three days, 1 ft., or 0.3 m, of ash fell on Kodiak Island, about 150 km from the erupting volcano.

Pinatubo, 1991 (VEI = 6)

Mount Pinatubo in the Philippines had not undergone a major eruption for at least 500 years. However, the occurrence of minor eruptions and many earthquakes in April and May 1991 suggested that a major eruption might soon occur. By the time the major eruption happened on June 15, 1991, over 60,000 people had been evacuated from the areas most at risk, and this undoubtedly saved many lives. In spite of these efforts, nearly 900 people were killed by the eruption. Most deaths were due to ashfall causing roofs to collapse, and damage caused by hot ash flows and mudflows.

Santa Maria, 1902 (VEI = 6)

The Santa Maria volcano is near the Pacific coast of Guatemala. Before 1902, the volcano had been dormant for at least 500 years. The 1902 eruption devastated much of the southwestern part of the country. In 1922, eruptions began again. Several of these eruptions caused hot ash flows and mudflows, which caused loss of life.

Other Relatively Recent and Significant Eruptions

Mount St. Helens (VEI = 5):
Last Major Eruption in 48 Conterminous United States

In May 1980, a volcanic explosion removed the top of Mount St. Helens in Washington. This volcano, part of the Cascade Range, formed about 50,000 years ago, and has been sporadically active since then. The eruption on May 18 resulted in about 60 deaths and caused ash to be deposited over large areas of Washington, Idaho, and Montana. In eastern Washington, more than 300 km from the volcano, ash deposits totaled more than 7 cm; trace amounts of ash were deposited as far to the east as Oklahoma. The force of the explosion devastated an area near the volcano about 30 km by 20 km. In part of this area, trees were completely destroyed; beyond this area of complete devastation all trees were knocked down, with each tree pointing away from the explosion.

The amount of ash produced by the 1980 eruption of Mount St. Helens was about 1,000 times the amount produced by the 2010 Eyjafjallajökull eruption in Iceland, but less than 1/100th the amount associated with the 1815 Tambora eruption.

The 1980 Mount St. Helens explosion provides examples of a variety of problems that may result from volcanic activity:

- *Wildlife and habitat destruction.* An estimated 7,000 large game animals and many thousands of small animals and birds perished around Mount St. Helens.

- *Natural resources destruction*. The timber blown down could have built nearly a quarter of a million homes.
- *Agricultural destruction*. Seven percent of some crops as far away as 150 km were destroyed when volcanic dust coated leaves, inhibiting photosynthesis.
- *Cleanup*. One town, Yakima, for example, population 51,000, spent 10 weeks and $2.2 million removing ash. It was 130 km away from the volcano.

Eruption of Eyjafjallajökull Volcano in Iceland in Spring 2010 (VEI = 2)
Air travel in spring 2010 was disrupted for weeks by volcanic eruptions in Iceland. Over 100,000 flights affecting millions of passengers were canceled because planes were grounded to avoid risking damage to their engines by abrasive airborne volcanic ash produced by the explosive eruptions of Eyjafjallajökull volcano in southern Iceland.

Eyjafjallajökull volcano had last erupted in 1823. Beginning about a year before the 2010 eruptions, GPS measurements indicated that the ground below the volcano had moved several centimeters, apparently the result of magma rising under the volcano. This movement provided hints of renewed activity, as did an increase in minor earthquake activity recorded in that area in February and March 2010. The first eruptions occurred in March 2010. They filled low areas with lava, melting adjacent snow and ice. Explosive eruptions began in April, producing clouds of volcanic ash and dust, some of which drifted over Europe, interfering with air travel. These eruptions melted more snow and ice near the volcano, and the resulting flooding destroyed roads and farms. Residents were evacuated from the general vicinity of the volcano due to the threat of flooding and hazards of ash deposits.

In spite of the problems caused by the 2010 Eyjafjallajökull volcanic eruptions, this series of eruptions was minor compared to other historic and prehistoric eruptions (VEI = 2). A minor eruption of this approximate magnitude is likely to occur somewhere on Earth each year. Reports from the Smithsonian Institution's Global Volcanism Program suggest that the Eyjafjallajökull eruption produced only about 1/100,000th the amount of ash produced by the eruption of Tambora, which was the most explosive eruption of the past 200 years.

Volcanic Eruptions— A Long-Term Perspective

Studying volcanic processes and hazards to try to prevent disaster might seem reasonably straightforward: identify past behavior of volcanoes, interpret volcanic products and processes, monitor present conditions, and empower community leaders to take actions necessary to protect people and property. Unfortunately, shortfalls of time, funding, knowledge, and logistics make hazard mitigation far from simple. The major problem is that volcanoes and volcanic eruptions are extremely complex. So far, we cannot determine with confidence when eruptions will occur or how devastating they will be. Another problem is that as the world's population has increased, more and more people are living on the slopes of potentially hazardous volcanoes and in nearby areas.

Throughout history, people have recognized that volcanoes destroy human life and structures. Much less known is that volcanoes also could be thought of as making positive contributions to human and other lives:

- Primeval volcanic episodes may have provided initial sources of Earth's air and water.
- Volcanic ash contributes nitrogen and phosphorous to soil and increases fertility.
- Volcanoes create terrestrial landscapes on which ecosystems form and evolve.
- Emissions from volcanoes are important sources for industrial materials like pumice, ammonia, and boric acid.
- Thermal energy in volcanic areas is harnessed for industrial and domestic uses (e.g., Iceland, Italy, United States, Mexico, Japan, and New Zealand).
- Remnants of volcanoes such as the Hawaiian Islands and Cascade Mountains provide opportunities for recreation and scenic enjoyment.

While volcanoes are powerful natural forces that inspire awe—and sometimes fear because of their destructive potential—they are nonetheless an integral component of Earth's ecological cycles.

Conclusions

Volcanic activity during Earth's history has played a major role in building Earth's crust and lithospheric plates. This activity also contributed to or caused the formation of Earth's atmosphere and oceans. Depending mainly on the composition of the magma, some eruptions of molten rock do not form volcanoes but spread great distances. Others form volcanoes with relatively gentle slopes. Finally, there are the explosive eruptions that create volcanoes with steep slopes. Because of where many people live, volcanic eruptions are a potential hazard that we must respect.

Earthquakes

Earthquakes: What They Are

Thinking about what happens when materials are bent or deformed can help in understanding earthquakes. If you slightly bend a thin strip or rod of metal and then release the pressure, the rod will return to its original shape. The metal underwent temporary, or elastic, deformation. If the strip is bent more, it might retain its bent shape after pressure is released. If so, the metal underwent what is called plastic deformation. Should you continue bending the metal, at some point it will break or rupture. When metal or another solid material is bent, some of the energy required to bend it may be stored in the object; when the object breaks, this energy is released (**Figure R3.1a, b, c**).

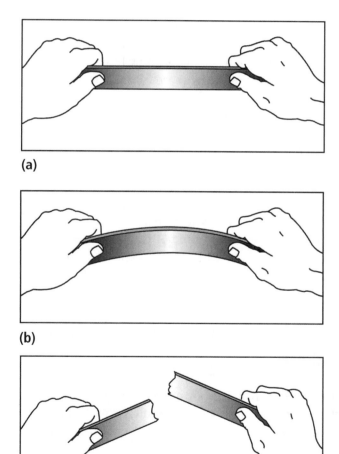

(a)

(b)

(c)

Figure R3.1
Figure (a) shows holding a strip of metal.
Figure (b) shows bending the metal.
Figure (c) shows the result of bending the metal to the point that it breaks.

Almost all solid materials behave the same way as the metal strip described above, including the rocks that make up Earth's crust and lithospheric plates. The sudden release of energy, which results from the breaking or slipping of deformed rock within Earth's crust, causes earthquakes. The released energy is transmitted by earthquake—"seismic"—waves through adjacent rock; these waves cause the shaking that geologists associate with earthquakes.

Earthquakes: How and Where They Happen

Interactions between lithospheric plates usually cause the rock deformation that leads to earthquakes. Most major earthquakes occur near plate boundaries where plates converge or diverge. Eighty percent of the world's recorded earthquakes occur in areas bordering the Pacific Ocean, along the boundary of the Pacific plate. About 15% of earthquakes occur in a zone that extends through the Mediterranean Ocean and eastward into India and China. Significant earthquake activity also occurs at the mid-ocean ridges, such as those in the Atlantic, Pacific, and Indian oceans. These areas of major earthquake activity, along plate boundaries, also have high incidences of volcanic activity.

We often think of California as a location where earthquakes are likely to occur. Earthquakes do often occur in California, along the San Andreas Fault and other fault zones. In 1989, the Loma Prieta earthquake in San Francisco registered 7.1 on the Richter scale. It damaged much of the downtown area, and caused a World Series baseball game to be stopped. But, earthquakes also occur elsewhere in the United States, including locations far from plate boundaries. These are where ancient fault zones exist in the interior of the North American plate. Some of the biggest earthquakes to affect the United States have occurred in the east: Cape Ann and Boston area, Massachusetts, 1755; New Madrid, Missouri, 1811 and 1812; and Charleston, South Carolina, 1886 (magnitude 7.3).

Earthquakes, Rock Movement, and Faults

When rock is displaced or moved during an earthquake, that movement either creates what is called a fault, or rocks are moved along an existing fault. A fault is a break or fracture in rock where the rocks on both sides of the fracture have moved with respect to each other; the rocks are named according to how they have moved along the fault. Although simple diagrams (like the ones in this Reading) usually show faults as planes, in reality they are irregular surfaces. If the fault is oriented so that the mass of rock on one side of the fault is above the fault zone or plane, that mass or block of rock is called the hanging wall block; if there is a block of rock below the fault, it is called the footwall block.

Figures **R3.2** and **R3.3** illustrate the faults that result from compressional forces (pushing toward one another) and extensional forces (pulling away from one another) acting on the Earth's crust. Other faults are characterized by mostly lateral movement of the rock along the fault (**Figure R3.4**). The San Andreas Fault is one of the best known examples of the type of fault with lateral movement.

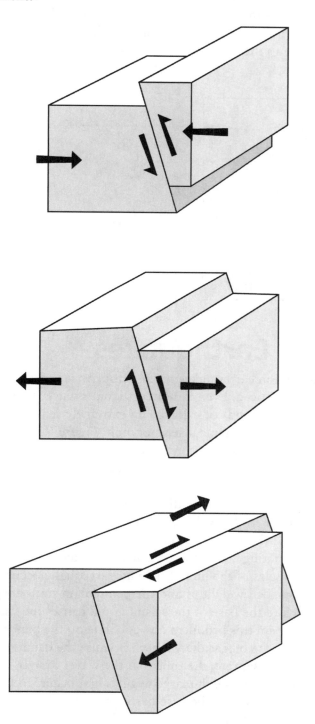

Figure R3.2
Compressional forces, indicated by the horizontal arrows, cause the hanging wall block to move up relative to the footwall block (note that the movement is relative—either or both blocks could move). This is a reverse fault. When the angle of the fault plane is shallow, it is a special case called a thrust fault.

Figure R3.3
Extensional forces, indicated by the horizontal arrows, cause the hanging wall block to move down relative to the footwall block (note that the movement is relative—either or both blocks could move). This is a gravity fault (also sometimes called a normal fault, but this is a poor term as other faults also are "normal.")

Figure R3.4
Stress may produce lateral movement along the fault. Such faults are called strike-slip faults.

Earthquake Focus and Epicenter

The subsurface point where the rock has fractured and movement has occurred is the focus of the earthquake. The point on Earth's surface directly above the focus is the epicenter. The release of energy occurs at the focus and radiates in all directions as seismic or earthquake waves. These vibrating waves become less and less powerful as they move away from the focus. The epicenter is generally where seismic waves will be felt most, although that is not always the case. **Figure R3.5** shows the relationships among the focus, the epicenter, and seismic waves.

Figure R3.5

This is a sketch of a cross-section of the upper part of Earth. It shows the focus where an earthquake originated, and a spot at Earth's surface—the epicenter—directly above the focus. The circles represent seismic waves moving outward from the focus.

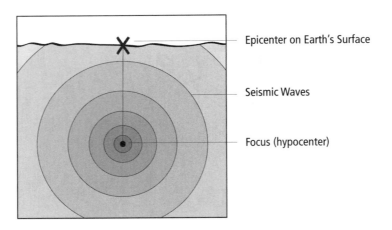

Epicenter on Earth's Surface

Seismic Waves

Focus (hypocenter)

Detecting Earthquakes

An estimated one million earthquakes occur throughout the world each year, although most are unnoticed. Even minor earthquake waves that cannot be felt by people can be detected and recorded by an extremely sensitive device called a seismograph. A typical mechanical seismograph (**Figure R3.6**) consists of a rotating cylinder or drum with a recording chart mounted on its outside, a heavy weight, a pen for marking on the chart, and a support and base on which to mount everything. The heavy weight is hung from a support above the drum, and the pen is in contact with the rotating recording chart on the drum. The base is attached to Earth's crust (lithosphere): if the crust shakes, the base also shakes. If there is no earthquake, the pen draws essentially a straight line on the rotating chart (there normally is background noise that does result in tiny wiggles of the line). When an earthquake occurs, because of inertia of the suspended weight, it and the pen remain stationary. But, the movement of Earth and the base of the seismograph causes the chart to move under the stationary pen; this produces a wiggly line on the paper—the more severe the earthquake, the bigger the wiggles. Because the drum turns continuously and turns at a known rate, the time that the waves arrived is indicated by the place on the paper where the large wiggles first occur. Today most seismographs are electronic, but they are based on principles similar to the older mechanical seismographs.

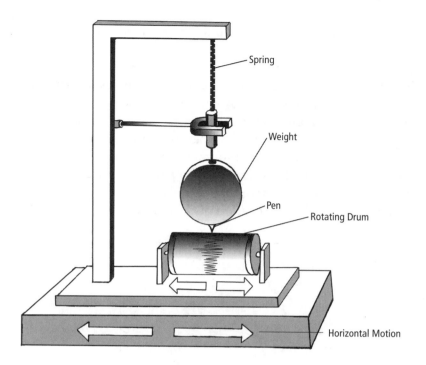

Spring

Weight

Pen

Rotating Drum

Horizontal Motion

Figure R3.6
This is a sketch of a seismograph that records one component of horizontal ground motion (E-W or N-S). At a seismograph station, there would be at least two other seismographs, one to record N-S or E-W motion, and one to record vertical motion.

P, S, and L Seismic or Earthquake Waves

There are three main types of seismic waves:

- **Primary Waves (P-waves).** The most rapidly moving (7–8 km/sec) of the three types of waves, P-waves arrive at a given location before the other wave types. They travel through Earth's interior, and are able to pass through both solids and liquids.
- **Secondary Waves (S-waves).** The second-fastest type of wave (4–5 km/sec), these waves arrive at a given location after the P-waves. S-waves also travel deep within Earth's interior, but they travel through solids only.
- **Long Waves (L-waves).** L-waves move slowest of the three wave types, about 3 km/sec. L-waves travel along and just beneath Earth's surface.

All three of these seismic wave types are generated simultaneously at the earthquake focus and radiate outward. Because of their different velocities, they are recorded at seismographs at different times.

On a seismograph chart, the first indication that an earthquake occurred is a series of short wiggles on the chart that represent the arrival of the P-waves. The S-waves are recorded next, followed by the arrival of the L-waves. In actual practice, two seismograph units are set up at right angles to one another to register north-south and east-west components of horizontal seismic movements. A third unit measures vertical movement. Because the P and S waves travel with known velocities, the difference between the arrival times of these waves establishes how far away from the seismograph the earthquake occurred.

Topic: seismographs
Go to: *www.scilinks.org*
Code: PSCG213

(Reference tables of data from thousands of previous earthquakes are used to make this determination.)

If three or more widely spaced seismic stations are able to determine their individual distances from the epicenter, concentric circles drawn around each on a map will locate the epicenter by determining the single point where the three circles intersect. **Figure R3.7** shows how an earthquake epicenter can be determined using data from three seismograph stations. The station to the west is 1,500 km from the epicenter, the southernmost station is 1,000 km away, and the station to the northeast is 1,200 km from the epicenter. Circles with these radii are drawn on the map; there is only one point in common to all circles, and that has to be the location of the epicenter.

Figure R3.7
Determining the location of an earthquake epicenter by knowing the epicenter's distance from three seismograph stations. The point in common to all circles is the epicenter.

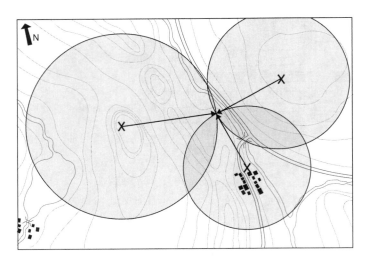

Measuring Earthquakes

Until about 1980, earthquakes were generally evaluated using either the Richter magnitude scale or the Mercalli intensity scale. The Richter scale, devised in 1935 by American geophysicist Charles Richter, evaluates an earthquake's magnitude by using the size of the wiggles recorded on seismographs as they respond to ground motion caused by the earthquake. This scale reports magnitude based on the measured maximum ground motion. The assigned moment magnitude or Richter scale magnitude is always adjusted for distance of the seismograph from the epicenter so that all seismograph stations report the same magnitude for a specific earthquake. The Mercalli intensity scale, developed in 1902 by Italian volcanologist Giuseppi Mercalli, evaluates an earthquake based on what is felt at specific locations and the extent of earthquake damage at these locations. The moment magnitude scale is based on the amount of energy released, and this is the scale used today by the U.S. Geological Survey. The magnitude obtained for a specific earthquake usually is about the same as obtained using the Richter scale. Media commonly report earthquake magnitudes as Richter scale values, although today they actually are based on the moment magnitude scale.

Using the moment magnitude or Richter scale, the smallest earthquake a person might feel would be assigned a value of about 2. These scales are logarithmic, meaning that each unit of increase (from two to three or from four to five, for example) corresponds to a tenfold increase in the amplitude of the ground motion. Magnitude also can evaluate the energy released by an earthquake. On these scales, each unit increase represents about a 30-fold increase in released energy.

Seismographs also detect other types of explosions. They can be used to detect and monitor testing of nuclear bombs. Atmospheric nuclear explosions are banned by international treaty and are relatively easy to detect. Underground nuclear explosions are more difficult to detect, but with adequate distribution of seismographs, usually detection is possible. Determining if a seismic event was due to an earthquake or a bomb explosion requires doing a detailed analysis of the seismic wave patterns.

The Mercalli intensity scale recognizes different levels of destruction, ground motion, and impact on humans by assigning a number between Roman numerals I and XII. The intensity of an earthquake varies from location to location and is influenced by the earthquake's magnitude and depth, the distance of the location from the earthquake, local geological conditions, and construction practices. Because intensity is more useful than magnitude as a measure of destruction, the construction and property insurance industries rely on the Mercalli scale. We can also use reports from diaries, letters, and newspaper articles to determine Mercalli intensities for historical earthquakes. However, because the moment magnitude and Richter scale magnitude are measured remotely, these values quickly provide information about the relative size of earthquakes around the world. This probably explains why the moment magnitude scale has been so readily adopted by international media. **Table R3.1** provides some perspective about the relative energy released by earthquakes.

Table R3.1: Relative Energy Releases by Explosives, Tornadoes, and Earthquakes

Magnitude	TNT Equivalent	Example
1.0	6 ounces	--
2.5	63 pounds	--
4.0	6 tons	Small atomic bomb
4.5	32 tons	Tornado, average size
5.5	500 tons	Earthquake, Massena, New York (1944)
6.5	31,500 tons	Earthquake, Coalinga, California (1983)
7.5	199,000 tons	Earthquake, Hebgen Lake, Montana (1959)
8.0	6,270,000 tons	Earthquake, San Francisco, California (1906)
8.5	31,550,000 tons	Earthquake, Anchorage, Alaska (1964)

Source: Adapted from FEMA. 2000. Tremor Troop: Earthquakes—A Teacher's Package for K–6. Revised Edition. FEMA Publication 159. *www.fema.gov/library/viewRecord.do?id=1632.*

Tsunamis

Tsunami is a Japanese word for "wave." These are unusual waves that usually are triggered by earthquakes that cause a sudden shift in part of the seafloor. (In addition, erupting volcanoes and submarine landslides also may shift part of the seafloor and cause tsunamis.) Tsunamis are often called seismic sea waves, and have incorrectly been referred to as tidal waves. (Tides are predictable and are due to gravitational attraction of the Sun and Earth's moon.) Tsunami occurrences have been distributed as follows: Pacific Ocean, 63%; Mediterranean Sea, 21%; Atlantic Ocean, 5%; Caribbean Sea, 4%; Indian Ocean, 6%; and Black Sea, 1%. Devastating tsunamis occur in the Pacific Ocean region about once every 10 years.

Table R3.2: Devastating Tsunamis Between 1810–2010 That Caused 1,000 or More Deaths

Year Month/Day	Quake Magnitude	Cause (Nonquake)	Location	Maximum Wave Height, Meters	Deaths	Minimum Injuries	Minimum Houses Destroyed
2004 12/26	9.0		Indonesia	50.9	227,898	?	?
1883 08/27	–	Volcanic Eruption	Indonesia, Krakatoa	35.0	36,000	?	?
1896 06/15	7.6		Japan	38.2	31,122	13,247	11,000
1868 08/13	8.5		Chile	18.0	25,000	?	?
1976 08/16	8.1		Philippines	8.5	4,456	5,366	?
1933 03/02	8.4		Japan	29.0	3,022	?	5,851
1854 12/24	8.4		Japan	28.0	3,000	?	15,000
1992 12/12	7.8		Indonesia	26.2	2,500	500	31,785
1877 05/10	8.3		Chile	24.0	2,477	?	?
1899 09/29	7.8		Indonesia	12.0	2,460	300	?
1998 07/17	7.0		Papua New Guinea	15.0	2,183	1,000	?
1923 09/01	7.9		Japan	13.0	2,144	166	868
1946 08/04	8.1		Dominican Republic	5.0	1,790	?	?
1819 06/16	7.7		India, Kutch	?	1,543	?	?
1946 12/20	8.1		Japan	6.6	1,362	?	1,451
1944 12/07	8.1		Japan	10.0	1,223	2,135	3,059
1960 05/22	9.5	Volcanic Eruption	Chile	25.0	1,223	?	?
1815 11/22	7.0		Indonesia	?	1,200	?	?
1861 02/16	8.5		Indonesia	7.0	1,105	?	?
1906 01/31	8.8		Ecuador	5.0	1,000	?	?
1951 08/03	6.0	Volcanic Eruption	Nicaragua	?	1,000	?	?

Source: Data from NOAA National Geophysical Data Center: *www.ngdc.noaa.gov/hazard/tsupub.shtml.*

A tsunami travels rapidly across the ocean with a velocity of about 800–900 km/hr. In the open ocean, these waves are difficult or impossible to see because they normally are less than a few centimeters high. However, as a tsunami approaches a coast, the increasingly shallow seafloor interferes with the circular water motion that characterizes waves, and this interference affects the wave's behavior. Wave height and steepness increase until the wave becomes unstable and breaks. The maximum height of the wave above sea level is called run-up, and on rare occasions these heights can reach 30–50 m or more.

In December 2004, an earthquake of magnitude 9.1 near Sumatra in Indonesia created a tsunami that killed more people than any other tsunami in recorded history. Approximately 228,000 people died, and over 1 million people lost their homes at least temporarily. People who lived far from the earthquake's epicenter along the coastlines of Thailand, Sri Lanka, India, and East Africa could have had adequate time to go to higher elevations to avoid the effects of the tsunami. Unfortunately, at that time there was no tsunami warning system for the Indian Ocean region, and there was no effective way to warn people in those coastal areas about the tsunami hazard created by that earthquake. The result was a huge loss of lives and property. Estimated economic losses were over $10 billion (amount in U.S. dollars).

In the Pacific Ocean region, there has been a tsunami warning system in operation since 1949. The National Oceanic and Atmospheric Administration (NOAA) operates the Pacific Tsunami Warning Center with an international network of seismograph and tidal stations around the Pacific that send information by satellite to Hawaii. When an earthquake occurs or an unexpected change in sea level is recorded at a tidal station, the Center analyzes the data looking for indications that a tsunami could have been generated. If a tsunami is indicated, a warning is immediately sent to all populated coastal areas in the Pacific Basin.

The extremely rare event of the impact of a large asteroid in an ocean also could trigger a tsunami. Approximately 65 million years ago, an asteroid at least 10 km in diameter struck what is now the coast of the Yucatan Peninsula in Mexico. The explosion caused by the impact formed a crater about 200 km in diameter, and there is speculation tsunamis many thousands of meters high were generated. Fortunately, since that impact about 65 million years ago, no asteroid larger than about 5 km has reached Earth, and this on average probably happens only about every 10 million years.

Earthquake Damage

As building construction materials and methods improve, architects and engineers design and construct buildings that are less likely to be damaged or destroyed by earthquakes. **Figure R3.8** shows some of the ways seismic waves affect buildings. While no construction design can be absolutely earthquake-proof, new materials and procedures can increase human safety and reduce property damage. For example, we now know that if an earthquake occurs in an area of soft sediments, such as landfills or sedimentary basins, the damage to buildings will be greater than in an area of solid rock. Accordingly, in many parts of the world, there now are restrictions or prohibitions regarding building in such areas.

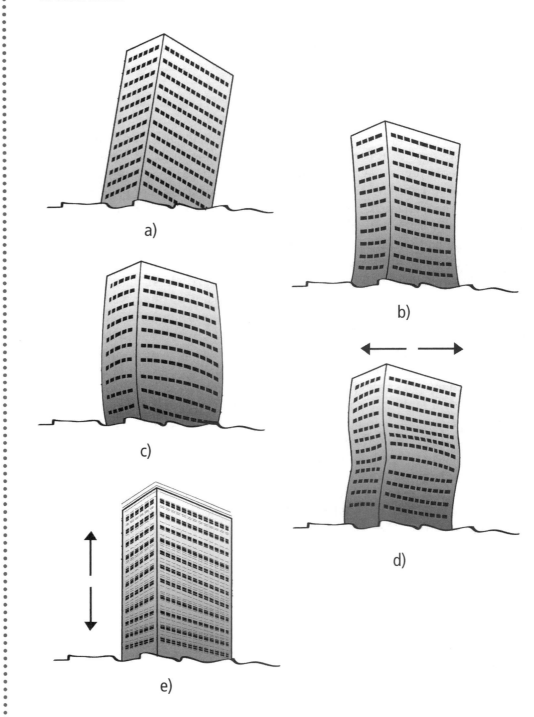

Figure R3.8
Some ways that earthquake waves affect buildings. Some of these changes are short-lasting, while others are permanent.
(a) The building may slide.
(b) Part of the building may contract. **(c)** Part of the building may expand.
(d) The building may shake.
(e) The building may bounce.

Figure R3.9 shows some earthquake-resilient construction designs. Devices that cushion or separate a structure from its foundation absorb earthquake shocks. Now buildings can also be constructed with shear or interior walls that provide additional support; as well, construction materials can be designed to bend temporarily rather than resist and break in response to shaking caused by earthquakes.

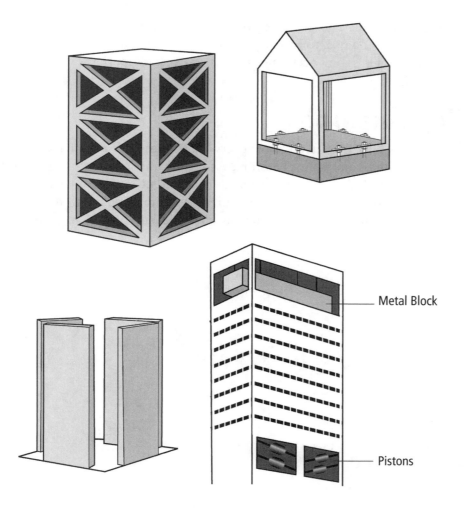

Metal Block

Pistons

Figure R3.9
These are design features that help withstand earthquakes: **(a)** cross-bracing; **(b)** building attached well to foundation; **(c)** shear walls for additional support; **(d)** metal blocks and pistons to act as shock absorbers.

Earthquakes can and do occur in many parts of the United States. It is a good idea to have safety response plans ready to be put into immediate action in both classrooms and homes. Teaching students about why earthquakes happen provides an excellent opportunity to teach them about civic responsibility, humanitarian aid, and organizations that engage in disaster relief. The Red Cross and the Federal Emergency Management Agency (FEMA), for example, are excellent resources for information. They often will provide free information about natural hazards, emergency preparedness, and response for classroom use.

Earthquake Prediction

We cannot yet accurately predict earthquakes. (A successful prediction must accurately give the location, magnitude, and time of occurrence of a future earthquake). A very few earthquakes have been predicted, but failed predictions far outnumber the successful ones. Earthquakes are complex phenomena that occur in different kinds of rocks under different conditions. There are so many variables and uncertainties that it may never be possible to make many successful predictions. The best a geologist, seismologist, or other Earth scientist usually can do today is to be reasonably confident from available data that an earthquake will "soon" occur along a particular fault, perhaps within several years or decades.

Conclusions

Earthquakes have occurred almost everywhere, although most have occurred at and near plate boundaries. Therefore, essentially any location might experience an earthquake. Although it is not possible to predict earthquake occurrences accurately, and thus always take measures to minimize damage and loss of life, it is possible to make structures such as buildings and bridges more resistant to damage by earthquakes.

Rocks and Minerals

Plate Tectonics, Rocks, and Minerals

Earth's plates consist of rocks composed of many minerals, plus a thin covering of soils. Developing an understanding of the relationship between the most obvious aspects of geology—minerals and rocks—and the unifying theory of plate tectonics may seem difficult at first. Plate tectonics describes how, and by what mechanisms, Earth's surface has been and is being transformed on a large scale. We often think of continental movement, mountain building, volcanoes, and earthquakes as those aspects of geology explained through plate tectonics. However, rock and mineral types, locations of mineral deposits, and rock formation and transformation also can be understood when studied in the context of plate tectonics. Plate tectonics provides a link between rock and mineral specimens that can be studied in the classroom, and the geologic history that led to their development.

Minerals

A mineral is a naturally occurring, inorganic crystalline material with a unique chemical combination. Different combinations and atomic arrangements of elements give each mineral its characteristic properties, such as color, hardness, shape, density, and cleavage. Although about 3,000 different minerals have been identified, most are extremely rare. About 95% of Earth's crust is comprised of only 10 to 15 different minerals or mineral groups. The following relatively short list of minerals and mineral groups comprises the primary ingredients of rocks:

Feldspar—a group of similar minerals; they make up roughly 60% of Earth's crust

Quartz—approximately 10% of Earth's crust, found in many different rocks; sandstones can be nearly all quartz

Pyroxenes—mineral group with many members; common dark-colored minerals

Amphiboles—another mineral group with many members; common dark-colored minerals

Mica—mineral group; includes biotite and muscovite, common in igneous and metamorphic rocks

Garnet—another mineral group; diverse in occurrence and color

Clay—mineral group; sediments and sedimentary rocks; produced by weathering of feldspars

Calcite—major constituent of sedimentary rock limestone, and metamorphic rock marble

Dolomite—similar in occurrence to calcite, but sedimentary rock is called dolostone

Olivine—uncommon at Earth's surface because it weathers easily; common within Earth

This website from the Smithsonian Institution provides good information on creating your own classroom exhibit of rocks and minerals: *www.smithsonianeducation.org/educators/lesson_plans/minerals/lesson1_main.html*. From this page, it is possible to go to other useful links about minerals. The U.S. Geological Survey also provides helpful information about minerals and their use as resources. This link is titled "Do We Take Minerals for Granted?" and can be accessed at *http://minerals.usgs.gov/granted.html*. Additional interesting mineral information can be found at this web page as well.

Rocks

A rock normally is an aggregate of mineral grains, although a few rocks are formed of fossils, fragments of fossils, or fragments of rocks. Different types of rocks form in different ways.

Igneous rocks result from the solidification or crystallization of molten rock. They may form at Earth's surface (where molten rock is called lava) or below Earth's surface (where molten rock is called magma). Two common igneous rocks are granite and basalt. They differ in their mineral composition and mineral grain size. Granite forms several kilometers below Earth's surface, where the insulating properties of the surrounding rocks cause magma to cool slowly. This allows for the growth of large mineral grains. Basalt forms at or close to Earth's surface, where rapid heat loss results in relatively small mineral grains.

Sedimentary rocks form from rock fragments, minerals, or fossils that are compressed beneath the weight of overlying sediments. They also form by chemical precipitation of minerals dissolved by water. Sedimentary rocks form at low temperatures at or very close to Earth's surface. Common sedimentary rocks are sandstone, limestone, and shale.

Metamorphic rocks are those in which the original mineral composition, grain size, or grain shape has changed as a result of exposure to moderately high temperatures, high pressure, or both. Most metamorphic rocks form below Earth's surface. Marble, slate, and schist are common metamorphic rocks.

Over time, or in response to changing conditions, rocks may change from one type into another. The rock cycle depicted in **Figure R4.1** summarizes the steps by which one rock type transforms into another. The counterclockwise arrows indicate changes in rocks and rock materials that may take place. The words next to the arrows refer to processes by which the changes are accomplished. Shortcuts, indicated by interior arrows, may occur in this cycle. For example, igneous rocks can be metamorphosed to form metamorphic rocks by heat and pressure, or sedimentary and metamorphic rocks may undergo weathering to become sediments and/or dissolved mineral material. (The dissolution of rock material during weathering and the possibility of that material being precipitated to form sedimentary rock is not included on **Figure R4.1** in order to keep the diagram relatively simple; examples of such chemically precipitated rocks are some limestones that form in oceans and salt [halite] deposits that can form in desert lakes or in an isolated part of an ocean.)

Topic: minerals/rocks
Go to: *www.scilinks.org*
Code: PSCG222

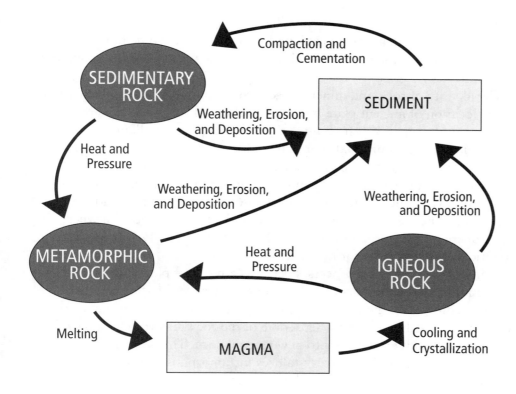

Figure R4.1
The rock cycle. Rock types plus magma and sediment are in capital letters. Processes that alter rocks or sediments are in capital and lower case. Arrows indicate how one type of rock material may change as geological conditions change. These changes need not occur, or they could take many millions of years to happen.

Strictly speaking, before you can accurately identify a rock, you must know what minerals are in it. If a rock has decomposed or weathered, even geologists may have a difficult time recognizing those minerals and determining what rock it is—or what it used to be. It is usually easy to tell when rocks and minerals have been weathered; they may crumble when handled and their surfaces may be dirty or covered with what appear to be brownish stains. Typically, geologists examining a weathered rock will break it with a hammer to expose a fresh or unweathered surface. The geologists will then study the rock's minerals with a magnifying glass and scratch grains with a knife blade to determine hardness. By identifying minerals, they can give the rock a provisional name. If the rock needs further study, geologists might use a specialized (petrographic) microscope using polarized light or analytical instruments that provide chemical data to identify the minerals and thus definitively name the rock.

The identity of a rock or mineral usually provides clues as to the type of environment where it formed, which is often quite different from Earth's surface. For example, a typical granite that is now exposed at Earth's surface probably crystallized at a temperature of about 700°C, at high pressures, and at a depth within Earth of at least 4–10 km. That rock, now on the surface of Earth, was exposed when the overlying rocks were eroded and weathered away. This action is part of the uplifting process on Earth's crust. Limestone provides another example of a rock that indicates what an environment was like in the past: A coral-containing limestone that is found today on land in a relatively cold climate originally formed in a warm, shallow ocean. (That is where we find most corals living today.) Assuming the limestone formed where it is now found, the environment at that location must have changed significantly since the time the rock formed. (An alternate explanation could be that something, perhaps a glacier, transported the rock a long distance to a new location with a different environment.)

The identity of rock and mineral specimens also may provide information on the location of ancient plate boundaries. Unusual rocks and minerals may form at specific types of plate boundaries. For example, peralkaline volcanic rocks, which have an unusual chemical composition, currently are forming at several active divergent plate boundaries where continents are pulling apart (e.g., East Africa Rift). Rocks of similar composition that are approximately 700 million years old occur in the central and southern Appalachian Mountains. These rocks are believed to mark the time and location where an early supercontinent began to split into North America and Africa, with the Atlantic Ocean gradually forming between them.

Many of the rock cycle processes occur as a result of plate motion and interaction. At subduction zones, where one plate slides beneath another, seafloor sediment on the underlying plate is carried along with oceanic crust down into the asthenosphere where some of the rock may remelt. Some of this material will recrystallize into new igneous rock. The heat that is released as the molten rock cools and recrystallizes metamorphoses adjacent rocks. High pressures created when two plates push together or "collide" also can metamorphose any sedimentary, igneous, and metamorphic rocks at the plate boundary.

Conclusions

Specific minerals and rocks form in response to specific environmental conditions. Locating and recognizing these minerals and rocks is how past environmental conditions on Earth are determined.

Careers in Geology and Geosciences

What Is Geology?

Geology is the study of Earth's materials, especially rocks and minerals. It includes the processes that form and change these materials, and the history of Earth and its life.

What Does a Geologist or Geoscientist Do?

Geologists and geoscientists work in diverse areas of science, including geology, geophysics, paleontology, mineralogy, geochemistry, hydrology, oceanography, environmental science, soil science, and even some areas within atmospheric science, planetary science, and meteorology.

The knowledge and skills of geologists and geoscientists are applied to many problems and questions relating to Earth, of which these are just a few:

- How have meteorite or asteroid impacts on Earth's surface affected Earth?
- What areas are most at risk of damage from earthquakes and volcanic eruptions?
- Can earthquakes and volcanic eruptions be predicted?
- How does the makeup of Earth's interior affect what happens at Earth's surface?
- Is it safe to put potentially hazardous liquid wastes in underground rock?
- Can risks of damage to buildings by landslides be reduced?
- What natural energy resources will be available in 10 years? 50 years?
- Can the location of coastlines be expected to change in our lifetimes?
- Can water shortages be avoided in areas of rapidly growing population?
- How do we know that Earth is about 4.5 billion years old?
- How are fossils and types of rocks used to determine ancient environments?
- When and how did the Appalachian Mountains form?
- What is the geology of other planets and moons?

Where Do Geologists and Geoscientists Work?

Some geologists work mostly outdoors doing fieldwork, while others work mostly in labs or offices. It is not unusual for a geologist to divide work time between fieldwork, lab, and office. Fieldwork sometimes is done in beautiful and interesting parts of the world.

Most geoscientists are employed by petroleum companies to explore for oil and natural gas. Many geoscientists work at the U.S. Geological Survey, state geological surveys, and other government agencies where they develop and protect water resources, look for mineral resources, assess geologic hazards, and participate in environmental cleanup and protection.

Universities, colleges, and schools have a significant number of geologists and geoscientists on their faculties. Other geologists, especially those with considerable professional experience, are self-employed as consulting geologists providing advice to property owners and industries.

What Education Is Needed?

A minimum of an undergraduate degree in geology or geoscience is required. For most fields, a good background in math, chemistry, and physics also is needed.

Online Information About Careers in Geosciences

The American Geological Institute has prepared an informative brochure, "Careers in the Geosciences," that provides additional information about what geoscientists do and where they work:

American Geological Institute. 2002. Careers in the geosciences. *www.agiweb. org/workforce/brochure.html*.

The New Mexico Network for Women in Science and Engineering has a good website entitled "Geology," which includes what life is like as a geologist, and what one needs to do to become a good one:

Rodriguez, M., and G. E. Pena-Kues. 2010. Geology. 3rd ed. New Mexico Network for Women in Science and Engineering. *http://nmnwse.org/careers/HTML/C14GEOLO.HTM*.

Topic: geology and geoscience careers
Go to: *www.scilinks.org*
Code: PSCG226

Resources

This material was completely updated and revised by the authors for this new second edition. It is not meant to be a complete representation of resources in geology, but should assist teachers in further exploration of this subject. The entries are subdivided into the following categories:

- **Activities.** This category includes collections of hands-on activities and multidisciplinary units.

- **Audiovisual Materials.** Media materials listed in this section include DVDs and CDs.

- **Books and Booklets.** Textbooks and booklets are included in this category.

- **Information and References.** This category lists additional resources such as periodicals, bibliographies, catalogs, maps, reference booklets, and reports.

- **Internet Resources.** Starting points for exploration of online resources in geology. Each entry has an address (URL) for the website, plus a brief annotation about it.

- **State Resources.** Each of the 50 states of the United States has its own geological survey, and most can provide materials that can be of significant use to teachers and students.

Activities

National Association of Geoscience Teachers
(Activities; 2006; middle school, and the like.)
A variety of inquiry-based, hands-on educational activities, lab demonstrations, and so on. Available online for downloading.

Activities in Planetary Geology for Physical and Earth Sciences
(Activities; 1998; 5th grade–college)
Product Number: EG-1998-03-109-HQ
Activities in 223-page online book grouped into five units: (1) introduction to geologic processes, (2) impact cratering activities, (3) planetary atmospheres, (4) planetary surfaces, and (5) geologic mapping. Second edition of NASA SP-179, first printed in 1982. Additional teaching resources can be accessed through the website at right.

National Association of Geoscience Teachers
NAGT, c/o Carleton College B-SERC
One North College Street
Northfield, MN 55057
tel. 800-344-6909 or 516-576-2270
fax 516-349-9704
http://nagt.org/nagt/teaching_resources/activities.html

NASA
Public Communications Office
NASA Headquarters, Suite 5K39
Washington, DC 20546-0001
tel. 202-358-0001
fax 202-358-4338
www.nasa.gov/audience/foreducators/topnav/materials/listbytype/Planetary.Geology.html

Audiovisual Materials

Planet Earth Series
(DVD or VHS; l986; middle-high school)
Older but classic series include
The Living Machine (60 min.)
Explores the theory of plate tectonics
The Blue Planet (60 min.)
Investigates the ocean depths
The Climate Puzzle (60 min.)
Looks at changes in climate
Tales from Other Worlds (60 min.)
Explores other planets and moons
Gifts from the Earth (60 min.)
Examines Earth's mineral and energy resources
The Solar Sea (60 min.)
Investigates the relationship between Earth and the Sun
Fate of the Earth (60 min.)
Discusses theories about the global consequences of a "nuclear winter" and an "ultraviolet spring"

Annenberg Media
P.O. Box 55742
Indianapolis, IN 46205-0742
tel. 800-532-7637
fax 317-579-0402
e-mail: AnnenbergMedia@fpdirect.com
www.learner.org

Audiovisual Materials
(cont'd)

National Geographic Society
(DVDs; dates of copyright vary; middle-high school)
Alaska's Deadliest Volcano
Huge 1912 eruption of Katmai
Volcano!
Volcano: Natural Inferno
Doomsday Volcano
Santorini eruption 3,600 years ago
In the Shadow of Vesuvius
Story of an historic and devastating eruption
Born of Fire
Volcanoes, earthquakes, and their relation to plate tectonics
Amazing Planet: Explosive Earth
Volcanoes, earthquakes, and tsunamis
Forces of Nature
Volcanoes and earthquakes
National Parks Collection (7 discs)
Natural wonders of our parks
L.A.'s Future Quake
Earthquakes in California

Geological Society of America Explore Geoscience CDs
(CDs; dates of copyright vary; middle school)
Active Geology Paper Models CD-ROM
Paper models to help students understand plate tectonics
Explore Deep Time
Geologic time, relative ages, ages based on radioactive decay
Explore Earthquakes
Activities, facts, images, models
Explore Plate Tectonics
History of theory, evidence, images, 3-D cutouts
Explore Tsunami
Activities, images, links, cutout model
Explore Volcanoes
Activities, images, models, and the like. Both an elementary and a secondary edition.

National Geographic Society
Education and Children's Programs
1145 17th Street NW
Washington, D.C. 20036-4688
tel. 800-627-5162
http://shop.nationalgeographic.com/ngs/category/dvds

Geological Society of America
3300 Penrose Place
P.O. Box 9140
Boulder, CO 80301-9140
tel. 303-357-1000
fax 303-357-1070
www.geosociety.org/educate/cds.htm

Books and Booklets

Laboratory Manual in Physical Geology, 8th Edition
(Activities; 2009; high school)
Busch, R. M. This manual is set up in lab report format. However, it also contains numerous maps and colored photographs. Laboratory topics include rocks, minerals, topography, water, winds, landforms, earthquakes, and plate tectonics. (336 pages)

River Cutters, 2nd Edition
(Activities; 1999; sixth–eighth grades)
These activities model rivers as dynamic, ever-changing systems; investigate erosion, pollution, toxic waste, and human manipulation of rivers. These activities introduce the passage of geologic time. (120 pages)

TOPS Learning Systems
Rocks and Minerals #23
(Activities; 2009; 6th–12th grades)
Task Oriented Physical Science Program (TOPS) hands-on activities on minerals, rocks, and soils, and suggestions for organizing and presenting them. (88 pages)
AND
Pressure #16
(Activities; 2009; 7th–12th grades)
Activities on various aspects of pressure; 32 activities. (80 pages)

Physical Geology
(Book-hard; 2010; college)
Plummer, C. C., et al.: Introductory geology textbook covering a broad range of topics.

Pearson Education
K12 Customer Service
P.O. Box 2500
Lebanon, IN 46052
tel. 800-848-9500
www.pearsonschool.com

GEMS, Lawrence Hall of Science #5200
University of California
Berkeley, CA 94720-5200
tel. 510-642-7771
fax 510-643-0309
www.lhsgems.org

TOPS Learning Systems
10970 S. Mulino Road
Canby, OR 97013
tel. 503-263-2040
fax 503-266-5200
e-mail: rmarson@topscience.org
http://topscience.org/home.html

McGraw-Hill Companies
P.O. Box 182604
Columbus, OH 43272
tel. 1-800-2MC-GRAW (1-800-262-4729)
fax 609-308-4480
www.mhprofessional.com/category/?cat=5312

Books and Booklets
(cont'd)

Earth–Portrait of a Planet, 4th Edition
(Book-hard; 2011; college)
Geology text for undergraduate, nonscience majors. New edition has current coverage of all major topics, especially earthquakes (including the disaster in Haiti in 2010), volcanoes, and climate change. Google Earth exercises provide virtual field trips over the entire world.

Golden Guides for
    Fossils
    Geology
    Rocks and Minerals
    (and other titles)
(Book-soft; dates of publication vary; middle and high school)
Each pocket-sized volume contains illustrations and descriptions of common, important, and interesting examples. Books also include range maps, descriptive text, and more. (160–360 pages) Note: These useful books are now out of print, but they are still available from some suppliers. If WARD'S no longer has the volume that you want, it can be worth searching and trying to locate it elsewhere. WARD'S also can supply other Earth science books and teaching materials.

Volcanoes
(Book-soft; 1985, new illustrations 2008; elementary)
Branley, F. M.: "Let's-Read-and-Find-Out" book. This story explains how volcanoes are formed and how they affect the Earth. Elementary reading level.

W.W. Norton & Company
500 Fifth Avenue
New York, NY 10110
tel. 212-354-5500
fax 212-869-0856
http://books.wwnorton.com/books/Index.aspx

WARD'S Natural Science Establishment, LLC
5100 West Henrietta Road
P.O. Box 92912
Rochester, NY 14692-9012
tel. 800-962-2660; 585-359-2502
fax 585-334-6174
e-mail: customer_service@wardsci.com
http://wardsci.com

HarperCollins Publishers
10 East 53rd Street
New York, NY 10022
tel. 212-207-7000
fax 212-822-4090
www.harpercollins.com/index.aspx

Information and References

Geological Highway Maps

The American Association of Petroleum Geologists has produced geologic maps of 12 regions of the United States. Maps highlight the geologic history of each region and contain a brief discussion of fossils, minerals, and gemstones.

Investigating Earth Systems (IES)

(Information; 2001–Dynamic Earth, and Rocks and Landforms modules; sixth–eighth grades)

This is a standards-based, Earth science curriculum developed by the American Geological Institute. There is a text that can be purchased for the curriculum, but their website provides many links to information on rocks and landforms, dynamic planet (use of models, Earth's interior, plate motion, mountain formation, earthquakes), and other Earth science topics. To access useful links, go to the IES modules.

Geology Research and Information: U.S. Geological Survey

Website with links to U.S. Geological Survey programs: earthquake hazards, volcano hazards, landslide hazards, mineral resources, and energy resources, among others. Links also provided to latest earthquakes and volcanic activity, and the like. Publications and data also available.

GeoRef

(Database; for North America, coverage is 1669–present; all levels)

Most comprehensive database in the geosciences; contains over 3.1 million references; over 100,000 added each year: geoscience journal articles, books, maps, conference papers, reports, and theses. Available on the web, online, or on GeoRef CDs.

American Association of Petroleum Geologists
P.O. Box 979
Tulsa, OK 74101-0979
tel. 918-584-2555
fax 918-560-2665
http://bookstore.aapg.org

American Geological Institute
4220 King Street
Alexandria, VA 22302-1502
tel. 703-379-2480
fax 703-379-7563
www.agiweb.org/education/ies/index.html

U.S. Geological Survey
USGS National Center
12201 Sunrise Valley Drive
Reston, VA 20192
tel. 703-648-5953
http://geology.usgs.gov

American Geological Institute
4220 King Street
Alexandria, VA 22302-1502
tel. 703-379-2480
fax 703-379-7563
www.agiweb.org/georef

Information and References (cont'd)

EARTH
(Magazine; monthly; high school-college)
Very readable monthly geological sciences newsmagazine by the American Geological Institute, formerly published as *Geotimes*. Includes current news about earthquakes, volcanoes, environmental problems, and other important developments in Earth sciences. Contains information about media and other resources for teaching. Individual issues can be purchased online and downloaded.

American Geological Institute
4220 King Street
Alexandria, VA 22302-1502
tel. 703-379-2480
fax 703-379-7563
www.earthmagazine.org

Earth Science Week
(E-newsletter; monthly; high school-college)
Free newsletter with information about Earth science and Earth science education.

American Geological Institute
4220 King Street
Alexandria, VA 22302-1502
tel. 703-379-2480
fax 703-379-7563
www.earthsciweek.org/newsletter/index.html

Journal of Geoscience Education
(Periodical; five times per year; college)
Formerly the Journal of Geological Education, this National Association of Geoscience Teachers publication contains articles about teaching and learning of geosciences at undergraduate and precollege levels (including middle school): pedagogy, assessment, and philosophy.

National Association of Geoscience Teachers
NAGT, c/o Carleton College B-SERC
One North College Street
Northfield, MN 55057
tel. 800-344-6909 or 516-576-2270
fax 516-349-9704
https://www.webassociationmgmt.org/nagt

Geology.com Website
(Website, current; middle-high school)
Earth science news and many links to Earth science topics, satellite images, maps; information about what geologists do; links for teachers; online store for tools and supplies for geologists, teachers, and others. Website maintained by Dr. Hobart M. King.

Geology.com
http://geology.com

Information and References (cont'd)

ScienceNews
(Periodical; biweekly; middle-high school)
Science digest periodical that often contains articles pertaining to geology and recent geological findings.

U.S. Geological Survey Catalog of Maps
(Catalog; annual; all levels)
U.S. Geological Survey catalog of geoscience maps, including topographic maps, photo image maps, satellite image maps, geologic maps, hydrologic maps, maps of planets and moons, land use maps, and more.

U.S. Geological Survey Teacher Packets
(Packet; various publication dates; elementary-high school)
Good background material for teachers as well as for students. Can download.
Topics of packets include
Geologic Age (Grades 7–12)
Global Change (Grades 4–6)
Volcanoes! (Grades 4–8)
What Do Maps Show? (Grades 5–8)
Exploring Maps (Grades 7–12)

ScienceNews
Editorial Offices
1719 N Street NW
Washington, DC 20036
tel. 800-552-4412 (subscribe)
e-mail: editors@sciencenews.org
www.sciencenews.org/view/home

U.S. Geological Survey
USGS National Center
Reston, VA 20192
http://ngmdb.usgs.gov

U.S. Geological Survey
USGS National Center
12201 Sunrise Valley Drive
Reston, VA 20192
tel. 703-648-5953
http://education.usgs.gov/common/TeacherPackets.html

Internet Resources

The Internet is filled with resources pertaining to geology that are appropriate for student use. Keyword searches yield the best results. Examples of sites include

Digital Library for Earth Science Education (DLESE)

DLESE, which is now operated by the National Center for Atmospheric Research (NCAR), provides access to high-quality Earth data sets and imagery, lesson plans, and the like; support services for educators; communication networks to facilitate interactions and collaborations.
www.dlese.org/library/index.jsp

Earth Science World Image Bank

Online images that can be downloaded and used for noncommercial purposes
www.earthscienceworld.org/images/imageuse.html

EarthScope

This is a National Science Foundation program to study the structure and evolution of the North American continent with hundreds of seismometers, GPS stations, and other scientific instruments. Students, teachers, and the public can participate.
www.earthscope.org/eno

Electronic Volcano

Information on active volcanoes
www.dartmouth.edu/~volcano

Federal Emergency Management Agency (FEMA)

Information and activities about the causes and effects of earthquakes
www.fema.gov/library/viewRecord.do?id=3558

Franklin Institute

Resources for educators: general geology, volcanoes, earthquakes, rocks and minerals, lesson plans
www.fi.edu/learn/index.php

Geologic Time

Online edition of a book from the U.S. Geological Survey: relative ages, ages in years, geologic timescale, age of Earth
pubs.usgs.gov/gip/geotime

Global Volcanism Program, Smithsonian Institution and U.S. Geological Survey

Weekly reports on volcanic activities around the world, with maps and detailed reports of individual eruptions
www.volcano.si.edu/reports/usgs

Heat from Within—Earthly Insights Into Planetary Volcanism

Links to volcanic activity, including on other planets; other related links. Website provided by the Lunar and Planetary Institute.
www.lpi.usra.edu/education/fieldtrips/2006/resources.html

Incorporated Research Institutions for Seismology (IRIS)

Information for teachers and students about earthquakes
www.iris.washington.edu/hq

NASA Website for Educators

Images, featured articles, teaching materials, and more.
www.nasa.gov/audience/foreducators/index.html

National Science Teachers Association (NSTA)

News, services, publications, and more.
www.nsta.org

Internet Resources
(cont'd)

National Oceanic and Atmospheric Administration (NOAA)
NOAA educational resources, and links to other useful information
www.education.noaa.gov

Nature-Watch
Supplies and activity kits for learning about nature
www.nature-watch.com/index.php

NOAA National Geophysical Data Center—Educational Resources in Oceanography and Earth Sciences
Links to many useful sources of information
www.ngdc.noaa.gov/mgg/education.html

NOAA National Geophysical Data Center—Natural Hazards
Tsunamis, earthquakes, volcanic eruptions, wildfires: data and images
www.ngdc.noaa.gov/hazard

Pacific Tsunami Warning Center
NOAA site that provides warnings, as well as information about past tsunamis
www.weather.gov/ptwc

PALEOMAP Project
Animations showing the distribution of Earth's continents in the distant past, and where they may be in the future. Can be downloaded; also available on CD. Prepared by Dr. C. R. Scotese.
www.scotese.com/earth.htm

Pangaea Puzzle Activity
Download, cut out continents, and see how shapes fit together; from U.S. Geological Survey
http://volcanoes.usgs.gov/about/edu/dynamic-planet/wegener/puzzlepieces.pdf

Scientific American
Articles and news on science
www.scientificamerican.com

Seismic Sleuths: Earthquakes—A Teacher's Package for Grades 7–12
Units with activities on causes of earthquakes, Earth's structure, seismic waves, preparedness with respect to earthquakes
www.fema.gov/library/viewRecord.do?id=3558

Smithsonian Institution
Activities and information about minerals; additional information via links on site
www.smithsonianeducation.org/ educators/lesson_plans/minerals/index.html

This Dynamic Earth: The Story of Plate Tectonics
Online edition from the U.S. Geological Survey on what plate tectonics is, how the theory developed, and what evidence supports it
http://pubs.usgs.gov/gip/dynamic/dynamic.html

U.S. Department of Energy
Activities and lesson plans for topics related to energy
www.energy.gov/foreducators.htm

U.S. Geological Survey Earthquake Hazards Program
Significant earthquake information, up to the present; access to information and maps showing where earthquakes occurred
http://earthquake.usgs.gov

U.S. Geological Survey Mineral Resources Program
Information about mineral resources: where they come from, future supplies, possible environmental impacts
http://minerals.usgs.gov/granted.html

U.S. Geological Survey National Map Viewer
View any area in the United States, topographic map or satellite image, at different scales and with overlays showing different types of information (structures, boundaries, transportation, and the like).
http://viewer.nationalmap.gov/viewer

U.S. Geological Survey Photographic Library
Free viewing and downloading entire USGS photographic collection of national parks, volcanoes, earthquakes, and more.
http://libraryphoto.cr.usgs.gov

Volcano World
Resources on volcanoes for students and teachers
http://volcano.oregonstate.edu

Windows to the Universe
National Earth Science Teachers Association (NESTA) website with links to information on Earth and space science, including content specifically for teachers. Material for students is written at different reading levels in both English and Spanish.
www.windows2universe.org

State Resources

Each of the 50 states of the United States and Puerto Rico operate their own geological survey, and most states publish a wide variety of materials relating to geological features, geological activity, and how these relate to state citizens. Many of them have publications especially for teachers and for classroom use. Below is a list of the state surveys along with contact information for each.

Alabama Geological Survey:
www.gsa.state.al.us
420 Hackberry Lane, Tuscaloosa, AL 35486-6999. tel. 205-349-2852.
e-mail: info@state.al.us

Alaska Division of Geological and Geophysical Surveys: *www.dggs.dnr.state.ak.us*
3354 College Road, Fairbanks, AK 99709. tel. 907-451-5000, fax 907-451-5050.
e-mail: dggs@dnr.state.ak.us

Arizona Geological Survey:
www.azgs.state.az.us
416 West Congress, Suite 100, Tucson, AZ 85701. tel. 520-770-3500,
fax 520-770-3505.

Arkansas Geological Commission:
www.state.ar.us/agc
Vardelle Parham Geology Center, 3815 West Roosevelt Road, Little Rock, AR 72204.
tel. 501-296-1877, fax 501-663-7360.
e-mail: agc@mail.state.ar.us

California Geological Survey:
www.conservation.ca.gov/CGS/Pages/Index.aspx
801 K Street, MS 12-30, Sacramento, CA 95814. tel. 916-445-1825, fax 916-445-5718.
e-mail: cgshq@consrv.ca.gov

Colorado Geological Survey:
http://geosurvey.state.co.us
Colorado Geological Survey, 715 State Centennial, 1313 Sherman Street, Denver, CO 80203. tel. 303-866-2611.

Connecticut Geological and Natural History Survey: *www.ct.gov/dep/cwp/view.asp?a=2701&q=323438&depNav_GID=1641&depNav*
Natural Resources Center, Department of Environmental Protection, 79 Elm Street, Hartford, CT 06106-5127. tel. 860-424-3583.

Delaware Geological Survey:
www.udel.edu/dgs
University of Delaware, Delaware Geological Survey Building, Newark, DE 19716-7501. tel. 302-831-2833, fax 302-831-3579. e-mail: DGS@mvs.udel.edu

Florida Geological Survey:
www.dep.state.fl.us/geology
903 West Tennessee Street, Tallahassee, FL 32304-7700. tel. 850-488-9380, fax 850-488-8086.

Georgia Geologic Survey Branch:
www.ganet.org/dnr/environ/aboutepd_files/branches_files/gsb.htm
To purchase publications: *http://ggsstore.dnr.state.ga.us/shopping/start.php?browse=1*
2 Martin Luther King, Jr. Drive, Room 400, Atlanta, GA 30334. tel. 404-656-3214, fax 404-657-8379.

Hawaii Department of Land and Natural Resources:
www.hawaii.gov/dlnr
Division of Water and Land Development P.O. Box 373, Honolulu, HI 96809. tel. 808-548-0400.

Idaho Geological Survey:
www.idahogeology.org
University of Idaho, Moscow, ID 83843. tel. 208-885-7991. e-mail: igs@uidaho.edu

Illinois State Geological Survey:
www.isgs.illinois.edu
615 East Peabody Drive, Champaign, IL 61820. tel. 217-333-4747.

Indiana Geological Survey:
http://igs.indiana.edu
611 North Walnut Grove, Bloomington, IN 47405. tel. 812-855-7636. e-mail: igsinfo@indiana.edu

Iowa Geological Survey Bureau:
www.igsb.uiowa.edu
109 Trowbridge Hall, Iowa City, IA 52242-1319. tel. 319-335-1575, fax 319-335-2754. e-mail: webmanager@igsb.uiowa.edu

Kansas Geological Survey:
www.kgs.ku.edu/index.html
The University of Kansas, 1930 Constant Avenue, West Campus, Lawrence, KS 66046-2598. tel. 785-864-3965.

Kentucky Geological Survey:
www.uky.edu/KGS
228 Mining and Mineral Resources Building, University of Kentucky, Lexington, KY 40506-0107. tel. 859-257-5500, fax 859-257-1147.

Louisiana Geological Survey:
www.lgs.lsu.edu
Department of Natural Resources, P.O. Box G, University Station, Baton Rouge, LA 70893. tel. 225-578-5320, fax 225-578-3662. e-mail: chacko@vortex.bri.lsu.edu

Maine Geological Survey:
www.state.me.us/doc/nrimc/mgs/mgs.htm
Maine Department of Conservation, State House Station 22, Augusta, ME 04333. tel. 207-287-2801. e-mail: nrimc@state.me.us

Maryland Geological Survey:
www.mgs.md.gov
2300 St. Paul Street, Baltimore, MD 21218. tel. 410-554-5500.

Massachusetts Executive Office of Environmental Affairs:
www.magnet.state.ma.us/envir/eoea.htm
Executive Office of Environmental Affairs, 251 Causeway Street, Ninth Floor, Boston, MA 02114. tel. 617-626-1000, fax 617-626-1181.

Michigan Department of Environmental Quality, Geological Survey Division: *www.michigan.gov/deq*
P.O. Box 30256, Lansing MI 48909-7756. tel. 1-800-662-9278, fax 517-334-6038.

Minnesota Geological Survey: *www.mngs.umn.edu/index.html*
Minnesota Geological Survey, School of Earth Sciences, University of Minnesota, 2642 University Avenue, St. Paul, MN 55114-1057. tel. 612-627-4780.
e-mail: mgs@gold.tc.umn.edu

Mississippi Department of Environmental Quality, Office of Geology: *www.deq.state.ms.us/MDEQ.nsf/page/geology_home?OpenDocument*
P.O. Box 20307, Jackson, MS 39289-1307. tel. 601-961-5171, fax 601-961-5660.

Missouri Division of Geology and Land Survey: *www.dnr.mo.gov/geology*
Department of Natural Resources, P.O. Box 250, Rolla, MO 65402. tel. 1-800-361-4827.
e-mail: dnrgsrad@dnr.mo.gov

Montana Bureau of Mines and Geology: *www.mbmg.mtech.edu*
Montana College of Mineral Science and Technology, 1300 West Park Street, Butte, MT 59701. tel. 406-496-4167.

Nebraska Conservation and Survey Division: *http://csd.unl.edu/surveyareas/geology.asp*
University of Nebraska–Lincoln, Institute of Agriculture & Natural Resources, 113 Nebraska Hall, Lincoln, NE 68588-0517. tel. 402-472-3471.

Nevada Bureau of Mines and Geology: *www.nbmg.unr.edu*
University of Nevada–Reno, Reno, NV 89557-0088. tel. 775-784-6691.
e-mail: nbmginfo@unr.edu

New Hampshire Department of Environmental Services: *www.des.state.nh.us*
29 Hazen Drive, P.O. 95, Concord, NH 03302-0095. tel. 603-271-3503, fax 603-271-2867.

New Jersey Geological Survey: *www.state.nj.us/dep/njgs*
P.O. Box 427, 29 Arctic Parkway, Trenton, NJ 08625. tel. 609-292-1185, fax 609-292-1185.

New Mexico Bureau of Mines and Mineral Resources: *http://geoinfo.nmt.edu*
Leroy Place, New Mexico Tech, Socorro, NM 87801-4796. tel. 575-835-5420.

New York State Geological Survey: *http://nygeosurvey.geology-forum.com*
3136 Cultural Education Center, Albany, NY 12230. tel. 518-474-5816.

North Carolina Geological Survey: *www.geology.enr.state.nc.us*
Division of Land Resources, 1612 Mail Service Center, P.O. Box 27699-1612, Raleigh, NC 27611. tel. 919-733-2423, fax 919-733-0900.

North Dakota Geological Survey: *www.state.nd.us/ndgs*
600 East Boulevard Avenue, Bismarck, ND 58505-0840. tel. 701-328-8000, fax 701-328-8010.

Ohio Department of Natural Resources, Division of Geological Survey: *www.ohiodnr.com/geosurvey*
4383 Fountain Square Drive, Columbus, OH 43224-1362. tel. 614-265-6576, fax 614-447-1918.
e-mail: geo.survey@dnr.state.oh.us

Oklahoma Geological Survey: *www.ou.edu/special/ogs-pttc*
University of Oklahoma, 100 East Boyd Street, Suite N131, Norman, OK 73019. tel. 405-325-3031, fax 405-325-7069.

Oregon Department of Geology and Mineral Industries:
www.oregongeology.com/sub/default.htm
800 NE Oregon Street, Suite 965, Portland, OR 97232. tel. 503-731-4100,
fax 503-731-4066.

Pennsylvania Department of Conservation and Natural Resources, Bureau of Topographic and Geologic Survey:
www.dcnr.state.pa.us/topogeo
Department of Conservation and Natural Resources, 3240 Schoolhouse Road, Middletown, PA 17057.
tel. 717-702-2017.

Puerto Rico Department of Natural and Environmental Resources, Bureau of Geology:
Box 5887, Puerta de Tierra, PR 00906.
tel. 809-725-2526, fax 809-724-0365.

Rhode Island Geological Survey:
www.uri.edu/cels/geo/GEO_risurvey.html
Office of the State Geologist, Department of Geology, The University of Rhode Island, 9 East Alumni Avenue, 314 Woodward Hall, Kingston, RI 02881.
tel. 401-874-2191.

South Carolina Geological Survey:
www.dnr.sc.gov/geology
5 Geology Road, Columbia, SC 29210.
tel. 803-896-7714.

South Dakota Geological Survey:
www.sdgs.usd.edu
Department of Water and Natural Resources, Akeley-Lawrence Science Center, University of South Dakota, 414 East Clark Street, Vermillion, SD 57069-2390.
tel. 605-677-5227.

Tennessee Department of Environment and Conservation, Geology Division:
www.state.tn.us/environment/tdg
Tennessee Division of Geology, 401 Church Street, Nashville, TN 37243-0445.
tel. 615-532-1500.

Texas Bureau of Economic Geology:
www.beg.utexas.edu
University of Texas at Austin, University Station, Box X, Austin, TX 78713.
tel. 512-471-1534/7721.
e-mail: begmail@begv.beg.utexas.edu

Utah Geological Survey:
http://geology.utah.gov
1594 West North Temple, P.O. Box 146100, Salt Lake City, UT 84114-6100.
tel. 801-537-3300, fax 801-537-3400.

Vermont Agency of Natural Resources:
www.anr.state.vt.us/dec/geo/vgs.htm
Vermont Geological Survey, 103 S. Main Street, Logue Cottage, Waterbury, VT 05671-2420.
tel. 802-241-3608, fax 802-241-4585.

Virginia Division of Mineral Resources:
www.dmme.virginia.gov/ divisionmineralresources.shtml
Department of Mines, Minerals, and Energy, P.O. Box 3667, Charlottesville, VA 22903.
tel. 434-951-6342.

Washington Division of Geology and Earth Resources: *www.dnr.wa.gov/ResearchScience/ GeologyEarthSciences/Pages/Home.aspx*
1111 Washington Street SE, Room 148, P.O. Box 47007, Olympia, WA 98504-7007.
tel. 360-902-1450. e-mail: geology@wadnr.gov

West Virginia Geological and Economic Survey: *www.wvgs.wvnet.edu*
Mont Chateau Research Center, P.O. Box 879, Morgantown, WV 26507-0879.
tel. 304-594-2331.

Wisconsin Geological and Natural History Survey: *www.uwex.edu/wgnhs*
University of Wisconsin-Extension, 3817 Mineral Point Road, Madison, WI 53705.
tel. 608-262-1705, fax 608-262-8086.

Wyoming Geological Survey:
www.wsgs.uwyo.edu
Box 1347, University Station, Laramie, WY 82071. tel. 307-766-2286.

About the Authors

Paul D. Fullagar

Paul Fullagar is professor emeritus of geological sciences, University of North Carolina at Chapel Hill (UNC–CH). He received an AB in geology from Columbia College, Columbia University in 1960, and a PhD in geology from Illinois in 1963. He then taught geology at Old Dominion College (now University) until 1967; he also conducted research at NASA (Goddard Space Flight Center). In 1967, he went to UNC–CH, where he was on the faculty for 40 years, and department chair for 16 years. Fullagar also was codirector of programs that encouraged members of underrepresented groups to have science careers by providing research opportunities and mentoring.

Fullagar established the Isotope Geochemistry Laboratory at UNC–CH. His current research uses isotopic compositions of rocks, glasses, and skeletal remains to determine sources and history of these materials, and the age of geological materials. Studies include evolution of the Appalachian Mountains, formation of islands and seamounts in the Hawaiian Islands area, sources and distribution of ancient glasses, and migration of ancient people (e.g., Vikings, Mesoamericans, Europeans).

Introductory-level courses developed and taught by Fullagar include geology, planetary geology, and Earth and environmental sciences. Upper-level and graduate courses include mineralogy, petrology, and isotope geochemistry. Fullagar's activities in preuniversity Earth science education include teaching workshops for middle and high school teachers, and serving as co-principal investigator for the project that resulted in the first edition of *Project Earth Science: Geology*. Fullagar also developed and taught an online Earth and environmental science (EES) course to prepare teachers to teach the EES course now required in North Carolina.

Nancy W. West

Nancy West is a geoscience educator in Fort Collins, Colorado. She received an AB in geology from Princeton University in 1979 and an MAT from the University of North Carolina at Chapel Hill (UNC–CH) in 1991. Her studies include graduate coursework in geology and fieldwork, petrologic, and chemical analysis of a Miocene welded tuff from the Mojave Desert. She has also worked as a geologist for a geotechnical company.

Ms. West has taught geology at UNC–CH, chemistry and geology in high school, geology for Thomas Nelson Community College, and science education courses at Duke University and the College of William and Mary (W&M). She has cotaught the Geology of Virginia for Teachers at W&M and a high school geographic information systems course.

In addition to teaching, Ms. West has developed Earth science curricula for a middle and high school National Science Foundation project, the North Carolina Leadership Network for Earth Science Teachers. This project emphasized conducting field studies with students on campus. She has other experience with curriculum—and professional development—as the Williamsburg–James City County Public Schools' science curriculum coordinator. Recently, she has been the curriculum specialist on the Virginia Demonstration Project at W&M, a project to enhance middle school students' interest in STEM careers, using problem-based learning, which features LEGO® robots.

Upon moving back to the West in 2009, Ms. West started a consulting company, Quarter Dome Consulting, LLC. When not working on projects such as *Project Earth Science*, she is hiking, snowshoeing, bicycling, bird-watching, reading, and enjoying her return to the land of mountains where rocks are exposed.

Index

A

active volcanoes, 20, 34, 152
Activity Planners, 16, 30, 40, 54, 64, 76, 86, 98, 110, 120, 134, 148, 158, 172
Activity Summary. *See* Summary, Activity.
age of Earth, 87
age of rocks, 36, 55, 59, 63, 143, 185, 193
ages of rock layers, 173, 174, 177, 182, 183
Alaska earthquakes, 1, 165, 166
Alaska volcano (Katmai), 20, 29
Alaska Volcano Observatory (AVO), 20
All Cracked Up (Activity 4), **40–52**
Alternative Preparation, 13, 71, 117
aluminum oxide (Al_2O_3), 19, 28
American Geological Institute, 226
American Red Cross, 169
ancient magnetism.
    See paleomagnetism.
Andes Mountains, 196
andesite rock, 19, 20, 21, 25, 27, 28, 29
Answers to Student Questions, 15, 28–29, 39, 52, 63, 73, 95–96, 108, 118–119, 131–132, 146, 156, 169–170, 185–186
anticlines, 175, 176, 177, 183–184, 185–186
Apollo 8, 101
Appalachian Mountains, 145, 146, 185, 198, 225
Arctic Circle, 177
Arrangement of Map Panels To Make World Map (Figure 1.1), **2**
art and volcanic products, 156
assessing Earth's models, 50
Assessment, 15, 29, 39, 52, 63, 74, 84, 96, 108, 119, 132, 146, 156, 171, 186
asteroids and tsunamis, 217
asthenosphere, definition, 42
asthenosphere layer, 42, 43, 47, 48, 99, 100
astronauts and Silly Putty, 101
atlas, using, 2, 13
Azores (volcanic mountains), 201

B

Background (Activities), 1, 31–32, 41–43, 55–56, 65–66, 77–78, 87–88, 99–100, 121–122, 135–137, 149, 159, 173–174
Bacon, Francis, 190
Baja California earthquake (2010), 159
basalt (igneous rock), 19, 20, 21, 25, 27, 28, 29, 76, 78, 81, 82–83, 222
basins, ocean, 2
bathyscaphe, *Trieste*, 65
beach sand, 82
beauty, discussion, 38
belts, mountain, 1
boundaries, plate, 11, 25, 26, 197–198
breakup of Pangaea, 134–146
Brigham-Grette, Julie, 177
budgeting for Activity, 72
building construction and earthquakes, 158–171, 217–219, 220, 225
buildings made of rock, 84

C

caldera of volcano, 200–201
California earthquakes, 1, 14, 165, 166
Canada, volcanoes, 20
candy bar as model of tectonic plates, 110, 112, 113, 115, 117, 118, 119
Candy Bar Tectonics (Figure 10.1), **112**
carbon dioxide (CO_2), 153
Careers in Geology and Geosciences (Reading 5), **187, 225–226**
Cascade Mountains, 149, 196, 201, 205, 207
Cascadia earthquake (1700), 14
CAT (computer-aided tomography) scans, 131
cause of plate motion, 195–196, 198
chain of volcanoes, 30, 34, 35, 149
chain of volcanoes, formation, 37
Challenger Deep, 65
characteristics of Earth's interior, 48
characteristics of rocks, 76–84
Characteristics of Solids and Liquids (BLM 9.1), **103**
Charleston, SC, earthquake (1886), 14, 163, 210
chemical components of rocks, 16
chemical composition of lavas, 199
chronology, geological, 185
Cincinnati Arch, 183
Clemens, Samuel L., 73
climate change and glaciers, 108
climate change and volcanic activity, 156
coal and electricity, 90
coal and sulfur, 90
collision of plates, 136
Color Guide for Continents (Table 12.1), **137**
color of rocks, 20, 82, 83
Common Objects Made From Earth Materials (Table 8.1), **95**
communications during earthquakes, 163
comparing rock samples, 84
Comparison of Major Compositional Layers in Egg and Earth (Figure 4.2), **43**
compass, magnetic, 62
composite volcano (stratovolcano), 200–201
compositions of Earth's layers, 48
computer models, 51
computer software, earthquakes, 13
computer-aided tomography (CAT) scans, 131
concept maps, 108, 116, 156
conclusions. See Questions and Conclusions.
conglomerate (rock), 76, 78, 81, 83
Connections, 14, 16, 28, 39, 51, 63, 73, 84, 95, 108, 118, 131, 145, 156, 169, 184
construction against earthquakes, 217–219, 220
continent movement, 134–146
continental collision and mountain ranges, 11, 117, 198
continental drift theory, 42, 117, 135–137, 189, 190
continental rock, 55, 61, 63
continental separation, 191–192, 193
continental splitting (rifting), 135–137
continents, positions. See positions of continents.
Convection (Activity 11), **120–132**
convection cells, 120, 125, 129, 130, 195–196
Convection Cells Activity setups (Figures 11.1–11.5), **122–125**
convection currents, 121–122
convection, definition, 121
Convection Experiments Data Sheet (BLM 11.1), **127**
convection oven, 130, 131
convergent boundaries, 17, 19, 20, 25, 26, 29, 88, 135, 136, 197–198
convergent boundary, definition, 17

R

S